Guides' Tales Of Adventure

Guides' Tales Of Adventure

Hunter's Information Series ®
North American Hunting Club
Minneapolis, Minnesota

Guides' Tales Of Adventure

Library of Congress Catalog Card Number 90-60992
ISBN 0-914697-29-3

Printed in U.S.A.
8   9

Contents

Dedication

To North America's
Men Of Adventure

Acknowledgments

Guiding big game hunters in North America's most desolate country is, arguably, the most dangerous profession on earth. This special edition compiles exclusively for NAHC members some of the most life–threatening, exciting and just plain funny stories from big game guides all over the continent. The story–telling ability of these seventeen men, combined with the exclusive art of Larry Anderson and the behind the scenes work of the NAHC staff, have made this a work which we are proud to include in the NAHC Hunter's Information Series.

Thanks to: NAHC Publisher Mark LaBarbera, Editor Bill Miller, Hunter's Information Series Managing Editor Jay Strangis, Associate Editor Dan Dietrich, Editorial Assistants Debra Morem and Tara Graney, Vice President of Products Marketing Mike Vail and Marketing Manager Linda Kalinowski.

Steven F. Burke, President
North American Hunting Club

Art & Photo Credits

Every illustration in *Guides' Tales Of Adventure* is an original pen and ink sketch specially commissioned from well–known wildlife artist Larry Anderson. Anderson's work frequently appears in *North American Hunter* and other NAHC publications. Anderson, from Des Moines, Iowa, also painted the NAHC's 10th Anniversary print, *Right Day, Wrong Stand*.

Photos in the "Men Of Adventure" section were provided by the outfitters and guides.

Foreword

E very hunt is an adventure. Whether an NAHC member plans and
saves to hunt grizzly in Alaska or throws a few shotgun shells in his
pocket and cuts across the back field to hunt rabbits, the outing is likely
to produce memories that will last a lifetime. If we pay close enough attention, every hunt is a source of excitement, humor, thrills—sometimes
even danger.

Few people are privileged to have a share in as much of the adventure
of hunting as are the guides and outfitters of North America. They are in
the field virtually every day of the season. They take the good clients and
the bad clients as they come. To them "the office" is some of the most
unforgiving country on the continent. For a lot of them "life insurance"
is nothing more than a clear head and faith in The Almighty.

Most of all, guides and outfitters are out there putting it on the line
for their clients every day. It takes a special kind of person to set off into
the wilderness with a complete stranger. Put yourself in the shoes of the
hunting guide and imagine the questions that must run through his mind
every time he sets out with a new client—"Can this guy shoot?"; "Is he
any good in the woods?"; "Can I count on him not to freeze when the
chips are down?" In most cases the client has had a great deal more opportunity to research his guide than the guide has had to research his client.

In the wilderness, even the routine can quickly become an adventure.
From one of my own hunts, I remember standing by watching as my

guide moaned and retched on a British Columbia sand bar miles from base camp. What put us in that situation? Earlier he had accidentally swallowed gasoline while siphoning fuel for our outboard motor! In the wilderness, the simple can instantly become the dangerous.

The adventures in this book are of all flavors. There are the humorous sort like the tale of the human mole who burrowed under the snow because he feared a bull moose would charge him, and the story of the hunter who missed the same pronghorn so many times he threw his bow at the buck instead. Some are thrilling like the guide who jumped down into an abandoned mine entrance with a bear he *thought* was dead. Some are thought-provoking like the legend of the mountain hermit. And some are simply factual reporting of the unbelievable but true, like the murderous grizzly attack which Darwin Carey survived and the story of a hunter whose enticement to take a trophy Dall sheep came down to a tin of apricots.

As you step into these tales of adventure, you'll find that some of the most dangerous situations were created by bad judgment or bad shots. It is easy to sit in a soft chair next to a fire in a safe, secure home and pass judgment. But as experienced hunters, you and I know the unfortunate fact is that even the most well-planned, well-executed hunt can result in a shot that's not true. Factors beyond anyone's control can waylay the best plans of hunter and guide. We also know that in survival situations, decisions must be made based on the best information available at the moment. Snap decisions may prove wrong, but they are sometimes better than no decision at all.

The main purpose of this edition in the Hunter's Information Series is to provide you with pure adventure. Because each story is straight from the mouth of a North American hunting guide or outfitter, giving you the vicarious thrill of "being there" is easy. There's no one better to tell the stories than the men who actually lived them.

The second purpose is to enhance the appreciation of the opportunity to share adventure and excitement which hunting guides and outfitters provide for all of us. As the guiding/outfitting industry faces stifling government regulation and economic hardship, a pat on the back for these guys is overdue. So from the members of the NAHC, this book is another way to say "thanks for sharing the adventures."

Steven F. Burke, President
North American Hunting Club

Don't Let
The Coyotes Have Me

by Duane Wiltse

"Duane, would my heart bother you if I went to the mountains for elk season with you this fall?"

"Of course not, Art, why should your heart bother me?"

"Well, I mean because of my heart attacks, you know."

Now that flip answer, offered so easily weeks ago, thundered into my mind as I stared at Art's crumpled and twisted body lying in the jumble of rocks at my horse's feet. I had ridden Surprise, my big Appaloosa gelding, unmercifully hard the last hour to get to the scene of the wreck. Still mounted and panting from the exertion that accompanies all efforts at 9,000-foot elevation, I exclaimed, "What's the matter, Art?"

"My damn leg's broke, Duane," he gasped.

"What do you mean your leg's broke? What happened?"

"I mean it's busted, smashed to smithereens and hurts like hell, damn it. Get off that horse and give me a hand. I'm hurt bad."

While Hansen Murray, one of my hunting guides, and I splinted Art's leg with sticks and neckerchiefs, I remembered Art had barely survived the last of his three heart attacks. And that was when he was at home in Cody, Wyoming, only minutes from the West Park Hospital. Right now he lay on a steep, boulder-strewn mountainside in the head of Burnt Timber Creek, some 35 miles west of Cody by car and another 15 miles south, up the Elks Fork River by horse. If he suffered another attack up here because of shock, excitement or fatigue, he would die. We were many hours of hard horseback riding from the nearest phone and farther yet from the possibility of any medical assistance.

Hansen and I used sticks to scratch out a reasonably level spot to lay Art and discussed what we'd have to do to save his life. The accident had happened about noon. It was 1:10 p.m. already. Darkness and the early autumn chill that comes with it to the high country in September were going to be our immediate enemies.

Quickly we decided that Hansen would stay with Art. I would ride to camp and return with blankets, food, water and, most importantly, Art's heart medicine. Russell Tompkin, our wrangler and best horseman, would make the grueling three-hour ride to the telephone to call the Park County Search and Rescue helicopter stationed in Greybull, about 60 miles east of Cody.

Art grabbed my pant leg. "Duane, whatever you do, don't forget my medicine. I am not feeling very good at all," he whispered as I prepared to mount up. His steel gray eyes were moist with pain and fear.

Art was 56 years old, not a large man, maybe five-foot, eight-inches tall and 150 pounds soaking wet, but tough—very tough—both physically and mentally. He'd been orphaned at an early age, played semi-pro baseball around the Big Horn Basin during his late teens and early 20s, worked on farms and ranches and hunted elk in the Big Horn and Beartooth Mountains all his life. But right now he needed help—medical help—and lots of it. With every passing moment his situation grew more critical.

I spurred Surprise. He sensed my feelings of urgency and responded instantly, leaping and clawing at the mountain, sometimes nearly out of control as he headed back toward camp at a too-fast pace. There's going to be a lot of good horse flesh abused before this night is over, I thought.

I knew Art didn't have much chance surviving the torturous hours that lay ahead and my heart ached for him. My human limitations frustrated me. If only I could fix it for him, like he was always fixing broken things around camp for me.

That's where he should be right now, I thought, around camp fixing things and catching trout for supper. Not laying out there in the cold rocks all busted up, gritting his teeth against the pain racking his body and being worried sick about his pump quitting.

But we had all gotten carried away with yesterday's hunting success. And when Art said he'd like to go up and help pack out the meat I hadn't given it a second thought. Now we were in a real jam.

The rest of our horses were grazing on the flats along the Elks Fork River. As we came off the mountain in a cloud of dust and rolling stones, they threw their startled heads in the air, alerted eyes and ears riveted on the exhausted, foam-covered Appaloosa and sweaty rider.

I gathered the remuda and rode into camp at a high lope. The horses thundering into the corral brought Betty Gray, my cook, to the hitching rail with concern on her face. As I dismounted, a quick glance at my watch enforced my concern. It was 3:00 p.m. already.

Shouting, "Art's hurt," I thrust a list of supplies I needed into her hand, tossed her a pair of saddle bags and told her to hurry. By the time I'd changed mounts the bags were packed. Surprise hadn't moved from the spot where I had unsaddled him. He just stood spraddle-legged and head down, his sides heaving in and out. I hollered at Betty to take care of him as I spurred Big Red through the timber and toward the long climb back up to Art.

Russell had been riding a young green-broke colt that morning, so he was a few minutes behind me coming into camp for a fresh horse. Before I rode out of sight I saw him catch a medium-sized black horse we called Thunder. Thunder was half-Morgan, half-Mustang and all heart—exactly what Russell would need for his race to the trailhead. There, he would jump into his truck and drive to Hansen's cabin in Green Creek for the nearest phone, over some 15 miles of narrow, twisting mountain road that followed the north fork of the Shoshone River. Everything was going to take time—too much time, I feared. Russell left camp about 3:40 p.m.

His choice of Thunder for his pony-express-type ride illustrated his good judgment of horses. Russell has that indefinable quality that all exceptional race horse jockeys have—knowing how to "rate" or "pace" a horse so he finishes strong but spent. His plan was to save 40 minutes in the first 10 miles, then go for broke after the last river crossing over the remaining five miles.

Thunder had been rested for two days, so being fresh and full of green grass he was anxious to go. But Russell, knowing he had five river crossings to make and 15 miles of rough country to cross, wisely held him to a fast walk for the first half mile.

Thunder was warmed and loosened up by then so Russell let him out just a little into a nice ground-eating lope. The trail follows the Elks Fork River, which splashes and wanders its way from its birth in a little green meadow surrounded by sheer, cloud-shrouded cliffs at the base of Rampart Pass. The headwaters are secreted behind a very wild, narrow and steep canyon with a thunderous waterfall right in the middle. The fish, game and scenery in there are akin to my expectations of heaven. Sometimes tranquil enough to bathe in, most times wild, white and free, the river travels through about 30 miles of some of North America's most majestic mountains.

At its origin, the Elks Fork River is ankle deep and narrow enough to jump across. By the time Russell would make his fifth crossing, she'd be 50 yards of deep whitewater crashing over, around and through all sizes of rocks and boulders. The streams and rivers rise dramatically during a sunny day in the mountains. By late afternoon and early evening a lot of snow has melted and traveled down the 20 other streams that feed the Elks Fork. It was mid-afternoon when Russell left camp. Thunder would have to swim portions of the last crossing.

As they approached the first crossing, Thunder just naturally dropped back into his trot and then to a slow walk as he stepped into the water. Russell allowed a pause for a short drink. The first three miles were uneventfully behind them. As they came out of the river, Thunder responded willingly as Russell nudged him back into the lope. He felt good under Russell—relaxed, but alert, breathing deeply as he weaved in and out of the timber from shade to bright sunlight, he maintained his rhythm uphill and down. Under the shimmering golden yellow leaves of the aspen trees that grew along the river bottom, through the tall, black green fir, pine and spruce trees that stabbed their cone-clustered tops into the pure blue sky, they rode. The sound of the rushing river only a few yards to their right drowned out the sound of their hoofbeats as they approached the easiest river crossing.

Suddenly the tranquil scene was shattered by an explosion of sound and movement slightly ahead and to the right of horse and rider. Thunder snorted, then bolted sharply to the left, leaving Russell clawing leather to stay aboard. Russell just barely gathered the white-eyed, nostril-flared mount under him as two grizzly bear cubs dashed across the trail and up the slope to his left. Then real grief arrived—a very angry 600-pound, hump-backed sow grizzly.

The silver-tipped hair on her neck and shoulders standing on end made it plain the sow was on the fight. The glare from her piercing yellow eyes and the growly snarl that leaked from around her bared fangs as she crossed a few yards in front of Thunder, told Russell what was coming next. Time seemed to be suspended, but it was only a couple of heartbeats until she had checked the safety of her twins and, with an ominous woof, turned to challenge the innocent yet threatening intruders.

Russell sensed there were only two choices. First, he could wheel Thunder, who was frozen in his tracks, and race back up the trail he had just come down, hoping Mama only made a fake charge, as grizzlies are sometimes prone to do. But there were two bad flaws in that option: if it was not a false charge she'd catch them all too soon, and while Russell could probably save his own life by getting up a tree, he'd lose his horse in the fight and several hours time trying to reach a phone. If it was a false charge, Big Mama might still hang around the site fuming and fussing about the intrusion, requiring a lengthy and time-consuming detour. It was apparent that Art would be the loser all the way around.

The second option called for bold action and split-second timing. The crossing looked tantalizingly close, a scant 100 yards ahead. The enraged silvertip was 30 yards to the left and slightly ahead. The instant she switched her attention to momentarily check her offspring, Russell spurred Thunder and let out a rebel yell.

Nothing, but nothing, runs at a grizzly. Startled by the sudden aggressiveness and hampered by naturally poor vision, the bear stood up on her hind legs. Her hesitation gave Thunder the edge he needed to get past her with powerful thrusts of his massive hind quarters, and dash for the crossing.

But the griz recovered quickly—too quickly.

Fifty yards, 40 yards, 30 yards to the crossing, but the bear was closing fast. At 20 yards the trail swung out within 10 yards of the river bank, but was a good 20 feet above a deep pool in the river. At that point the trail turned left and dropped sharply into a small ravine that led to the water's edge where the river was wide and shallow. The bear was snapping at their heels and, with a powerful lunge, she would pounce on them from the ravine bank the moment they entered it. There was nothing to do but go for broke as they reached the left turn in the trail.

Russell held Thunder right, spurred and yelled again. The edge of the undercut bank crumbled beneath them as Thunder leaped into space. In a shower of black dirt, green grass and mountain flowers, they struck the water about midstream. They were both swimming before either surfaced.

As they struggled up the stony bank on the other side of the river the sow, standing on the freshly scarred bank, gave them one more spine-chilling growl, then turned and ambled back toward her cubs. Both man and horse breathed a sigh of relief as they warily watched her slowly dissolve into the timber, her massive head lolling from side to side.

The grizzly was gone, but Russell was more worried than ever. Instead of a confident strong horse under him, Thunder was now a tired, hurting animal. The all-out 100-yard dash and swim after nearly six miles of loping spent the reserves Russell was saving for the last crossing and final five miles to the truck. And worse yet, Thunder was favoring his right front leg. Somehow during the race he had injured his right shoulder. They rested only a moment as Russell sat on a rock and poured the water from his boots. Then they walked. When Thunder was limbered up again Russell caught a stirrup and swung into the saddle.

"Fun and games are over, for a while at least," he said as he urged him along the trail. "Let's get back to work."

It was 5:30 p.m. by the time I returned to the scene of the accident astride a very tired and lathered horse. It had been slightly more than four hours since I had left for water, medicine and other survival supplies. The intense, unrelenting pain and paralyzing tension had already taken a terrible toll on Art's physical and emotional reserves. I dismounted and was stumbling over the steep boulder-strewn site, canteen in one hand and heart medicine in the other, before Big Red could come to a complete stop.

Together Hansen and I raised our ashen-faced friend's head and shoulders off the cold stony ground. He gratefully gulped the cool water and pills, and questioned me urgently about the helicopter. I had no answer for him.

As he sank back to the stones he said, "I don't feel very good. I hope they are in time. Promise me one thing, Duane," he pleadingly whispered.

"Of course, Art. What is it?"

"If the helicopter can't get into this canyon and I don't make it, you'll pack me out on horseback. You won't let the coyotes have me."

"What the heck is he talking about, Hansen?" I asked. "Coyotes getting him?"

With grave concern etching his face, Hansen replied, "He's been hallucinating the past half hour or so."

"Well, there won't be any coyotes or any other critters picking his bones, I'll promise you that," I replied emphatically. "What the hell happened here anyway?"

"Frosty blew up on him," was the answer, "'course it was Art's own fault. He got the lead rope under Frosty's tail."

"Yeah. So?"

"Well, he was leading that old gray mare packhorse you call Hungry. The one that's always got to have every clump of green grass along the trail."

"Go on," I urged.

"Well, she'd jerked the lead rope out of Art's hand several times, making him dismount and recatch her. Gave him a couple of bad rope burns in the process, too. So he got mad and wrapped the rope around his hand so she couldn't get loose."

"That was a damn fool greenhorn thing to do, Hansen! Why did you let...."

"Now hold on a minute, Duane. I had my hands full with my own pack horse switchbacking up this steep sucker. I didn't know he had done it until it was too late. As he made one of those sharp switchbacks right down there, Hungry swung her head out for some grass and slipped the rope under Frosty's tail. Without looking back, Art jerked the lead rope to retrieve her head and attention. But with that rope taught and tight under the root of Frosty's tail, Art got more of Frosty's attention than the mare's and the rodeo was on.

"With that rope wrapped around his hand, Art was in trouble. By the time he got rid of the rope and packhorse, Frosty was burnt so bad he thought he was afire and bucking for all he was worth trying to put it out. There were a lot of rocks and boulders kicked loose and rolling down the mountain when Art was thrown. He landed on his butt and back, with his left leg braced against that big, solid boulder over there to keep from going all the way over the edge, but another boulder about the size of a washtub came crashing down on him, just missed his head by inches and smashed his leg to a pulp just above the ankle. I could hear the bones in his leg breaking from clear up there where the elk lay."

As Sheep Mesa to the west of us devoured the sun, our spirits and chances of getting the helicopter in before dark began to dissolve.

Art seemed to be feeling a little better. Just having his medicine seemed to comfort him. At least he wasn't talking about the coyotes getting him any more.

Hansen built a fire for warmth and for a signal while I gathered a good supply of dry firewood.

We had estimated that Russell would have arrived at the truck parked at the trail head about the same time I had returned with the water and medicine—5:30 p.m. That should have put him on the phone to the S & R boys by 6:00 p.m. at the latest. Darkness arrived up there about 8:00 p.m. Allowing some scramble time, plan time and flight time, the helicopter should have arrived around 7:00 p.m. with an hour of light left to load and fly Art to the hospital.

But it didn't. Seven-thirty came and went. Eight o'clock brought deepening dusk as well as coyote howls echoing off the canyon walls as the varmints gathered for the night's hunting. But no helicopter.

Art was afraid he wouldn't be able to hold any food on his sick stomach, so he hadn't eaten since his 5:00 a.m. breakfast. Now he lay on a foam pad wrapped in blankets next to the fire, staring into the blue-black sky as little, sparkly, bluish-white stars began to appear all around us, as if by magic. The pain and anguish were clearly visible in the whites of his eyes. The passing of only five minutes seemed to be at least an hour to him as he repeatedly asked the time. Eight-thirty, and still no helicopter.

By now we were worried about Russell. Something must have happened. Hansen and I sat hunched on the steep slope, our down vests and down coats pulled tightly around us, our feet to the fire and waited and prayed and waited.

By the time Russell had led Thunder back to the trail, the horse's breathing was nearly normal and the limp was slight. But the vigor was gone out of both of them as Russell caught his left stirrup and swung into the saddle. Both horse and rider took a good look behind them. Again Russell walked Thunder for a ways, hoping the horse could regain some of his strength and composure, get warmed up and go back to his ground-eating lope. But Thunder was a bundle of raw nerves now, no longer tugging at the bit. He saw bears with big teeth and claws in every branch that rustled in the breeze, every shadow, every song bird that burst from the grass along the trail. Sighing and snorting, he aggravated his shoulder with each encounter. His lope was no longer strong and fluid, but labored and gimpy. The farther they went, the more often Russell got off and walked, leading the head-down, limping, coal-black horse.

It was 5:30 p.m. when they crossed the river the fourth time. The water was high and swift. Thunder was just barely able to keep his footing. Russell knew there'd be no such luck at the last crossing so he got off and walked Thunder the entire two miles between the two crossings to rest him as much as possible.

By the time they reached the swollen fifth crossing, Thunder's mental attitude was pretty much back to normal. He was still very tired and sore, but he knew the corrals, hay, grain and rest were a scant five miles away and he began to be anxious to get there. As he lost his footing just short of midstream and began swimming through the boulder-strewn, debris-laden, riley water, Russell slipped out of the saddle on the upstream side and held tightly to the saddle horn with his left hand while fending off sharp, slippery boulders with his right. They were swept nearly 20 yards downstream before gaining their footing again along the far bank.

By the time Thunder had caught his breath and Russell had poured the water out of his boots again, it was 6:15. He gathered his horse under him, gave him his head and said, "We've got to be at the corrals by 7:15, Thunder. Can you do it?"

We never knew if it was his empty stomach or the urging in Russell's voice that Thunder responded to, but, pain or no pain, that fantastic mustang heart of his took over and he went back to work. Yard after yard, mile after mile, he ate up the distance. Head high, eyes flashing, mane flying in the wind, the little black horse covered with white lather burst into the corral area at 7:14 on the dot. He stood in the middle of the corral, head between his front legs, mouth open, sides heaving, waiting to be unsaddled and cared for after the phone call.

At 8:45 p.m. the chopper made a pass over the signal fire that looked so tiny in this big, vast, beautiful but black wilderness. Art was nearly beside himself with relief and excitement. The fact that they didn't even try to land shook us all up.

"What's the matter now?" we demanded of each other. Without some kind of constant communication, such as radios, successful rescues are very difficult and rare. All we had was a signal fire.

Ten o'clock. The only thing that had happened since the chopper left was that it had gotten darker and colder.

It was comforting and encouraging to know professional medical talent and attention was nearby, but where? We hadn't even heard them since the one flyby. Had they even seen the fire? If they had, why didn't they try to land? If they hadn't seen the fire, why weren't they flying around out there looking for us, like you read about?

By 11:00 p.m. Art was getting feverish and we were all very restless. Where was that helicopter?

Art took the last two aspirin we had at 11:30 and reminded me of my promise about the coyotes. There was a faint light beginning to glow in the sky to the east of us behind Wapiti Ridge. Slowly but surely the big, bright, beautiful, orange harvest moon began to grow above the 11,000-foot ridge that encompassed us. It seemed so clear and close one should be able to reach out and touch it. We watched in revered awe as it grew into its full roundness and bathed us in its beautiful terrestrial light.

Within 15 minutes we could hear the helicopter returning. So that was it! They had to wait for the moon to get high enough to illuminate the rescue area. Within a few moments they landed on a small plateau about 600 yards above us.

Soon Art's personal physician from Cody and another medic were at his side, checking his vital signs and administering the much-needed professional care so vital before he could be moved. They quickly replaced our makeshift splint with one far more adequate and strapped him onto a stretcher. By 12:15 a.m. the arduous assent to the chopper began.

The accident had taken place one-half mile short of the head of Burnt Timber Creek. We were on the north side of the drainage about 600 yards below the top of the ridge that intersected Wapiti Ridge, forming the main canyon. The climb to the little grassy meadow the helicopter landed in looked deceptively easy. Yet, in all my years of guiding and hunting that high country, there had been very few hunters that could make the climb in less than one hour. They were only carrying rifles.

The stretcher, heavily laden with an injured man and carried by four tired men in the dark, represented no small task. You could stand flat-footed, stretch your arm out and touch the ground with your fingers at eye level anywhere en route to the chopper.

On hands and knees we carried, pushed and pulled Art inch by inch, foot by foot, yard by yard over those boot-shredding rocks. No one escaped the cuts and bruises to hands and knees the mountain demanded as penance. As we struggled on above timberline our temples throbbed, our lungs burned and our rubbery thighs screamed for oxygen from the rarified 10,000-foot air. But the mountains ask no quarter and grant no quarter, and are as unyielding to men's demands as they are beautiful to our senses. It was 3:00 a.m. when the exhausted rescue team gained the plateau with their precious cargo. There was very little talk or exhilaration. The men were professionals and tired, and Art's condition was still very unstable. As soon as the stretcher was secured to the struts outside the chopper, they all disappeared into the night amidst a whir of flashing red and green lights.

Art's heart survived the ordeal none the worse for wear. He was on the operating table from 4:00 to 8:00 a.m., as surgeons gingerly inserted three stainless steel plates with 14 stainless steel screws to repair the shattered bones. They assured him that even though he was going to lose all flexibility in his ankle and that he could never hunt the mountains again, he was very, very lucky to be alive.

I wonder what they would have thought if they had seen him the next fall, hobbling up the sage brush draw behind our elk camp, taking pot shots with his old .30-30 Winchester at a camp-robbing coyote. He looked like Chester of that old TV western, "Gunsmoke."

Once the steel was all removed from his ankle, he regained about 90 percent flexibility and regained the ability to hunt and fish the mountains as well as ever.

There will always be a very special place in our hearts and memories for Thunder—the proud little half-Morgan, half-Mustang coal-black horse with the big heart.

He died that night.

A Lion For Henry

by Patrick Meitin

F eathery snow filtered from the woolly clouds obscuring Sherman Mountain from my view. I guessed it was just ahead, somewhere in the white yonder. I turned Popeye up a familiar ridge and toward home. We had been in the saddle since daybreak.

Wally, Blue, Ace, Chomps and Doxy all followed at the horses' heels in single file, with drooping tails, wandering little. One hundred yards behind, Henry's horse stopped to nibble from a dry sunflower weed, reins limp, hung over the saddle horn as the rider sat, hands in pockets watching the steed eat. I looked over my wet shoulder and under the felt hat, heavy with accumulated snow.

"Kick that damn horse! You're gonna spoil him, letting him do what he wants all the time. Let's go get something to eat!" I yelled back.

The hot meal of bacon and eggs inhaled in the morning darkness had long been spent. Shifting first one way, then another in the saddle had long since quit remedying the problem of a sore posterior, and my shoulders ached under the weight of a daypack.

Henry's lion hunt had started with a good omen. The much-needed snow, imperative to tracking the quarry, had arrived with him. Henry smiled from beneath his nicotine-stained moustache when I met him at the airport, saying that snow had followed him around the country this week. In his trips about the country on business, he reported snow in Cincinnati, Buffalo, Seattle, even Tucson. "It never snows there!" Henry said.

Henry was a big man, gray hair escaping from the boot-heel hole on the rear of his baseball cap. He showed his years only in the color of his hair and the erosion on his face. His teeth were white and straight. His handshake had a bite to it. His six-foot, stocky frame was simply clothed for a man who had entered the ranks of millionaire many years ago: worn blue jeans, a simple tan shirt, and red suspenders embossed lengthwise with "Oregon Farmer," which I thought strange for a man who lived in Vermont.

After years of guiding people, I had learned to pick out the hunting clients, and Henry Hunt had fooled my best instincts. First, I would consider where the hunter was arriving from. West coasters, with white cotton pants, fluffy striped shirt, deck shoes worn with argyle socks and a brand new felt safari hat, or an outfit of a pseudo cowboy, would head straight to baggage claim, nervous and fidgety. They would have a tan. Southerners would talk with everyone and smile. Northerners, with zip-up heeled boots, and sickly white skin from lack of sun, talked to no one, walked with purpose, weaved through the crowds hurriedly, without touching a soul or blocking another's passage. Any hunter, with the exception of the Californian, would be last from the plane, or nearly so. All would dress casually, while most other men their age emerging from the corridor might have on suits for business. One might notice the cameras slung over their shoulders or a more subtle hint, such as elk ivory or claw of some animal hung from a gold chain around their necks. All would inevitably retrieve a hard case safely carrying their bow or firearm.

Henry wore farmer's clothes and well broken-in hiking boots. He did not bring his bow with him, but opted to use whatever I had, a very odd trait as far as particular, fussy hunters go. He had flipped his luggage easily into the rear of the pickup, not allowing me to carry but the smallest carry-on. When I asked what he wanted to eat he said, "Anything at all," and continued to eat whatever was offered to him, at any hour of the day or night. He sat well in the saddle, although horses were alien to him, never complaining of a sore rump or aching knees. He always had an encouraging word when the lion spoor eluded us or the truck slid from the road and became stuck; always a joke when the ride ran long and darkness came. We hunted hard, slept fewer hours than we really wanted. Henry never lingered in bed, and I never had to wait on him in the morning. He shared his Cuban cigars, breaking one in two if he had only one in possession, and he shared his French cognac. I wanted Henry to get his lion.

Each day we had gone out in the cold of morning, saddling horses by lantern light, loading the trailer and driving on slippery roads until we reached our destination, or got stuck in the truck. Some days we rode out from the house, hoping to intersect the track of a ranging mountain lion, hoping to curb his hunger on a hapless mule deer. It snowed daily, indiscriminately, night and day, a foot one day then only a few inches the next, none of it melting during the cold days or freezing nights. We finally stuck the horse trailer in a snow-filled ditch, where it would have to stay until the snow ceased and someone could be hired to rescue it with a tractor. We rode out from the house each day, traveling larger, wider circles, but we had found no fresh tracks in the ever-deepening snow. Riding in darkness the sixth evening, talking very little, sensing my disappointment, Henry reassured me that tomorrow would be the day.

"Seventh days have traditionally been magic for me," Henry began. "Once, while on safari in Kenya, back in the 1950s when they had real safaris, we hunted greater kudu six days straight—didn't see a thing. The Kikuyu tracker said it was on account of the hyena dung he had found in the camp. He said that, according to old ways, if a hyena entered your camp and left its mark, a "thahu," bad luck or a curse or such, would follow. After the insistent urging of some of the native African blokes, and considering my desire to live life to the fullest—those were my younger days—we paid a visit to the local "mathanjuki," a witch doctor, African style. He charged me $10 to lift the curse. I paid him, because I thought he most likely needed it more than me. It was quite an affair, very entertaining. The old chap chanted hocus-pocus, rattled small horns, piled beans into little piles and so forth. He told me the curse was lifted and that I shouldn't sleep in my tent, but under the stars, to complete the purification. Hell, I couldn't take a chance after such a convincing ceremony—I slept outside."

"Did you get your kudu?" I asked, knowing the answer. For why would he go to the trouble of telling such a tale if there weren't a point to it?

"Well, I'll be damned if I didn't get my kudu the next day. Late in the evening my native hunter tracked down a great beast, which I took with one quick shot through the thorns. I forget where he goes in the books now. The white hunter with us said it was the best kudu he had seen in years—of course, I would expect him to say as much."

"Say, how 'bout we nip off to town tonight and throw back a few martinis!" Henry's voice was suddenly exuberant. "We've been going at this hard, boy, we need to relax. Get our nerves ready for tomorrow—the seventh day."

"Maybe look up the local mathanjuki!" I chuckled. "Sounds like a plan."

The town bar was full of cold, bored people that night. Unable to make the rounds to the farther towns, the local bar would have to do.

Henry was an immediate success with the local women, knowing the polka, and the jitterbug and the cotton-eyed Joe. He instructed the bar maid on the proper construction of a dry martini, and the drink became instantly popular with the town's folk, who thought a Corona beer exotic. Every rancher there invited us to hunt their spreads if we needed the space. We left town early, by mining town standards, and went to catch some sleep. We slept well, dreaming of howling hounds, lion growls and snow.

My eyes were open suddenly, before the alarm would have a chance to sound off, a habit formed after awakening at the same hour each morning many days in succession. I rolled out of bed to throw some fuel into the wood burner and put the coffee on. I could hear Henry sliding into his pants. The hounds, who slept in the house when hunting and during nasty weather, began to stir. Chomps walked into the kitchen yawning widely, looked up at me and wagged his tail.

"Looks like that pup's ready to go. Say, how do you like your eggs?" Henry asked digging into the fridge. "And say, here's some bacon, too. Might's well begin the day right. I feel good about today. I slept very well—for an old man. How 'bout yourself?"

"Yeah, I slept good, dreamed of lions all night."

Day number seven wasn't turning out to be the magic day we had been hoping for. The day had started out on a good note, with the skies semi-clear and still. We saw many mule deer while riding, some nice bucks, bouncing stiff-legged the way mule deer do when alarmed. Then we saw nothing. The wind picked up and the snow started again—big, sticky flakes that coated clothing and trees. By 1:00 in the afternoon Henry and I were wet, chilled and far from a warm place to rest. Once the dogs had opened on a track, sending our pulses into double time, but it was only the track of a bobcat and it was soon lost in the drifts.

We stopped for some hot tea and to build a fire to warm ourselves. I carried a light backpacker stove, tea bags, matches and tin cups for just such occasions. There is no better way to warm the body than from the inside. My knees were giving me pains anyway. We pulled up in a sheltered wash at Trujillo Canyon and staggered off the horses, every joint with a separate ache. Blue greeted Henry with a wet hound-dog kiss, and Henry roughed him around a bit, just playing.

The quick stop turned into an hour discussion on the current state of affairs in the local game department and its relations with guides and outfitters. We discussed ranching and trying to make a living at outfitting in today's world.

"I envy you," Henry said. "I would give it all up tomorrow to be out here day after day. The board would think I'd gone mad! I'm getting old

now and the money's getting to mean less. You spend your life building a fortune then have no time to spend it. But I'm in too deep to quit it now," Henry commented, his voice trailing off.

"Tough making a living out here these days," I said quietly. "Funny, everyone in town thinks I'm rich, doing nothing but playing all the time—wish it were true. We better get on with it," I said, looking into the sky at the big flakes coming down. "It's coming down thicker."

Sherman Mountain was growing larger now, the young rock column wreathed with low clouds—young only in geologic years. Pieces of Sherman Mountain lay tumbled in disarray at its base, as large as houses and trucks and compact cars. I wondered how many mountain lions Sherman Mountain had witnessed pass beneath its base over the past thousand years. The pockmarks in the trail ahead filled with snow, but gave away the passing of the ultimate predator. Instinctively I knew something was about to begin.

The thought barely passed my brain when Doxy threw her head up, sniffing at the air. Chomps, Ace and Blue attacked the ground where the smooth depressions dotted the whiteness, threw their heads up and proclaimed to the world they had found a lion. Wally and Doxy dove into the middle of the pile of hounds and completed the chorus. The track was smoking hot and the dogs headed up the hill toward Sherman Mountain.

"Grab a dog! Grab a dog! Grab a dog!" I screamed as I flew off my horse. "Doxy, come!"

"We've got a hot one here, old boy!" Henry said, grinning widely, dragging two hounds down toward the horses. "Just in time!"

"Do something with those horses. I'll get Doxy up there to make sure we get it going the right direction. Man, we've got a good one here—the dogs smell it in the air!" I shouted down the hill over my shoulder.

The dogs went wild at the ends of their leashes, howling like banshees. Henry chased Popeye down the hill, grabbing at the loose reins dragging behind him in the snow. Sambo stood still, watching the circus around him unfold, a veteran of many hunts, baby-sitter of dude hunters who were new to horseback riding.

In the powdery snow the depressions gave little hint of its destination, only that the lion did exist. We would have to rely on the instinct and razor-sharp nose of my number-one hound. Doxy stuck her nose into one of the depressions, powdery snow blown out with each puffing sniff. She opened loudly, jumping into the next depression, then bounded over the hill, screaming at the top of her lungs. The rest of the hounds were turned loose and the chase was on. We ran back to the horses, collecting leashes, hooking them around our chests like bandoleers, and tying the horses more securely to assure our ride would be there when we returned. We would go on foot into the wasteland below Sherman Mountain.

I fumbled with the knots holding the take-down recurve scabbard to the saddle. I bit my glove off, struggled with the knot, then retrieved my Fuma from my pocket and hacked the scabbard off. The saddle-leather scabbard that held the Bear Custom Take-Down was worn smooth on the side that rode toward the carrier's back, the suede rubbed off from too many miles of hound chases. In an attached pouch were six, newly-sharpened Zwickey broadheads and a half-dozen wood arrow shafts were shoved into a side slip. I handed this to Henry then ran over to my horse to throw a rain slicker over the seat of the saddle. The hounds suddenly began barking in a fevered pitch, higher into the rough and tumble at Sherman's feet. I hissed at Henry, holding my breath so I might hear a bit better.

"They've jumped the cat! We better get after it or they're going to loose us!" I said excitedly.

"That old boy must have passed while we where having a rest! Damn good planning on your part!" Henry spouted through a wild smile. "Let's get up there and have a look."

We made good time traveling uphill in the thin air of the high altitudes. The dogs barked steadily now, holding in one place just below the mountain. Each dog's voice floated down clearly: the chop of Blue's bark, Wally's long yowl, Ace's weathered howl, Doxy's piercing scream and Chomps...well, Chomps wasn't named Chomps by chance, he called his own name with each outburst. I began to worry as we rounded the top of a ridge and saw there were no trees in the area of the hounds. The sight shot adrenaline into my system and I ran ahead of Henry to reach the area. Lions bayed on rock ledges present a world of problems to an overly zealous hound. One could fall to its death trying to follow where only a lion can go, or be lured into a tight place and killed in ambush or any number of accidents that do not occur when the cat is safely up a tree. I caught sight of the dogs crawling in a maze of rocks, cliffs and water-carved chutes and caves, like mice in a wood pile. Blue barked from a ledge and God knows how he got there, Wally from another, barking into a hole. Chomps and Ace howled at the end of a blocked chute with 50-foot walls. Doxy was well off to one side dancing at the edge of another vertical chute filled with boulders. I went to her. When all else fails, I follow Doxy.

The area was a hellhole of rock and ditches big enough to hide a truck—well chosen by a cat that knew his territory well. Reaching Doxy I saw nothing but high ledges and jumbled rock. No sign of the cat. I took Doxy and began to circle the area, almost hoping the lion had slipped away from the maze. The snow surrounding the hole was clean and undisturbed, nothing had passed through. Henry had reached the area then and helped with gathering dogs. We let Chomps and Doxy loose and proceeded to search the area for sign of the cat. Henry had thrown the bow together and put the broadheads on the arrows, wearing the scabbard like a back quiver, the arrows sticking from the top. We crawled over the area like monkeys, descending into each dark hole, our flashlights throwing light into the corners, looking under rocks. Doxy again returned to the area where she was when I first arrived and barked into the darkness below. I hopped from rock to rock to investigate closer. Looking into the pit I saw nothing at first, so I climbed down the slippery chute to have a closer look.

The lion print in the snow patch atop the boulder was clear with sharp edges, but it was the only one. It was 20 feet below the ledge I was standing on and the only step into the floor below was another 25 feet. There was only a square-yard patch of light punching a hole into the darkness. I called to Henry and warned Doxy away from the ledge, as she looked over, ears dangling in front of her eyes. Henry arrived on the ledge looking down inquisitively:

"How in the world did you get yourself down there?" Henry asked. "You see the cat?"

"No, but I need you down here. You have your leashes?" I said, stopping short as I saw them. "I jumped down here, but it's a pretty good jolt. Hang over the edge, I'll give you a hand."

Henry threw down the bow and scabbard of arrows and turned and went to his knees. He slid over the edge on his belly. I reached up to get a foot and lowered him to within three feet of the ledge. I lost my balance and dropped Henry, grabbing at the chute wall to keep from falling, then grabbing the back of Henry's jacket. We hooked the dog leashes in a string and I harnessed myself in, looping one around my chest and under my arms.

"Lower me down, I'm gonna get in there and see what I can see," I said. Henry looked at me like I were crazy.

"Be careful down there—if that damn cat gets a hold of you, I can't do a thing about it," Henry warned.

The rope leashes cut into me as I was lowered, half-clinging to the rock, half-walking myself down. The snow where the lion track was imprinted was slippery and I straddled the rock when I got there, afraid of slipping into the dark bottom. There was a passageway beneath Henry that shot off into dark. I held my flashlight in my teeth to light up the empty crevice. I was able to wedge myself between the boulder, which had the track on it, and the chute wall and shimmy down into the darkness, my flashlight beam leading the way. I came to a short ledge 10 feet above the flat bottom and stopped to probe the darkness with my light. I looked up into the blinding slit of daylight 50 feet above to see Doxy, Chomps and Henry silhouetted, peering down at me. Henry's light sent a spark flashing occasionally from his outline. I reached down, slipping the loop of leather from the hammer of my .45 Colt Commander. Crawling to the low, undercut ledge above the bottom I stopped, hanging over the corner, peering into a recess going into the mountain.

The deep guttural growl that came from below my chin made my hair stand on end and my pistol appear in my hand without the thought crossing my mind. I rolled away from the edge, pistol in one hand and flashlight in the other, as the huge cat floated across the shaft of daylight on the floor, 10 feet away from my outstretched feet. The cat walked into the darkness of the mountain's guts and was engulfed by the blackness. The hissing and deep growls echoed from the dark recess as the cat met the end of the cave. The two green-gold embers of cat eyes burned in the rear of the black velvet hole as I aimed my flashlight down the shaft. I slowly crawled to the rock where the lions foot mark had been, watching my backside as I did so.

"I need to get you down here, I think there is just enough room to draw a bow!" I yelled up. The cat again voiced his disapproval of my presence, hissing in the amplified darkness. "Send that rope down!" I grabbed the dangling rope above my head and kicked my way up the rock face as Henry hauled me up.

"I saw him when he walked clear of the rock, he's a big fellow!" Henry exclaimed. Then he asked, smiling: "You sure you can get me down there without killing me?"

"Trust me!" I laughed.

He began tying the leash around his chest before I could begin to insist. He left his bow and arrows on the ledge next to me and slid off the rock backwards on his belly. I strained at the weight when he took the slack from the chain of leads. Setting down on the slick rock he slipped and nearly fell into the bottom, but was caught by the rope. I dropped the recurve then the arrows down to him.

"Here, catch this," I said, pulling my .45 from its holster. "Give me a minute, I'm coming after you." I found a corner of rock and hooked a loop of rope over it, jerking it to test its trustworthiness. "Hold on," I whispered to myself.

I repelled down the rock until I reached the end of the rope and hung, with my feet still four feet above the boulder. I dropped to the rock beside Henry and he grabbed my coat by the collar to help both his balance and mine. I flipped the rope several times until it finally snaked into the bottom, falling into a wad in my hands. Doxy whined and barked up top, wanting at the lion, or perhaps just worried of being left alone. I yelled at her, ordering her to get away from the ledge, but to little avail. The cat still growled from his dark hole in the wall. Tying Henry to the end of the rope, I again lowered him to where the cat and I had almost touched noses earlier, then handed down the bow and arrows. The cat screamed from the corner.

"It's a bit tight down here, old boy, but I think I can get one off," Henry yelled up. "But, damn, these are tight quarters!" he said again. "My God, that fellow's not happy, keep an eye out good man!"

Henry set his flashlight on a ledge pointing into the notch, setting the lion's eyes afire again. He knocked an arrow, drew until his elbow met rock, eight inches of arrow still protruding from the bow riser, and let the shaft fly. There was a solid, hollow crack and the cat went crazy in the hole. Henry saw lights again and set another shaft into the hole. Again there was a hollow crack. Then nothing. "I think I have killed the beast—there's nothing moving down there!" Henry exclaimed, after a quiet minute.

"Wait a while, that's not a place to be screwing around! Where'd you hit him?" I said, not looking at him, but watching the hole where the lion was.

"I think I took the critter between the eyes—he just went out with that last shot—his eyes, I mean!" Henry's voice echoed out of the bottom.

We waited for five or ten tense moments, minutes that seemed much longer than they actually were. I watched over the sights of my Colt, Henry over an arrow on a dented string. There was not a stirring from the darkness where the lion had been. The only sound heard was the faint howls from the hounds tied outside. Doxy and Chomps even quit barking momentarily. After a long wait, Henry shot an arrow into the corner of the recess. A hollow thud returned from the corner. "Did you hear that? The old boy is dead!" Henry shouted up.

"Wait a minute! Don't move, I'm coming down!" I said, urging the pistol back into the holster. I shimmied into the bottom, joining Henry on the crowded ledge. Shining the lights into the hole revealed only darkness; there was no sign of cat. We waited a few more minutes, listening intently, our eyes straining to catch movement in the velvety darkness.

"I guess you killed him, but damn I don't..."

"Lion—lion—lion!!!" Henry screamed, backing into me.

The following seconds went in slow motion. Struggling with the pistol, the lion growing larger as he came closer, I fell to my knees. I grabbed the .45 handle, flipping the hammer catch with my thumb at the same time. I pushed Henry into the rock wall at my left, the pistol coming up under his right arm. As the pistol jumped, blocking my vision for just a bit of a second, the lion stumbled to his chest. The lion regained his footing, coming again in a desperate rush. The .45 jumped again, the fire of the muzzle jumping half the darkness between the cat and the hunters. The cat fell on his back, pushed over by 350 foot pounds of energy from a 200-grain hollow point. The 160-pound cat lay still, 10 feet away, and winded his last sad bellow. My ears began ringing and Henry fought to remove a hot brass that had bounced down his shirt. The hounds at the top of the crevasse went wild, Chomps jumped to the first level. I ordered him to stay. My elbow was throbbing from being knocked into the chute side while drawing on the cat, and I slumped to the floor, rubbing the sore elbow.

"You shot him very pretty, chum!" Henry said smiling and sliding down beside me.

"Sorry I had to shoot your cat."

"Well I won't accept your apologies—that damn cat was going to have us for dinner, you silly bloke!" Henry scolded, although I knew he was being pleasant.

I noticed for the first time the arrow hanging from the great cat's neck and another nasty slice above the animal's left eye. I wondered what had happened to the third arrow. Crawling to the rear of the hole where the cat had hidden I found the arrow wedged into a tight crack in the rock. The odds of another shot like that were one in a thousand.

"Yeah, these Zwickeys are tough, man—to stick in rock and all!" I joked.

"Say, have you given any thought as to how we might get ourselves out of this damned crack in the rocks, old boy?" Henry quizzed, looking up at the slit of weak light.

"Somehow, I think we might manage." I said. "Trust me!"

Almost Dark And
An Empty Saddle

by Dan Cherry

L ooking back, it had been a long season—a long dry one. Dry in more ways than one.

The winter had been mild without much snow, even in the mountains, and that summer the rain just hadn't come. Not that Montana gets much rain anyway, even in a normal year. But that year the rain didn't even come in June or September, the only two times you usually count on it—if you can ever count on it in that country. There was talk of shutting the woods down for a while, stopping all logging and hunting until we got some rain or snow.

The hunting was tough, too, mostly because of the drought. Not that the critters weren't there; they just got tougher to get. It did seem like there weren't as many around most of the time. They didn't leave much sign, and no one could figure out where they had gone. The ones that were there stayed in the thick stuff close to water with little desire to leave and, dry as that thick stuff got, it was impossible for hunters—and guides—to stay quiet. It was a dry year for hunters all through that country.

We'd gotten our share, I guess—about as many elk as the other outfitters did. Even got one real dandy, the opening day 6x8 that Scatter had put his hunter on after chasing it around all morning. He'd get it to bugle once in a while, just enough to let him and his hunter stay with it as it moved its harem away. The big boy bugled once too often, moved his cows the wrong way and, the next morning, they packed him into camp.

We'd gotten a few deer, too—a couple of pretty decent bucks. Deer hunting had been a little better than elk hunting, with the mulies staying higher and more in the open. But even the deer seemed scarce that year. Good bucks had been relatively few, and pretty far between. Now we were down to the last day of the last hunt of the year.

Even the last hunt had been a long one. We'd finally gotten some snow, and this good cold snap had brought the elk out more into the open. One of the hunters got a pretty fair buck on the first morning out, so we cleaned and left it ready to pack, then got back on our horses to hunt elk. About a mile up country we crossed good tracks and left our horses tied in a lodgepole pine stand to trail the elk up the steep, rocky slope. It was mid-afternoon by the time we spotted the herd on a semi-open bench. My lead hunter saw them the same time I did, but, in the few seconds he took to turn and say so, a good bull had sensed us, jumped and taken the whole herd with him. We straggled into camp well after dark.

The second day was similar, and with equal results. A temperature of minus 16 degrees brought elk into the open to feed and to catch what warmth they could from the direct light of the sun. I spotted two five-point bulls and a cow bedded in a meadow three-quarters of a mile away. But as we worked in for a shot, three cows and a calf spooked and ran between us and the bulls, and our plans were thrown awry. The hunter tried a long shot, which fell short. We packed his buck into camp that night—again without elk.

The rest of the trip went the same way, just like the season had. The other hunters shot small bucks, and they glimpsed a few more elk, but, for the next six days, no one got a shot, or even a look, at a bull—not even a spike. The weather had warmed considerably, and the elk had become their reclusive selves again. They just weren't moving anymore.

We rode out that last morning hoping things would change and we'd get on something good. The year was wearing on, and migration would start any time. Kevin, another guide, had planned to take two hunters up-river that morning, and I took one downriver, hoping we'd catch something on the move. We said goodbye and good luck, and rode out for one final try.

We found fair tracks that led us to fresh tracks and, within a few hours, had knocked down a pretty good five-point bull—big enough that we could pack the head and cape into camp with the horns riding down on either side of the saddle.

Rather than let it freeze overnight, I would finish the caping in camp. Could have been there early, too, if we'd tried, and gotten pack horses and an extra guide to help. They expected us early, since it was the last day out. There were no extra days left for packing game into camp, so

anything we got we'd have to get by noon and be in shortly after for pack stock.

But doubling our tracks twice would be pointless, we figured. Since the bull had dropped near the trail and we'd pack out the same way tomorrow, the quarters could be picked up right there. So we did all the cleaning, skinning and quartering, which takes a while when you take time first to cape the unwieldy beast, and then dragged the quarters to the trail, covering them with pine and spruce boughs.

It was mid-afternoon when we finished the chore and went back up the ridge one last time. We had a rifle to retrieve, an elk head to pack and a four-mile jaunt back to camp.

I went and got our horses, rigged my riding saddle to pack like a decker and lashed the head onto my horse. Friday, the paunchy little imp of a gelding I rode stood still for the packing job, but, with just light nylon rope to lash with, I doubted how the elk head would ride.

Foaled on Good Friday—that's how they said my horse got his name. Friday really belonged to the boss' son, and he and some guides may have figured Bad Friday or Friday the 13th as the day of the horses birth. He was a good horse for packing, as long as the rest of the string stayed calm. But he'd been cut pretty proud when he was gelded—left with spunk enough to buffalo most of the herd and sometimes whoever climbed on him.

I had ridden out a few of Friday's crow-hops, but he'd never really tried to throw me. Scatter hadn't been so lucky. He took Friday hunting a few years back and, about the time they hit Blacktail Ridge, the cayuse started bucking. Bounced Scatter's binoculars into the rocks, shook his .338 out of the scabbard to boot—busted the stock when it bounced—then ran off for camp. Scatter had a three-mile walk to get him plenty steamed up.

I got Friday packed and we had headed toward camp for a couple of miles when Scatter pulled in behind us with a string of five or six horses. He'd been out on the trailhead most of the trip and was bringing in a load of hay. On the way he'd seen our pile of pine limbs marked with surveyors' tape, and said it looked like someone had gotten an elk. We told him it was a five-point and he congratulated the hunter.

When I led my horse around a bend, he got a good look at the head and didn't say much more, since he'd seen plenty of five-points before. We talked about hunting for the next mile and a half toward the tents.

It was getting on toward dark when we hit the cut-off into camp. Things were going fine until I stopped Friday 300 yards out and centered his load one last time. It happened that Scatter had Racket pig-tailed in the middle of his string—and if a horse in your string ever stepped over a halter rope, you could count on her being the one. She stepped over with a hind leg, of course.

A horse gets upset with a rope under its groin, and Racket tried to buck loose, which wasn't so bad except the whole string got excited. Piggin' twines broke, and the tail horse swung around and ran his packs into Friday. Being jabbed in the flank with a royal tine really can't be much fun, even for the most docile horse. And Friday wasn't the most docile horse.

A mountain horse usually heads toward camp when he's spooked or on the loose, since that's where he gets his hay and grain. And that's where Friday headed when he snorted and bucked, and his loosed lead rope slipped through my wet leather gloves. The nylon rope didn't hold, and he shook the elk head loose in the timber as he crow-hopped his way into camp. No doubt he flanked himself on the horns again and got frenzied up all the more.

Scatter and I got his string settled down, set the packs right and followed Friday, figuring we'd tend to the bronc when we got there.

We'd hadn't given it much thought, but, by now we were over four hours late, and the boys back in camp had been wondering where we were. There's no telling what speculation they raised as to why we hadn't come in, and nobody really said. But it had been a long, dry season and a long, hard hunt. Nobody figured we'd score; they figured to see us by noon.

We got into camp, unpacked the horses and pulled their saddles and pads. After graining the stock we put them in the corral and tossed out a few bales of hay. Everyone threw in a hand, and we made it pretty short work. I told the boss man we had a five-point quartered and ready to pack, and he seemed just a little relieved. We went out, found the head and dragged it in to be caped. Everyone's spirits were high.

When the work was all done and we sat down to chow, the details of our day's hunts were told. There were questions and stories, and the light-hearted banter that hunting partners share so well.

We heard their story too, how they'd waited and wondered about our whereabouts since noon. They said they heard Friday, all in a panic, come into camp on the run. He'd found the hitch rail that, for now, was his home and stood quivering, his reins hanging loose.

And maybe they were just razzing Kevin, since he was the new guide, and had taken their flack all trip long. But when he stepped through the cook-tent flap, they said, his eyes got a little bit white. Four hours late and almost dark, my infamous horse stood alone—snorting, frenzied and wild-eyed—while his empty saddle dripped blood to the ground.

Grizzly Attack

by Darwin Cary

E arl Boose, my stepfather, motored away from the riverbank as I slipped into the shoulder straps of my pack sack. The familiar pack felt good, not too heavy this time, containing only my down sleeping bag and a few personal items. From where Earl had dropped me off I had only a $2^1/_2$-hour hike into our fly camp on Charcoal Flats. There I would be joining my two guiding companions and our Stone sheep hunting party from Kansas.

The first half of the trail was the most difficult. It was a 1,000-foot, uphill climb. As I climbed, I stopped frequently to glass for sheep and goats. Quite often, I had seen rams in this area, but today saw only ewes and lambs. I continued to periodically watch the trail, well-traveled by horse and game. I noticed black bear, wolf and deer tracks all within a short distance.

I reached the height of land with little difficulty. On top, the trail plateaus out for about half a mile with meadows and moose wallows. Then the trail gradually descends off the mountain.

I was about $1^1/_4$ miles from the camp and making excellent time when I suddenly walked within 15 yards of the most beautiful blonde grizzly bear I'd seen in years. He looked to go about six-feet, six-inches and 450 pounds. He stood in the buck brush beside the trail watching my every move. I noticed his eyes were deeply set and that his ears perked forward. Unarmed, I continued down the trail.

Once one has spent some time in the wilderness and observed bears in their habitat, you soon acquire a great deal of respect for these power-ful animals. Throughout the years I've had several encounters with black and grizzly bears. Grizzlies, the dominant of the two, will often kill a black bear. With their great power, they have been known to carry away a carcass weighing double their body weight. With the speed of their blow they are capable of slicing open a 45-gallon steel drum. Once, dur-ing rutting season, I came upon two bull moose that looked as if they had been fighting. A sow grizzly with two cubs came along and I presumed had finished killing the moose; but she also charged us and the pack string, nearly succeeding in getting one of the horses. My hunter and I felt very lucky getting out of there unharmed. So you can see why I was concerned when I saw this beautiful bear.

I remained calm, but cautious. If one acts in fright or curiosity, bears will often loose their fear of man. I had walked a good 150 yards down the trail without looking back, when suddenly I heard the ground being torn up. I glanced back over my right shoulder and 30 yards back up the trail the grizzly was charging toward me at about 40 miles per hour. Ter-rified, I bolted for the nearest tree, a large jack pine.

As I jumped for the lower limbs, I felt the grizzly's teeth close around my right foot. Jerking it from his jaws, I continued to scale the tree for about 35 feet.

Scared half to death and in excruciating pain, I watched the griz climb the tree! These are the animals that aren't supposed to climb trees!

I contemplated jumping when the griz reached the upper portions of the tree, but realized I had a slim chance of making the 35-foot jump suc-cessfully, especially on one foot. I was sitting Indian-style, with my legs around the tree top, watching the bear climb closer and closer! The griz was hooking his paws over the limbs, using his wrists. He just wrapped his body around the tree for the last 10 feet. Suddenly, I was jerked from awe to realization when the griz snapped his jaws six inches from my kidneys. My buttocks hung just inches from his incisors! Fighting for my life, I stuck my left foot down the tree and repeatedly kicked the griz in the head. Every time I kicked him, he bit my leg. Screaming from pain and fright, I continued to fight. I could feel the flesh and tendons being pulled from my left leg. Weak from exhaustion and loss of blood, I couldn't hold on and found myself falling.

I landed on the pack sack which contained my eiderdown sleeping bag, and I am sure that is the only thing that saved me from breaking my back in the fall. I laid there, looking up at the bear, then noticed my watch said 7:12 p.m.

For the first few seconds on the ground I couldn't breathe. The wind had been knocked out of me.

Knowing I couldn't walk or run from the bear, I just laid motionless. "This is it," I thought, but instantly ruled that out, and repeatedly told myself the griz would leave me alone. The griz was slowly climbing down. I watched helplessly, continually telling myself he would leave me alone. When the bear was about 10 feet off the ground, I closed my eyes, not knowing if I would ever open them again. The last thing I remember hearing was the scratching of claws on the tree. How long I had my eyes closed I'd never know, but it seemed like forever.

When I opened my eyes I found myself alone.

Where had the griz gone and in what direction?

There wasn't any time left to waste. I looked at my left leg, feeling weak in my stomach. My whole left calf was gone, just tendons and flesh

hanging. Fortunately, it didn't appear to be bleeding extensively. Looking at my right foot, my heel was hanging and one-third of my sole had been ripped off. A large chunk of flesh was missing from the right side.

With over a mile to go, I thought I could possibly walk. Tearing off my pack sack and binoculars in frustration and hurling the glasses as far as possible, I tried to get up, but only collapsed. I tried again. No way.

With fear of the griz returning I started to crawl, knowing pain I'd never dreamed of. After crawling 10 feet, I collapsed. This went on and on. I'd gone maybe 50 yards and came across a stick large enough to use as a crutch. I tried to get up, but couldn't. Continuing to pull the stick with me, I found a second one, thinking for sure I'd be able to walk now. Crawling that $1^1/_4$ miles would be virtually impossible.

I successfully managed to pull myself up on the sticks. I took one step and collapsed flat on my face from the piercing, agonizing pain. Furious with fright, I discarded my walking sticks. I continued to crawl 10 to 15 feet and collapsed with fatigue. Knowing if I laid motionless for too long I'd never make it, I'd get up and go a little farther, another 10 to 15 feet, and collapse again. After a half hour, I decided I had better take another look at my legs.

The pain was unbearable, and why I hadn't bled to death, I'll never know. Deciding to wrap my legs, I removed a ball of twine from my shirt pocket. I also took out a note pad to write about what had happened when I thought, to hell with this, I'd tell them about it when I get there. So I pitched the pen and pad away. I removed my shirt and cut it up, wrapping it around my leg and tying it with the twine.

Once finished wrapping my legs, I continued on. I couldn't drag my feet because of the pain, so I crawled with them at a 90-degree angle. My knees started to ache and bleed. I tried to roll where the ground was clear, but I'd get exceptionally dizzy. I progressed on in fear. Every time a squirrel or bird moved, I jerked, fearing it was the grizzly, returning to finish the job. On and on, it seemed as though I'd never get there. About half a mile from the fly camp, I heard a horse. I contemplated catching up to it, but knew I'd never succeed. Horses are continuously on the lookout for wolves and, since I smelled of griz and blood, there was no chance they'd come near me.

I continued crawling over windfall and brush. A lifetime seemed to have passed by. I kept telling myself you can do it, you have to do it. But I kept thinking it would be five days before anyone missed me or passed over this trail.

My destination was the open face of a hill about a quarter of a mile from the fly camp. I could call out and from there I'd be heard. I continued on, still only 15 to 20 feet at a time. Just short of my destination I heard a coyote call. I have heard them before from the fly camp, but this one was behind me on the mountain.

I hollered "help" three times, and was out of breath. It was 9:20 p.m., and I had crawled for over a gruesome two hours. Having traveled over the trail many times I knew if help didn't arrive within 10 minutes I would have to proceed, which meant crawling down a very steep embankment, through a creek about 20-inches deep and 15-feet wide and up a gravel bed a couple hundred yards. I had my doubts about whether I would make it crawling through that icy water.

Within 10 minutes my two guiding companions, Stan Stewart and

Doug Zieffle, came to my aid. As they came up the trail I hollered, "Hurry up, the mosquitoes are eating me alive." They had been swarming all over like I was a piece of dead meat. The moment I saw Stan and Doug, my body relaxed and I started to tremble uncontrollably. They instantly put their coats over me. I briefed them on what had happened and Stan was immediately on the lookout for the griz with his .30-30 Win.

Doug went to the fly camp to get two horses, returning within 20 minutes. Taking Stan's .30-30 Win., Doug rode out for Sandpile to get help. By this time it was getting dark and riding back to Sandpile meant going back past the grizzly. There I was, shaking uncontrollably and reeking of griz and blood, and Stan was trying to calm a horse that has no love for griz and blood. Stan asked if I was ready, and hoisted me onto the horse by my belt. The horse didn't appreciate my predicament.

Hanging on for dear life, we started down the trail. My leg started bleeding profusely, and I was moaning in agonizing pain as the brush whipped against my raw legs. Stan lead the horse around as much of the brush as possible. Where the brush was extremely thick, he cut it away with his hunting knife. I found myself sliding off the horse as I was riding down the steep embankment, but managed to stay on by desperately clutching the horse.

At the bottom of the hill was a creek, and Stan started leading the horse through the water. Realizing how dry I was I asked for a drink. Using his hat he gave me two swallows, just enough to make me thirstier. Not knowing if water would help or hinder me, he only gave me a couple more swallows and proceeded on through the creek and up the gravel bed. At least here there wasn't brush to contend with.

Finally we reached camp, which consisted of two small tents. With Don's help, Stan carried me into the tent as Kitty and Anna looked on. They had arranged foam pads and sleeping bags upon which I was laid. I was in for the longest night of my life.

By this time I seemed to have lost track of time. Everyone did what they could to make me comfortable, even though we lacked the proper medical supplies. Kitty and Anna tried to comfort me with soup and cake to keep up my strength. Stan cut a clearing for the helicopter which we were expecting at daybreak. Don sat beside me most of the night as I was in and out of sleep.

Once Doug left, Stan rode bareback to Sandpile, normally a 2^1/2-hour ride, arriving there about 10:30 p.m. He immediately notified Earl, who tried calling Watson Lake then Fort Nelson on the single band radio, but he got no response.

This was the only means of communication with the outside world. Normally, radio communication is non-existent after dark, with the

chance of no radio communication until 8:00 a.m. Doug was instructed to ride to a neighboring outfitter who had an airplane, and could fly to Watson Lake at daybreak. Shortly after 11:00 p.m., Doug saddled his horse and started out on his 12-mile expedition.

Before long, Doug's horse lost the unfamiliar trail and became entangled in a swamp. Rather than try to fight the horse through the swamp, Doug got off, tying his horse to a tree, removed his .30-30 Win. from the scabbard and set out on foot with half the distance to go. He struggled through the night to arrive at his destination around 4:30 a.m. By 5:00 a.m. the plane was in the air.

Around 6:45 a.m. on August 10th the helicopter landed at Sandpile camp and picked up mother and Earl. Earl guided the chopper to the fly camp and, by 7:00 a.m., it was touching down within 50 feet of the tent in which I lay. As it was a small chopper, mother accompanied me to Watson Lake and Earl walked back to the base camp. I was then flown to Watson Lake where I spent $2^1/2$ hours, then on to Whitehorse. On arrival in Whitehorse, Yukon, I received seven pints of blood. I was there for three days stabilizing, then was sent to Vancouver General Hospital. After eight operations, including plastic surgery to both legs and six months rehabilitation, I'm back on my feet.

When Earl finished the fall hunt, mother and he came to see me in the hospital. We were trying to decide what caused the bear to attack, and both came to the same conclusion that he was just waiting for something to play with: at one time he had my whole foot in his mouth and, if he wished, could have smashed every bone in it. So when he came down the tree and saw me lying there motionless, he must have decided there was no more fun in playing with something not moving. During the whole ordeal, he never took a swat at me with his paws, which most bears do when they are fighting or mad.

The Prince's Tent

by Duane Wiltse

S uddenly the bodyguard burst through the tent flap, his black eyes flashing and his Colt .45 automatic leveled at my belt buckle. I stood stark still between the prince and his bodyguard, not daring to move.

It all began in the summer of 1973, when I received a discreet request to outfit an Iranian dignitary on a Shiras moose hunt into northwest Wyoming's Thoroughfare country.

The man's identity was to be kept secret because he would be traveling with only one bodyguard. But, I was assured, he was a world-class sportsman and he neither required nor sought special consideration. He was so tough and experienced, I was told, that he didn't even need a tent or a stove, and one pack horse would be more than enough to pack his gear the 35 miles from Eagle Creek trailhead to our camp near Bridger Lake. In other words, he was just a good ol' boy that was as handy as sliced bread and I'd be well paid for my services.

September is a beautiful time to be in the mountains. The streams are low and their gurgling, crystal-clear water beckons you to their banks for daydreaming. Deep, translucent pools entice you to fish for the prized cutthroat trout hidden there. The nights are crisp and studded with brilliant stars that remind one of exquisite diamonds showcased on a background of blue-black velvet. The melancholy singing of coyotes and the hair-raising challenge of bugling bull elk come drifting in on fragile air currents from miles away and echo just beyond the campfire's glow. One sleeps deeply in Wyoming's rarefied, September air.

Security is tethered to the musical tinkling of the horse bells. Even when the horses quit you, you are sure that you can still hear their bells. The days are bright with warm sunshine and full of promise. Powerful horses step quickly and excitedly beneath you, their heads up, nostrils, eyes and ears alert, receiving nature's messages carried on fragrant fall breezes.

Many people seek yearly renewal from these quieting yet strengthening experiences, and so it was that several of my hands insisted on making this hunt with me.

My cook, Red Arthur, was a man of medium height and frame, but with a head and face full of fire red hair and a nature and disposition to match. An excellent campfire cook, Red was a man who thought for himself.

Hansen Murray was a hunting guide of medium height and stocky build. A little older than the rest of us, Hansen offered maturity and experience, knowing the high country like a veteran hunter knows his favorite deer rifle. A man of impeccable manners, principles and reputation, Hansen made a highly successful hunting guide.

Horse wrangler Russell Tomkins was of medium build and height, but there was nothing medium about his horsemanship and horse-sense. The word "extraordinary" did not do Russell justice. He thought more like a horse than some horses I have known.

At 6 feet tall, 190 pounds and 17 years, Mark Wiltse was the oldest of my three sons, but still young and inexperienced. Mark was learning fast and loving every minute of it.

It was a two-day ride from the Eagle Creek trailhead on the Shoshone River's north fork, 50 miles west of Cody, Wyoming. Our route was to take us up Eagle Creek, over the pass, across the southeast corner of Yellowstone Park and, finally, down into the exquisitely beautiful, lush Yellowstone Valley where we would camp and hunt.

Two days earlier, I had sent Hansen, Russell and Red in with pack horses, grub and even tents, to establish a comfortable camp and to scout for moose.

Our objective was a large representative trophy for the national museum of the hunter's home country. The hunt was scheduled for 10 days, so while Hansen guided the prince, the rest of us planned to do the camp chores and to catch up on our trout fishing.

Mark and I were busily and naively saddling horses as we awaited the guest's arrival at the trailhead that fateful morning. Five riding horses were saddled and dozing at the hitching rail. I was adjusting the britching on the third and last pack horse, when I heard Mark say softly, "Uh oh, Dad. I think we're in trouble."

I followed his gaze to the overloaded, yellow Jeep station wagon that was inching its way toward us. Its rear bumper was grading in the potholes and ruts in the old dirt road that ended at the corrals.

The Jeep jarred to a sagging, sighing stop opposite us. Three men wearing crisp African safari clothing stepped out and approached us—the bodyguard, the Iranian prince and a loud American. The American introduced us, briefed us as to proper protocol in the presence of a prince and informed me that they had a lot more gear than could ever be packed on only three pack horses.

The Prince was of medium build and a tad short. He barely acknowledged us.

The bodyguard was big, very big, and he carried a Colt .45 automatic on his hip. He briskly marched up to one of the dozing saddle horses and began slapping the dust off the saddle with his noisy plastic rain poncho. He sure got all of the horse's attention!

The American was just plain medium, but diligently trying to impress and please the prince. He explained we were not to address the prince directly, but to convey all communication to the bodyguard first, and to refer to the prince as "His Highness." Under no circumstances were we to be in the prince's presence without the bodyguard.

"Hmmm." I thought to myself, "You may be right, Mark. This could prove to be a very educational trip for all of us."

While the guests were painfully deciding which one-third of the heavy gear we could actually pack into the wilderness, a forest ranger in a light green Chevrolet pick-up truck pulled in with an urgent message for me.

"Boy, am I glad I caught you," he said as he handed me a crumpled scrap of paper and curiously eyed the prince.

Hastily scribbled on the crumpled paper was a message from Hansen. "Make your overnight camp short of Eagle Pass," was all it said.

If I followed Hansen's instructions, our overnight camp would be far short of half way, resulting in a short first day's ride and a very long second day's ride to the main camp. But, getting a message to me at all required a great deal of effort on Hansen's part, so I figured it must be important. I reluctantly decided to follow his advice.

Earlier in the summer, Hansen had given me an old, green umbrella tent to use as a latrine tent in our elk camp during the fall hunting season. My plan was to experiment with the old tent on this trip and see if it would really work as a latrine. I didn't want to wait until I had a long line of urgent elk hunters to discover a snafu.

That day, we used the old green tent for a pack cover on the first packhorse and we tightened our diamond hitch around it.

When we rode into the first little meadow that afforded any grazing for our horses, the pass was still about an hour's ride ahead and the sun was about three hours from setting. I wanted to make a few more miles that afternoon and we had plenty of daylight to do it in. The big, stout, colorful Appaloosa gelding that I was riding was anxiously straining at the bit and throwing his head as he pranced around. His neck was bowed and he was trying to coax me to go on.

But, Hansen's message had been emphatic, and if I got over the top of the pass and for some unknown reason could not find enough grass to adequately feed my horses, they would suffer physically and I would suffer mentally. So, I signaled a stop and dismounted near a stand of tall, protected pine and balsam trees.

Shortly, the horses were unpacked, unsaddled, belled, picketed and turned out to graze on our little half-acre meadow.

Meanwhile, the three guests had been walking around on the carpet of pine needles, stretching their legs and enjoying the fragrant solitude.

The bodyguard strode over to where Mark and I were organizing our gear and covering our tack with pack covers.

"Where is the prince's tent, Duane?" he demanded.

Dumbfounded, Mark and I looked at each other. Several thoughts chased through my mind. We never set up a tent for ourselves for just one night on the trail. We had been told that the prince would live like the rest of us, that he enjoyed roughing it in spike camp. I should have suspected something when I was told a week before the trip to be sure to bring several gallons of bottled water for the prince because he wouldn't drink the natural water.

I had the old green umbrella, soon-to-be-latrine tent, but no sleeping tents.

With a poise and confidence that surprised both Mark and me, I stepped over to the musty old green tent and said, "Right here. We'll have it up for you in a jiffy."

"How does this thing go together, Dad?" Mark asked as we carried it to the flat spot that the prince had chosen to spend the night.

"I don't know. Hansen was going to show me when I got to camp. We'll just have to fake it," I replied.

No sooner had we gotten the prince's tent up than the bodyguard asked for his tent.

I was confused for just a moment again. There was plenty of room for four people to sleep in the prince's tent, even more if they were family or of the opposite sex, but as I began to understand my station in life as seen through the eyes of Iranian royalty, I tossed him a little orange pup tent. My kids played with that tent, but, because it had a floor and

zipped shut, I had brought it along to secure our groceries from mice and rain. Mark quickly set up the little orange pup tent for the bodyguard.

When Mark returned to the cooking fire that I was tending, he mischievously asked, "Where is *my* tent, Dad?"

A chunk of firewood glanced off a huge balsam tree as he ducked behind it.

The sun was setting the next evening when we rode across the marsh on the west end of Bridger Lake. As we approached a fork in the trail, a lone rider materialized from the darkening timber 60 yards to the right.

The bodyguard drew his .45 as Hansen met me at the fork.

"What's the matter with him?" Hansen asked, nodding toward the bodyguard.

"You haven't seen anything yet," I replied. "Why are you coming in from that direction?"

"Too much activity up on the other end. Something fishy is going on up there, so I picked a campsite back yonder in the timber. More privacy," Hansen answered.

A 15-minute ride through green-black timber brought us into a secluded meadow. Camp was a peaceful scene of grazing horses, two wall tents and a small, crackling fire that produced glowing coals for Red's excellent slit-trench style cooking.

The hands had figured that we would all sleep in one of the 12- by 14-foot tents and that the guests would all sleep in the other one, but the prince immediately claimed the empty 12- by 14-foot tent for himself. After making some disparaging remarks about not having a stove or a bed, he disappeared inside.

Hansen's eyebrows raised, but he said nothing as we set up the fine, old green umbrella tent for the bodyguard.

When supper was ready, the bodyguard served the prince in his tent and then retired to his own tent to eat in private, a practice they would follow for every meal of the hunt, except one.

After supper, the rest of us gathered around the cheery warmth of the campfire and brought each other up-to-date on our respective experiences of the last two days.

Russell reported that all of the horses were in fine shape—no sores or injuries from the trip and he would have several well-rested, well-fed horses saddled long before daylight to begin the hunt tomorrow morning.

In his typical, enthusiastic style, Red wondered what in the hell he was expected to do with the gallon of bottled water.

"The prince must have pure water to drink so when that gallon is gone, refill the plastic container at the creek for him," I replied.

The reflection of dancing flames in his eyes and the slight grin that parted his red beard can only be described as devilish.

I asked Hansen to explain the message that the forest ranger had delivered and why we weren't camped at our appointed campsite.

"Well," he said, "we stayed up there the first day and night, but there was a steady stream of people stopping by who wanted to see the prince. The Forest Service had even raked the area and cut and stocked some firewood. I understood that the prince was traveling incognito for security reasons and that area didn't look very secure to me, so I moved down here."

"The reason for the message," he went on, "was to save you the kind of grief we suffered at the hands of an over-zealous park ranger."

It seems that Hansen had camped at his favorite site just a couple of miles inside the Yellowstone Park boundary on the first night on the trail. It was raining hard, so the boys set up a tent. Just at dark, one of those people who works for the government "of the people, for the people and by the people" (a park ranger), on his way to his warm, dry cabin, stopped by and demanded that they break camp in the dark and rain and get off *their own* National Park property.

On the morning of the hunt, the horses were saddled and breakfast was ready by 5:30 a.m., but no hunter! At about 7:30, the bodyguard appeared and told us that the prince would want his tea first, hot and very sweet. Half an hour later a call for tea drifted out of the prince's tent and shortly thereafter came a call for warm water to wash his hair. Later still, he called for his breakfast.

Just before 10:00 a.m. the prince appeared, wearing crisp, clean, new Eddie Bauer duds with his .300 Wthby Mag. wrapped in protective oil skins and tucked under one royal arm. Now he was ready to stalk the cunning and deadly Shiras moose.

Because they had missed the first hours of daylight, Hansen requested sack lunches. That way they could stay out all day and at least get in an evening hunt, but the prince insisted on returning to camp at 4:00 p.m.

For four days we followed that same fruitless and frustrating routine.

On the fifth day, when Mark, Russell and I returned to camp with fresh cutthroat trout for lunch, we found Hansen saddling pack horses. That could mean only one thing. We gathered around Hansen to hear of the kill.

"Did he get a nice one, Hansen?" I asked.

"No, he's just a three-year-old with small horns," Hansen replied.

"I don't understand," I said, puzzled. "I thought the prince wanted a good bull for the museum."

"Seem's funny to me, too," Hansen said as he raised his sweat-stained Stetson to scratch his graying hair and squint into the sun, while measuring its distance to the horizon. "But I pushed the bull out of some willows and into the opening within 75 yards of the prince, and he put two bullets in his chest cavity, so I guess he must have wanted that moose. Let's eat some lunch and then all of us can go back up there. We have a lot of caping, quartering and packing to do yet this afternoon. Remember, they told us several times not to touch the trophy until they were through with picture taking. I haven't even gutted the moose yet. He is laying right where he dropped."

Hansen lead the way back to the kill astride his sorrel mare, Ginger. We were just coming up out of a boggy bottom and rounding some willows when we ran right into the three members of the hunting party. They were a mile away from the site of the kill.

"You'll never believe what happened!" the American exclaimed. Then they all started talking at once.

Shortly after Hansen left, they claimed, as they were preparing to take pictures, the moose suddenly sprang to life and raced off into the protective timber before anyone could do anything about it. Now they wanted Hansen to take them over by the lake, about two miles in the opposite direction, for an evening hunt.

We sat on our horses, eyeball to eyeball with the royal hunting party, momentarily stunned by their story.

"I think they're lying, Dad," Mark said softly.

"I think so, too," I thought to myself, "but how do I publicly call a foreign dignitary, a world class hunter and a guest of the U.S. government a liar, without creating some kind of international incident?"

Hansen broke the silence by agreeing to take the two Iranians to the lake. The American was to accompany Mark, Russell, me and the empty pack horses back to camp.

The creak of leather and the jingle of spurs was all that could be heard as we rode along the trail. Each man was engrossed in his own thoughts.

Two-thirds of the way back, I still didn't have a clear plan of action in mind, but I knew that I was going to start with that mousey American. He and I were going to have an understanding, by hell, and we were not going to leave a dead moose to rot.

Two strange horses were tied to the hitching rail when we arrived in camp. By the cooking fire, two forest rangers were having coffee with Red.

Before I could say anything to the American, the ranger began questioning me. Did we have a real prince in camp? Why hadn't we used the campsite that they had prepared for us? Where had we been for the last six days? When could they meet the prince?

The only information they had gleaned from Red was what was for supper and after about 30 minutes of double talk with me, they were convinced that they weren't going to meet the prince that day either.

As they rode out, the game warden rode in. I thought to myself, "Old Dave is good, but by God, he can't be this good. I don't even know where that moose is yet. What in the world does he want?"

Short and stocky, Dave rides a long-legged horse and gets up early every morning. Very little, if anything, gets past him.

After a casual, inquiring stroll around camp wherein he exchanged pleasantries with all the hands, he beckoned me over by his horse.

A stream of snoose juice exploded against a rock and was quickly followed by the question, "This old kid you're hunting, does he have a license?"

"You bet," I said. "A government permit."

More snoose juice. "You seen it?"

"Of course. Haven't you?" I asked.

"No, by hell, I haven't. The governor says it's none of my damn business who he gives those damn permits to." Two shots of snoose juice this time. "I suppose he'll be out hunting until well after dark," Dave said softly.

I nodded agreement.

"But, you've seen his license?" he asked piercingly this time.

"Yes, I have, and it is signed by the governor and everything," I answered.

After a little more thoughtful spitting and kicking dust, Dave swung into the saddle and reined his long-legged, well-cared-for horse toward the main trail.

"OK. That's good enough for me. I'll see you around. Good luck." One more spit before he rode out of sight and the evening shadows enveloped him.

Dave was barely out of sight when Hansen, the prince and his bodyguard rode in from the opposite direction.

Dismounting quickly and handing his horse's reins to Russell, Hansen said to me, "Come on, Duane. Let's go get some water."

The creek was about 40 yards from camp. Now, Hansen and I seldom pack water, but the seclusion of the stream accorded us our first opportunity to talk privately concerning the runaway moose. I was anxious to hear his thoughts.

"I'm sure that moose was dead, Duane. He certainly looked dead when I left him. Whatever you decide to do, we'll back you all the way to hell and back," Hansen said, concern showing on his weather-beaten face.

Hansen had confirmed my suspicions, now I had to act.

I had been studying the situation all afternoon and it didn't seem all that complicated. The man had killed his bull. He should tag it and take it home. End of hunt, end of story!

It is amazing to me how some people can complicate a simple solution.

The prince was startled and apprehensive when I entered his tent, uninvited and alone.

I was angry! Leaving an animal to rot while he hunted for a bigger one was going against everything I had been taught by my father about pride, sportsmanship and conservation, not to mention the fact that it was illegal and I could lose my hunting and outfitting livelihood for a long time.

I had been jacked around all afternoon by these foreign dignitaries, then the United States Forest Service and finally by the Wyoming Game and Fish Department, and now I was having trouble choosing my words carefully.

Looking the prince squarely in the eye, I blurted out, "I don't believe your story about the moose running away."

A long stony silence settled around us as we glared at each other.

The bodyguard was alone in his own tent. All of the hands were warming themselves around the campfire. No one knew where I was.

I heard Red call supper.

Finally, the prince broke the silence by stating evenly, "That moose is beneath my status as a world-class hunter. I can't take him home."

"I don't care if you take him home or not," I said, "but the hunt is over. Fill out your tag because we are packing everyone out of here tomorrow, including that moose. If you don't want him, I am sure that the hands will make good use of the meat."

Red called supper again.

"There are some other things we could do," the prince said loftily.

"Like what?"

"I could pay everyone extra to keep quiet about that bull and we could hunt until we find a bigger trophy," he replied.

I could scarcely believe what I had heard.

"There isn't a man in camp, including me, that would accept any amount of money from you under these circumstances. You would only insult us if you asked," I answered.

"Well then, I'll just order everyone to keep silent," he stated emphatically.

"That may work for you in the Middle East, but not here in the Thoroughfare," I shot back.

Suddenly the bodyguard burst through the tent flap, his black eyes flashing and his Colt .45 automatic leveled at my belt buckle. I stood stark still between the prince and his bodyguard, not daring to move.

Red disgustedly called supper for the third time.

The two Iranians spoke briefly to each other in their native tongue. Slowly, the bodyguard holstered his .45.

I breathed again.

The two of them were engaged in a lengthy discussion in their own language when Red's fourth summons to supper became obscene expletives. Red was just outside the prince's tent, and he knew nothing about the events of that afternoon. He was fed up with all the dawdling. Supper was ready and, by hell, he wanted it eaten while it was still hot.

Everyone was surprised to see the prince join us for supper around the campfire that night. Before we had left his tent, I had agreed to let the prince make a face-saving explanation concerning the end of the hunt.

Of course, the moose had started to sour, but we packed it all out anyway.

No pictures, no celebration.

Although the prince spent only one night in the old green umbrella tent, now, many years later, the latrine tent in each of our three wilderness elk camps is called "The Prince's Tent." And sometimes around the campfire, if the mood is right, our hunters will receive the answer to their query, "Why do you call the latrine tent 'The Prince's Tent'?"

In The Dark
Of A Bear Chase

by Judd Cooney

J erry and Sharron are the type of clients guides dream about booking. They come to the hunt full of infectious enthusiasm and every day of the hunt they get more excited. When they talk about being together, they mean *together*, whether it is going to a football game or sitting in the same tree stand waiting for a bear.

A pine squirrel visiting the bear bait to snatch a bite to eat aroused their excitment, so it was only natural that the gorgeous blonde bear that strolled into the small clearing really got their fires lit!

The tree stand in which they were sitting was one of my deluxe, permanent stands that is big enough for several people. Jerry was standing behind Sharron with the camera, ready to photograph her arrowing the bear. The bear didn't take long to get in the right position, and Sharron took even less time to get an arrow from her compound into the bear.

Instead of heading for the heavy timber in a blur like arrow-hit bears are supposed to, this bear jumped onto the tree by the bait, bawling and growling. He climbed up about 10 feet. He then jumped out of that tree and took to the one next to it, somewhat closer to the tree stand and repeated his act. All Jerry and Sharron could think was that she had really made the bear mad and he was looking for them. Jerry dropped the camera and tried to get his handgun out, only to see the bear finally disappear into the woods.

By the time I got to them, just after dark, they were about as hyper as two bowhunters could be. After hearing the story, I tried to pick up the blood trail, but could find very little to follow. In situations like this, I don't fool around; I have a couple of four-legged blood trailers that have saved losing countless wounded bears and can blood trail in the dark a lot faster than I can.

It didn't take me long to get my two top Plott hounds, a couple of eager, young dogs, and one of my guides on the three-hour-old blood trail. The dogs milled around where the bear was hit and then took off up a rocky ridge in pursuit. The plan was that I would follow the dogs and stay within hearing distance while my guide would keep my light in sight and watch out for Jerry and Sharron. As the chase progressed, the bear headed into some steep, oak-covered canyons and made a wide circle heading back toward the bait site.

Jerry and Sharron were struggling up and down the canyons in the dark, cussing bears, outfitters and oak brush that grabs everything that gets near it. They didn't realize the guide up ahead was keeping their light in sight and staying just far enough ahead to keep me in sight and the dogs in hearing. They had visions of spending the rest of the night wandering around, lost in the dark, so they were about to kill themselves trying to make time in the damnable oak brush and rocky slopes.

They were floundering up one particularly rugged, oak-covered slope with Jerry leading the way. He had Sharron's bow in one hand and the flashlight in the other. Sharron was hanging on to Jerry's belt to keep from sliding back down the slope.

Suddenly, Jerry let out a gasp and told Sharron not to make a sound. His gasping breaths and burning lungs were trying to extract the last bit of precious oxygen from the thin mountain air when he heard brush breaking just ahead of them. The wounded bear had obviously circled and was back-trailing himself right into their laps!

Jerry whispered for Sharron to hold tight as he dropped her bow and grabbed for a solid handhold on an oak limb. The snuffling animal breaking brush was almost on top of them so Jerry did the only thing he could to protect Sharron and himself. He grabbed the .357 Mag. on his hip! In order to get a hold on the pistol he had to let go of his flashlight, which rolled down the hill into the thick oakbrush.

This left them both hanging precariously from the limber oak bush, on the steep slope, with no footing, in the pitch black. Not the best of situations when you are about to be run over by a wounded bear. Jerry thought that by keeping quiet the bear might pass them in the dark, but suddenly it was on him. The furred nemesis hit him smack in the chest, almost making him lose his grip and sending them all tumbling into the canyon.

Fortunately, before he could get a shot off from his .357 Mag. in self

defense, Troubles, one of my young hounds, licked Jerry right in the face, and thereby saved his own life!

Once Jerry and Sharron got their tongues unstuck from their gullets and their hearts out of their throats, both of them and their new-found friend struggled to the top of the hill to continue the chase.

The dogs had trailed the bear nearly back to the bait before they treed it in a Ponderosa pine. Jerry and Sharron were almost back to normal by the time they found me, sitting under a nearby tree, contemplating the lot of outfitters in general and me in particular. As they plopped down in the pine duff by me I casually asked, "Sharron, what color was the bear you hit?"

"Oh, it was a gorgeous pale blonde that almost glowed when it walked up to the bait barrel," she bubbled with her normal enthusiasm.

Without saying a word, I turned my powerful light into the branches of the tree 30 feet above the bawling, baying hounds and lit up the good-sized *black* bear perched comfortably on the limb. Somewhere those two blankety-blank bears had switched places and we had chased and treed the wrong bear! We left the bear and tried to get the dogs back on the trail without success: they knew where the bear was and weren't about to leave it alone.

Later, Jerry's photo showed Sharron's hit to be high on the shoulder with little penetration. Within a week the "gorgeous" sneaky, double-dealing, blonde bear was back on the bait, eating free groceries and Jerry and Sharron were back home, regaling their neighbors with tales of bears attacking in the dark of the Colorado night.

"I Got Ammo! I Got Ammo!"

by Walt Earl
as told to Dan Dietrich

T here's a reason why I carry a .357 Mag. Whenever I guide one of my big game hunters, especially bear hunters, I pack a double-action Smith & Wesson in an accessible shoulder holster. A few years ago, I didn't.

In the early 1970s, I worked as a full-time government trapper and part-time big game guide. Base camp was located near Horseshoe Bend, Idaho. Out West, we hunt black bear just after they climb out from hibernation. The ravenous bruins are active in their search for food and their thick winter coats are yet to be rubbed.

In 1971 I had a bear hunter from Pennsylvania with me. I'll call him Joe. He wanted to take a black bear with his .44 Rem. Mag. handgun.

Joe had been in camp a couple days when a rancher called to say he had a sow bear killing his sheep. She had two cubs, and the rancher said he had already lost 15 sheep. That thieving streak marked this trio of bruins for extermination. As a government trapper/hunter, it was my duty to put an end to the rancher's loss of livestock.

I loaded four trail and tree hounds into the truck, and Joe came along to lend a hand. Joe strapped his .44 Rem. Mag. to his hip. I brought along what I always carried back then, a Ruger .22 Win. pistol.

We drove to the rancher's property, and parked the truck about a quarter mile from the sheep's "bedroom"—the place where sheep rear their young. The dogs were already excited and when their noses hit the ground they were hot on a trail. We took off in pursuit.

Back then, I had four hounds that I used in my work for the a government, and for hunting black bear and mountain lion with my clients. With me that day were Rocket and Sue, two redbone hounds; Rain, a Plott-blue tick cross; and Six Pack, a Walker-blue tick cross.

The four hounds followed a scent trail down past the sheep's bedroom and into the woods. Not far into the woods was a scattered pile of bloody sheep carcasses. The dogs were fast on a trail. From their anticipation and barking, I figured we must have surprised the troublesome bruins feeding on the carcasses.

No more than a half mile from the bedroom—three-quarters of a mile from the truck—the dogs treed two cubs. The sow went down into a patch of thick mountain laurel and hawthorne.

Putting an end to this marauding sow that was jeopardizing a farmer's economic livelihood would be tough. I didn't want to climb into the brush after the bear with a .22 Win. pistol, nor did I want to send this Pennsylvanian into his first close-quarters fistfight with a black bear.

Looking at the situation, we decided that the only way to bring the sow into the open would be to take the two cubs first. We decided that I would take the cubs with the Ruger .22 Win. That commotion, we hoped, would bring the sow out from the thicket. We agreed that Joe would bag the sow with his .44 Rem. Mag.

I pulled up my Ruger .22 Win. pistol and dropped one cub, then the other. The ruckus brought out the offensive side of the old sow. We could hear her fighting off the dogs with greater vengeance as she tried to get to us.

As we planned, Joe pulled his handgun from its holster, but then his face turned as white as an eggshell.

He looked at me. "I didn't load up!" he yelled. "The ammo's in the truck!" With that, he spun and sprinted up the hill. Seldom have I seen a flatlander move that fast!

As Joe skedaddled for ammunition I heard the sow crashing through saplings on her way out to greet me. The dogs were boo-barking and I knew that wasn't good. It meant that she had scared them good, and that they were now keeping their distance.

Holding what now felt like an adolescent's pea-shooter, I looked around. There was a fallen pine tree nearby. It was about $4^{1}/_{2}$ feet in diameter and about 80 feet long. It angled uphill. I ran over to it, jumped up and with arms outstretched like a tightrope walker scurried uphill to the farthest end. Near the end, a small spruce had grown up alongside the fallen pine; its delicate branches reached out and over the pine. I crawled behind that thin, green barricade and waited.

The sow charged out from the woods with the hounds 30 to 40 yards away. She went first to one cub and smelled it. She knew something was

up. Crossing my path, she charged over to the second. After sniffing it once, she lifted her head and swayed from side to side, looking for the culprit. I didn't move, and she didn't see me.

She went back toward the first cub and stopped where I had been standing when Joe had made his decision to take leave of this place. She put her nose to the ground and followed *my* trail straight to the fallen pine. She climbed up and walked straight down the trunk toward me and my pea-shooter.

Her head swaying, teeth popping, I held my shot. From behind the flimsy barricade of twigs, I took aim on her throat, and yelled for the dogs to take her. They moved closer, but didn't answer the challenge.

She stood 20 feet away, with all her attention focused on my throat. I had, in a way, brought a knife to a gunfight.

With eight rounds left in my 10-round clip, I pulled the trigger with my sights on the swaying bruin's throat.

One. Two. Three. Four. If anything, those rounds just angered her more.

Five. Six. Seven. Eight.

Click...

On the eighth shot something happened. Rocket, that old redbone hound, charged up into the bear, sinking his teeth into the sow's side. They both went flying from the log, claws flying and teeth snapping in midair.

I popped out my empty clip, and smacked in my only other clip. It had 10 rounds. As the hounds battled with the enraged bruin, I wondered what in the hell was taking Joe and his hard-hitting .44 so long.

The sow shook off the dogs and again charged toward my tree. I started popping her again as I heard Joe crashing down the hill. "I got ammo! I got ammo!" he yelled.

In words that shouldn't be printed I encouraged him to move his fanny a little faster.

Running on adrenaline, and that which separates a wild from a tame critter, she came at me fast. I yelled for the dogs and continued to pop her with my little .22 Win. In the background I heard Joe yelling, "Should I shoot her? Should I shoot her?"

There wasn't time to answer as I continued to send tiny bullets into the sow's throat. Again there was a collision as Rocket dove up into the sow. This time Sue was at Rocket's side and they both collided with the bruin. Teeth and claws and tails flew about as the trio tumbled off the log. My Ruger was empty.

With two dogs on her tail and more than a dozen rounds into her hide, the sow carried the battle into the hawthorne thicket.

Joe, a bit winded and adequately excited, came crashing to the tree. "I got ammo!"

We listened to the battle that Rain and Six Pack had now joined. In a short while it was over.

With a loaded .44 Rem. Mag. in his hand, Joe and I walked into

the thicket toward the dogs. We found the dead eight-year-old sow, and counted 14 holes in her hide. Most were scattered on her nose, head and front legs. One had traveled all the way back to her ham. We found two bullets that had reached the vitals and done the job. It was then that I decided to carry a Smith & Wesson .357 Mag.

As big game hunts sometimes do, this one had a happy ending. I was able to keep my hide intact and, two days after this experience, Joe bagged his own beautiful black bear with his .44 Rem. Mag. But I haven't seen the Pennsylvania handgunner since.

Second Chance Ram

by Bill Butler

C onsistently successful trophy bighorn hunters in Montana's rugged Beartooth Mountains strap on an organized, well-equipped backpack and head up the trail. This is not everyone's cup of tea. Hunting trophy bighorns this way is not the easy way.

The Beartooth Mountains have 23 peaks over 12,000 feet elevation; peaks of raw, jagged granite; glaciated valleys; high-hanging cirques; head walls 1,000 feet high; wind-blown plateaus; beautiful, emerald green lakes and ominous weather.

The Beartooths have never been known as an outstanding place to hunt bighorn rams. The country is extremely rough and there are not many sheep. You have to know which particular mountains to hunt and when to hunt. The better rams stay in the roughest country and winter on open, wind-blown plateaus at 9,000 to 10,000 feet. They come out to the low canyons where the ewes, lambs, and young rams winter, only to eat the fresh green grass of spring. Soon they are gone to the high country again.

I have killed five trophy rams here myself; three full curls, a seven-eighths curl, and a four-fifths curl. I have guided hunters to many more. I have been hunting these big rams since I was 18 years old.

Bob Housholder of the Grand Slam Club featured me in his newsletter one year. Soon afterwards I got a call from a hunter named Chuck—the last name doesn't matter here. He was from Minnesota, and he wanted to get started on a Grand Slam of North American wild sheep.

Wanting a bighorn first, he would be starting with the most physically difficult to hunt. It's more difficult to obtain a desert sheep license, but it usually proves to be an easier hunt.

We agreed on a price, he sent me a deposit and we set his 10-day hunt for early October. I told Chuck that a bighorn sheep hunt can be awfully rigorous and sometimes dangerous.

"The bad weather and big storms, like the equinox storm, or changing the season storms, can be extremely ominous," I advised. "They use to scare me when I was younger—big dark clouds, blizzards. Some years you get chest-deep drifts. Now I just set up a good camp and let 'em blow. Anytime before the middle of October, I will sit them out. They usually melt off and then you have an Indian summer for about a month. It is dangerous to hunt way back in the Beartooths anytime from mid-October on. There is always the chance of getting hit by really bad blizzards. If it gets too bad, we'll have trouble getting a bighorn ram which must have a three-quarter curl to the horns to be legal."

Hunting in early October instead of September usually gives you a better chance at a ram, because many of the sheep summer in Wyoming and are drifting toward the winter areas by early October.

So that Chuck would know what to expect when he got to Montana, I explained a few things about hunting bighorn sheep in my area. "My sheep hunting method calls for many miles afoot and plenty of hours glassing the slopes with a spotting scope. The main limitations to getting a ram is the miles you can cover. But the country is so rough that you can walk within a quarter of a mile of them and not see the sheep."

I shared with Chuck that I hunt slow and, from experience, know where to look for sheep. "Sheep will stay in the timber more than you think they will," I said. "People think of them up in the cliffs, but they are usually out on grassy slopes or in the timbered pockets. Our only link with the rest of the world will be a portable radio, to try to get weather reports. We will hunt out of a progressive camp, moving every day or two and hunting through the country. Freeze-dried food will be our menu and sometimes water might be in short supply."

The Beartooth sheep hunting districts are unlimited areas, meaning that the Montana Department of Fish, Wildlife and Parks can sell as many permits as there are people that want to hunt, and then close the season on 48-hours notice when the kill quota is met. This is a good program, because only a few sheep hunters are going to go after the rams in the back country. Many will buy a license, go up a mountain for a part of a day and never go sheep hunting again. Because of the roughness of this area, this is about the only way to get an adequate harvest. This type of hunt affords everyone who wants to hunt sheep the opportunity.

I told Chuck, a man in his 30s, to start jogging and get into the best physical condition he possibly could before fall.

That summer, I was at my home one day working with some rodeo bulls when Chuck showed up unannounced. He said he had been running a couple of miles every morning and had just decided to drive out, talk to me and look at the mountains that we would hunt. We talked a couple of hours and then I gave him directions to the mountains near where we would hunt so he could look around for a couple of days, camp and fish some. This he did and then returned home to finish his physical and mental preparation for our ram hunt.

I had one hunter, previous to this, that had come out to hunt. He paid his money for the 10-day hunt in full, but wanted to fly over the hunting area first, before we started in. A local pilot took him up in a Super Cub for a couple of hours and, at my instructions, flew him around over the hunting area. When the hunter got back on the ground he looked like he had seen a ghost. The vastness and ruggedness of the mountains scared him out. He said he had changed his mind and would just fish and do some photography around my place. He said he had a bad knee and did not think it would hold up in the rough country where we had planned to hunt. I tried to talk him back into the hunt, but to no avail. He fished a few days and then went home.

The autumn day for which Chuck had trained and eagerly waited finally rolled around. I met him at the airport in Billings. We had a good meal at a nice restaurant, what I call the "last supper". We then drove to my place and I had him empty all of his gear out on the floor in my living room. My backpack packed already weighed 60 pounds, and I still had some extra food to go in his pack. I had all of the camp in my pack: tent, fly, stakes, poles, stove, air mattress, medicine, first-aid kit, food, radio, spotting scope, flashlight, extra batteries, rain gear, cold weather gear, etc. I asked Chuck to leave anything that was duplicated at my house.

He went through his gear and I helped him pack his backpack for balance and convenience of access. We left nonessential gear. His pack was about 40 pounds. We got a good night's sleep and were on our way early the next morning.

On a previous hunt, I had seen two huge rams in a real jagged piece of real estate, a hanging meadow up in the cliffs. They were both record book rams and they both got away. Once I showed the rams to the hunters, they ignored my instructions and decided to make their own stalk. They were both self-important executives who thought they had a better way than what I offered. I watched as they botched a stalk and scared the rams out of the area.

I wanted to take Chuck back to this area to see if we could get one of these rams. We parked at the end of the road and set out for the high country. It wasn't all that far to where we wanted to hunt, less than 20 miles by the way we had to go. We followed a trail up the main canyon about nine miles, and then climbed up a very steep slope for less than a mile. The incline was as much as 70 degrees in places. We broke over into a beautiful basin at the foot of a high alpine peak of over 11,000 feet elevation. There were two small lakes here that did not contain any fish. There was some timber cover near one of the lakes that would make a sheltered camp.

I knew the place well as I had camped here before and had a hunter kill a fine, full curl ram here a few years before. The basin was empty of sheep now, though. The sky had a few clouds as we made camp, cooked supper and readied for the night.

In the middle of the night, a strong wind started, whipping the tent and protective trees around us. Then the first hard pebbles of snow hit us. The snow came heavily and the winds were blowing 60 to 70 miles per hour. I have a good tent, fly and poles, and was not worried. I turned over and went back to sleep.

The next morning, the sky was still overcast, but the snow had slowed. There were deep drifts, but only four or five inches of snow so far. We ate breakfast and secured some firewood in case of an emergency which, to me, would be if the storm kept up for several days.

I glassed the talus slopes of the basin and spotted three sheep, a ewe, lamb, and a one-half curl ram. They had come in during the night from one of the surrounding basins.

This had happened before on another hunt, but the rams were bigger the time before: we had gone to sleep with no sheep in the basin and when we awoke, there were two full curls and a three-quarter curl grazing on a grassy slope at the head of the basin. That time, we killed one of the full curls after a half-day stalk that took us out of our basin and back around on top of the rams.

Chuck and I waited out the storm all that day, spending our time glassing, eating and talking inside the three-man tent. Two large men and their gear in a three-man tent is somewhat crowded, but we had plenty of food, good survival gear and good sleeping bags. We did not make a fire; I almost never do when I am hunting because it is very unnatural and could spook game. I try to blend into the countryside like one of the animals when I am hunting.

Because we slept on and off throughout the day, we awakened many times during the night to hear the steady pelting of snow on the tent.

The dawn was gray and dreary, the same as the day before. We ate and Chuck went out to glass near camp. The cloud ceiling would raise

and lower allowing, at times, pretty good glassing of the basin we were camped in.

Chuck had been gone about 15 minutes when he came back into camp very excited. He said he had spotted a ram and wanted me to see if it was of legal size to shoot. I glassed it and discovered it was the same large half curl that we had seen the day before. I soon spotted the ewe and the lamb in a rock crevice a few hundred yards away. I glassed the basin for about an hour and found nothing more.

The storm quit about noon, and the sun broke through the clouds in places. We hurriedly packed up the camp on our backs and started up a very steep talus slope at the head of the basin. We climbed for 1,500 feet and got up in the clouds as we crossed the knife-edged ridge to reach another canyon that headed up against this same peak.

The snow had drifted over the rim and was corniced on the far side, a dangerous situation. Since the snow was fresh, I hoped that there would not be enough to cause an avalanche. There was a snow slide area that we were looking down, and I knew we had to go down it. We got over near the edge of the slide area where there were some larger rocks that angled out and away from the snow chute. The rocks were not part of the avalanche chute, and were solidly set into the mountain. They were extremely uneven, jumbled and slick with fresh snow. The avalanche chute next to the rocks was relatively smooth, with about one to two feet of fresh snow cover.

I planned for us to climb down the avalanche chute next to the large solid rocks. If an avalanche started, we could climb onto the larger rocks across from us to escape the devastating path of the rushing snow. I stared down the 1,000 foot chute a moment while I silently talked to my God.

"No guts, no glory," I said to Chuck as I burst through the snow cornice above the rocks on the side of the chute. We struggled through the deep snow on the jumbled, but solid, side rocks. We were climbing down backwards on the slick rocks on all fours. Some snowballs rolled down the chute next to us, but would stop quickly in the soft snow. The going was painfully slow on the rocks. I slowly inched my way onto the edge of the avalanche chute and stared down. I climbed carefully, ever cautious with total respect for the raw power I knew the mountain could unleash at any moment. Chuck was close behind me. We stayed only one quick spring away from the safety of the large solid rocks on the edge. We were far above the timberline now. The sky was becoming heavily overcast again and snow was starting to drift gently down upon us.

I could see down the canyon ahead of us as the clouds started to settle in. It was a beautiful sight, even though we were in a tense situation. We had not seen anyone else since we had left the vehicle. We were in an area with no trails and no lakes with fish in them, and there was little reason for people to get into this rough area. I had never seen another hunter in this area.

One misstep now and we might never be found. There had been others who ventured into these mountains to never be seen again, some even were lost in the summertime.

I took a real good look at the terrain ahead of us, and to our left at the base of the slide. I wanted to know exactly where to go from memory, especially if the cloud cover came clear down around us, making visibility extremely limited. I took a compass reading from where we were and planned our path ahead of time in case the sky did fall.

After what seemed like an eternity, we neared the bottom. I handed Chuck my camera to record the moment. The disappointing picture later was not quite as intense as the actual situation had been, since it showed me with a backpack on a totally white background.

Once safely away from the avalanche chute, we quickly walked to the head of this new canyon, a distance of maybe half a mile. We planned to go up through a narrow pass into the head of yet our third canyon of the day. As we came to where the canyon headed up, we quickly saw that the area was full of house-sized boulders, tumbled one on top of the another like a bunch of toy blocks loosely thrown together.

We methodically picked our way through this mess of oversized granite rocks that had peeled off both sides of the narrow cut. Some huge boulders would start to tilt as we would walk out on them, and we quickly retreated the way we had come to look for a different pathway.

We were getting quite weary as we left the last of the large rocks behind us. The ground now sloped down this new canyon toward timberline and another small lake. The incline was not as bad and it was a relief to step out and walk faster.

Darkness was gathering as we reached the welcome shelter of the timber surrounding the diminutive lake. We quickly set up camp and started supper (to call it dinner wouldn't have been appropriate).

We needed to eat a hot meal and get in our warm sleeping bags. Hypothermia was starting to set in as it usually did that time of evening, because of our wet, cold, hungry and tired condition. Your thinking becomes muddled when you get hypothermia and, knowing this, I always do my camp setup and cooking in the same routine. It is easier this way, even if you are slightly hypothermic, because you don't have to think as much.

I always wear wool outer clothing in the mountains because it is warm even when wet. I have rain gear if the weather gets too bad.

We had dropped quite a bit of altitude and the snow was not falling at this lower elevation. We had hardly spoken for the last several hours and, after a welcome warm meal, conversation was kept on hold as we quickly went to bed and to sleep.

By the next morning the snow had stopped altogether and the sun was peeking through the scattered clouds.

We were well rested because the nights are long when you sleep from dark to daylight. There is not much else to do at night but sleep. If you are not sleepy, you talk as long as you can, awaken a couple of hours before daylight, get up in time to eat and be ready to hunt by daylight.

The canyon we were in now was very narrow and deep, and ran approximately north and south. The sun would only shine on the canyon floor for a few hours each day causing the air there to be generally cold.

We climbed up the west wall of the canyon to a small basin, and we found some sheep beds there. This was where the two extra-large rams had gotten away from my previous hunters the week before. There were no sheep here now, though.

The sun had gone behind the ridge above us and the air was cooling quickly even though there were still three hours of daylight left.

There was a bunch of fairly large boulders at the bottom of the talus slope. We had glassed for several hours without spotting anything, so we ate some candy bars and decided to strike for camp as soon as we finished. We were getting extremely cold from sitting still for so long while we glassed. I heard some rocks rolling and started to search the horizon for movement, and I spotted two sheep that had just cleared the rim and were traveling fairly quickly down a finger ridge toward us. I pointed them out to Chuck, and he turned quickly to hide himself behind the boulder we were sitting on. Even at 400 yards the rams caught his movement. They stopped and stared in our direction. The largest ram was about a four-fifths curl and the other one was just short of a three-quarter curl. They moved over behind some boulders and stood looking at us with just their heads showing for two and a half hours. I studied them with the spotting scope set on 60 power because there were no heat waves to distort the view.

Darkness was approaching and we had to make a decision. I asked Chuck if he thought he could hit the ram at the 400-yard distance with his .270. I told him we could take the chance of finding the rams again tomorrow. He was shaking from many hours of cold and inactivity but wanted to try a shot because the sheep had seen us and might leave the area that evening.

He could see the head, neck and shoulders of the larger ram. He got as good a hold as he could in his cold, shaking condition and fired. He missed, undershot, and the rams started up through the rocks in their hobbyhorse gait as they jumped from rock to rock. The rams soon went over the rim and out of sight.

After missing the long shot, we dejectedly made our way back to the bottom of the basin and camp. It was dark at the bottom when we got there, but we heard some rocks falling from the top where there was still some daylight left. I got out my spotting scope and turned it on 60 power. Several hundred yards down canyon, on the other side of the finger ridge that the sheep had been on earlier, were the two rams. I had Chuck fix supper while I watched the rams until full darkness. I then locked the scope into position on its tripod, hoping to pick the sheep up at the same spot at first light.

The night went quickly and, as the light was just gathering the next morning, I was watching the ridge through the spotting scope. As the light brightened the area enough to see, I could make out both rams, lying in the same spot I had left them the night before.

I had Chuck fix breakfast while I kept a constant vigil on the two sheep. At about 9:00 a.m., the rams laid down for their morning naps after they had fed for a couple of hours.

There was still some snow on the ground so we put our white longjohns over our clothes to use as snow camouflage. We did not want the rams to see us two days in a row. The rams bedded on a small bench with some stunted pine trees for cover.

We climbed the steep slope slowly and carefully, pretty much in view of the sheep at all times. It was the only stalk we had because of the steep cliffs on each side of the sheep. When we reached the bench where the bighorns had been lying, they were nowhere to be found. Thinking that the sheep had climbed to a higher altitude, we decided to go even farther up the steep incline, which consisted of extremely hard, dry dirt. We had to scratch hand- and toe-holds to make our climb.

After another 20 minutes of climbing, I happened to look back down to where I had last seen the rams. There they were, standing in plain sight, in some scrub timber that only came up to their mid sides. They had apparently both been sleeping with their heads on the ground, making them invisible to us as we climbed past them. They were both staring wide-eyed at these white intruders. Maybe they thought we were mountain goats, since we probably smelled like goats by now!

I softly told Chuck that the rams were below us. He exclaimed, "What! How?" But when he looked, his eyes nearly popped out of his head. There was his dream sheep about 125 yards away, looking at him. We were both hanging onto the cliff with feet and hands.

In order for Chuck to shoot, he had to twist around while keeping his toes dug into the wall. I held him with one hand and held the cliff with the other hand. These kind of shots are usually not anticipated nor practiced ahead of time. The recoil of the shot jarred us, but we both deftly grabbed the cliff with both hands. Chuck's rifle was hanging on his arm by a sling.

We saw the young ram rapidly scampering away. The large ram had his spine broken, but was dragging himself down along the edge of a 300-foot cliff. Since the ram was moving too fast for Chuck to try another shot, we just clung to the face and waited as the ram moved down the cliff's edge for 150 yards. There, the animal turned, half-falling, half-sliding, and fell over the cliff's edge out of our sight.

We climbed back down the steep face as fast as we could. When we looked over the cliff's edge, we saw that the sheep had fallen only about 15 feet and was now laying about 100 yards farther down a grassy slope. Chuck humanely finished the animal with a well-placed lung shot.

The bighorn ram was beautiful, lying there in the snow with chocolate-colored hair, amber eyes, white muzzle and horns the color of fresh lumber that curved four-fifths of a full curl. We quickly took photos for the memory book.

I had been wearing my backpack with only plastic garbage bags in it to hold the boned meat. I quickly removed the animal's head and cape, boned the edible meat and put it in the garbage bags. We then made our way back to camp. It was early afternoon now and the snow was beginning to fall again. We ate a few candy bards for lunch and hastily broke camp, splitting the heavy meat between us. I tied the ram head and cape on top of my pack, which now weighed close to 100 pounds.

We decided that, due to the amount of snow, we would be unable to go back the way we had come. I had never been down this canyon before and was not sure if the way was passable.

There was an alternate way to get out if we could not traverse this canyon to the main canyon and a Forest Service trail. This way would be much shorter and, according to the topographic map, we would drop a lot of altitude quickly, lessening the danger from the on-going storm. The name of the canyon was Falls Creek. My greatest fear was that we would be rimrocked at a falls and have to go the alternate route, which would be about 20 miles.

We traveled as fast as we could and then the ground dropped off suddenly. We were climbing down an extremely steep slope, holding to small lodgepole pines saplings about four inches in diameter. We climbed, slipped and slid down this tough piece of God's country for a couple of hours. I had yet to see a level spot but, just as darkness fell, we found a small level area just large enough for the tent. The creek gurgled nearby as we set up the tent and made supper. We'd had a very tough, but satisfying day. There was no snow falling at this lower elevation, but the temperature was below freezing.

The next morning, we finished our descent before noon. We were now in the Stillwater Valley and stood looking at the thigh-deep river we had to wade to get to the Forest Service trail on the other side. We stripped off our shoes, pants and long underwear and, with a stick held downstream for balance, we eased across the bitterly cold stream. I don't think that I have known any greater relief than when we climbed out the other side, darned near frozen. We quickly dried and dressed.

When we tried to walk our muscles would cramp and we walked with jerky uneven steps. We soon limbered up, though, and walked the many miles out to the trailhead. We were now walking on a little-traveled highway and proceeded on until we came to a ranch about an hour after dark. Here I made a call for my dad to pick us up and take us the 20

miles back to my vehicle in the original canyon we started from. We slept in real beds, a well-earned rest.

You feel like you have run a marathon after one of these sheep hunts, and it takes several days for your body to adjust again. Chuck thought that he was in good shape, but lost an additional 10 pounds on the trip. He had bought a new .270 rifle especially for the hunt, but now it had rock scratches all over the stock and barrel, and it looked like a gun that had been hunted with for 20 years.

As Chuck was getting ready to leave on his flight home, he said, "I had no idea that getting a bighorn ram would be so tough. I hope the last three sheep in my grand slam aren't this tough."

Since then, Chuck has completed his grand slam, but none of the hunts were as arduous as his quest for a trophy bighorn ram.

The Great Denver Lion Capture

by Ron D. Moore

S truggling to climb the elm tree alongside the garage, I was hampered by my lariat. My friend, Tom Mitchell, had climbed onto the garage roof and was already in position. I straddled a limb, leaned back against the trunk, and surveyed the chaos below me. There were many hundreds of people, flashbulbs bursting and television cameras with bright lights. We were in a densely populated residential area of West Denver and although the police were there in force, they had lost all control of the situation. Ten feet out on a limb on which I sat, crouched a scared, 60-pound young female mountain lion. If she jumped, there wasn't a square inch of real estate on which she could land that wasn't covered with people.

The lion was in a clump of branches, making it difficult to throw the loop over her because the rope would keep hanging up on small limbs. My efforts, and the events on the ground, were making her extremely nervous. She was going to jump if we didn't get a rope on her soon.

My next throw struck the limbs again and the lion burst straight at me. There was no time to get out of the tree, so I twisted my upper body, grabbed another limb and leaned away from her. I could feel her push off my leg before she jumped onto the garage roof. The lion, with Tom in hot pursuit, ran toward the rear of the garage. I watched in horror as she leaped off the end of the garage and out over the sea of people.

It was 1964. I urged and cursed my old 1951 Willys Jeep station wagon down the highway through the Colorado Rockies. The back of the Jeep was full of hound dogs. The odor and floating dog hair was becoming unbearable. Top speed in the old Jeep was 45 miles per hour, and when traffic wasn't backed up behind me, people were passing me with looks and gestures that indicated I was not the most popular fellow on the road. I retaliated by banging my fist on the steering wheel and cursing the old Jeep. At age 22, I was not blessed with an abundance of patience.

I had a camp on Boulder Creek where I had been hunting for a month, but now I was headed for my parents' home to rest a week and sow a few wild oats before returning to camp. My parents lived in Westminster, a suburb of Denver. Pulling up beside their backyard, I found my mother busy hanging out clothes. She did little to conceal the look of dread on her face as I began tying up the hounds. I'm the eldest of four sons and my hunting, my hounds and my lack of a steady job had steadfastly guaranteed my position as the black sheep of the family. But mothers love even their black sheep, and I was greeted with a warm hug.

I spent two nights chasing cowgirls and drinking Scotch with friends at Ollie's Roundup, then accepted an invitation to play poker at Tom Mitchell's home on the third night. I was thoroughly enjoying my brief R & R.

Tom was a long-time friend and the game was low stakes, warm and friendly. His wife, Sandy, saw that there wasn't a shortage of food and soft drinks, which was a welcome change after two nights at Ollie's. We had played an hour when Sandy announced that I had a phone call. I couldn't imagine who would be calling me.

On the other end of the line was Gayle Boyde, a friend and Colorado Game and Fish officer. "How would you like to go lion hunting?" Gayle asked.

Thinking that he just wanted to go hunting while I was in the area, I launched into a barrage of excuses why I couldn't go for another few days. Gayle cut me off and said, "Good Lord, man, aren't you watching the television? We need your help; there's a lion loose in a residential area off South Sheridan Boulevard!"

I listened in disbelief as he filled me in. A guide from Canyon City had sold a young lion to a gentleman in Denver. The man had paid part of the money, but was unable to come up with the balance, so the guide sent an inexperienced friend to repossess his lion and his small cage. The would-be buyer had purchased a stainless steel feed pan and wanted it back, so the two of them opened the cage door and reached for the pan. The natural reaction of the lion was to spit and slap at them. Startled, they both jumped back and the lion hopped out and trotted away.

I hung up the phone, still struck dumb by what I had heard. The television stations were reporting the story and the location, and people were converging on the area. I called everybody in from the kitchen as I switched on the TV set. A reporter was saying that there was a ferocious lion loose in Denver. Television crews were heading for the scene and a camera was expected at the site soon. Tom and I went off to my parents' home and loaded four of my best hounds.

South Sheridan Boulevard is a six-lane main thoroughfare in West Denver. The farther south we traveled, the more congested the traffic became. We finally came to a complete stop six blocks short of our destination. Nothing in my life prepared me for what we found here. For six blocks in both directions, all six lanes were blocked. Most of the cars were abandoned, some with the doors standing open and the engines still running. We could see people with shotguns and rifles, and some were leading bird dogs and mutts.

These self-appointed lion vigilantes made me extremely nervous. Somehow Tom and I had to get ourselves and four hounds through them to the escape site, find Gayle and get the lion caught before someone was accidentally shot or trampled to death.

Tom and I had brought our lariat ropes, and we each took two hounds, running the ends of our ropes through their collars to lead them. This pulled the dogs too close and caused them to continually become tangled up, but we finally found Gayle. With him was the young man who had bought the lion and the fellow who had come to get it. Gayle seemed frazzled and worried. The other two looked as if they would rather be anywhere else in the world.

Gayle wanted to turn my hounds loose and let them find the lion. I refused, explaining that there were too many people with guns out there and any scent of the lion already had been trampled. I also wanted it understood that my price for subjecting myself to this Chinese fire drill was that, upon capture, I would own both the lion and the cage. They readily agreed, *if* I could just get them out of this before somebody got hurt or killed. I suggested that we start at the cage in the backyard.

We found it with the door still ajar. The night was now lit up by car lights, police lights and flashlights. At the rear of the yard was a short picket fence with a gate leading into a small enclosure that once had been used for a horse. Unused, it was now overgrown with weeds. On the other side of the fence, the houses continued unbroken by any open area. The two nervous lion handlers informed me that the lion had disappeared into the weeds.

By now, the police had lost their fight with the crowd and the yard was filling with people. We led the hounds into the enclosure while Gayle and the police did their best to keep the people behind us. I explained to Tom that we would go to the corner, then work our way along the high weeds to the rear fence. I reasoned that a young lion, scared and disoriented in a strange environment, would most likely seek the nearest cover and hide until she got things sorted out. We began working our way along the fence.

We had gone only a short way when the lion burst from the weeds 15 yards in front of us. We released the hounds and they fell in behind her in full bay. We ran after them, and the crowd was close on our heels. Two houses west was a backyard with a six-foot high solid cedar fence. The lion jumped the fence, caught the top and hung there for an instant before dropping inside the yard. As soon as she was out of sight, a small dog began barking frantically and we could hear a scream.

Grabbing the hounds, who were leaping on the fence in a futile effort to follow, we headed for the gate. Our entourage now had been joined by two television crews and several newspaper photographers. "This is getting crazy," I remember thinking, as I jerked the gate open. Inside, we were met by an overweight, middle-aged woman holding a white miniature poodle with little ribbons tied on its ears. She began shouting that

Andre, her poodle, had treed the lion. Next to the garage in a Chinese elm sat the lion.

Several Jefferson County deputies joined us and the news spread like wildfire. Soon the yard was filled with people, and more trying to push their way in. The deputies pushed them back from a small area around the tree, giving us a little breathing space. I told Gayle that we had to do something fast.

Two more Game and Fish men pushed their way under the tree. The older man took charge while Gayle advised him of the events that had taken place. Turning to me he asked, "Can you get the lion roped and tied up in five minutes?"

"Impossible," I replied.

"Well, then we will have to kill her," he said. "There is too much risk to the public involved."

I agreed with his decision, having had my fill of this madhouse. He turned and began pushing his way through the crowd. When he returned with his rifle, there were rumblings of disapproval from the masses which soon turned into angry shouts. This didn't go unnoticed by the Game and Fish man, but he had made his decision and he was going to carry it through. I attempted to change his mind. We were surrounded by a crowd that was getting out of control and, although I knew his decision was the right one, I reminded him that these people had seen too many Walt Disney movies and had strange ideas about wild animals. He said he could not take the chance of this thing going on any longer.

As he took aim, someone yelled "If you kill that lion, you #*%!, I'll kill you!" I'm sure he heard it, too, because he lowered the rifle and looked around at the crowd. We all exchanged concerned looks and the deputies became noticeably nervous. He raised the rifle again and the crowd began yelling. I was wishing I was someplace else. The crowd now considered Tom and me to be associated with the Game and Fish people. If things got out of hand, we could become targets of its anger.

Suddenly, a husky young man leaped past the deputies and hit the man who was going to kill the cat, knocking him to the ground. Four of the deputies jumped on the man and, with considerable trouble, subdued him. They did not arrest him, but quietly pushed him back into the crowd after he had quieted down. Tom and I helped the game department man to his feet. The crowd was really fired up now. We had to take the lion alive or there would be a riot.

We hurriedly devised a plan that I thought would pose the least risk to the masses. I took my belt off and ran it through all four of the hounds' collars. Selecting a strong-looking man from the crowd, I asked him to hold the dogs, telling him that, no matter what happened, he was not to release them. Tom would get on the garage roof with his rope, and I would climb a tree. When I got a rope on the lion, we would jerk her onto the roof where we would be able to tie her up away from the crowd. I waited until Tom got into position, then started to climb. That's when the lion leaped to the garage roof, ran across, and went airborne over the crowd.

Tom was running hard on the lion's heels and was unable to stop when he came to the end of the roof and fell into a pile of scrap lumber. I jumped onto the garage, then into the lumber with Tom. The lion had parted the crowd like Moses parting the waters. Miraculously, it had not landed on anyone.

Having no idea of what we were going to do, we jumped up and headed at a run in the lion's wake. Along the way, all four hounds ended up in front of us, minus my belt and the expensive buckle I had won at a rodeo.

With the hounds only steps behind her, the lion became confused and a chase ensued back and forth through a group of small plum trees.

We were helpless to do anything except watch as hounds and lion flashed in and out of the trees. She was too fast to catch with a rope. Several times she jumped onto a post and would have made it over the fence had it not been for my old red hound grabbing her and pulling her off. The crowd had pushed toward the action and was threatening to push us into the melee that was taking place at our feet.

As we watched, a man in a ski jacket, ski mask and gloves pushed past us and threw himself onto the lion and forced her to the ground. He had his hands around her neck and was hanging on for dear life. The lion was thrashing under him as the hounds got into the act and started grabbing at her. Tom and I regained our senses and jumped in, shoving the hounds back. We each grabbed a pair of lion feet and, as the man steadfastly held onto the lion's neck, we trussed up her legs. Finding a small stick, we put it in her mouth and tied it shut. She was at last recaptured, thanks to the daring guy in the ski outfit.

The mystery man turned out to be the young man who had bought the lion. We had lost track of him in the confusion, but he had become worried about the state of affairs he had brought about. He put on the get-up to protect himself from the lions claws and came back determined to sacrifice himself in order to recapture the animal. Years have passed and I can't remember his name, but he was an extremely brave and unselfish young man. Although she weighed only 60 pounds, there was enough lion to seriously injure any man.

The crowd's mood changed abruptly from anger to joy, and now it was cheering us. Until you have experienced it, you cannot imagine what it is like to be in the middle of that many emotional people when they are angry with you. It is something I don't care to experience again.

Dragging four hounds and carrying the lion we began pushing our way back to the cage. Everyone wanted to touch the animal, and this kept her excited and thrashing around, making progress very difficult. As if there wasn't enough confusion, the hounds kept up a steady baying. After what seemed a long time, we got the lion into her cage and removed the ropes. It may have been my imagination, but I thought I saw a glimmer of relief in her eyes.

The only way to get the crowd to leave was to get the lion out of there. The man sent to pick up the lion had parked his pickup on the street in front of the house. We decided we would load the lion and my hounds into his truck and, with the assistance of two sheriff's cars, try to reach my vehicle.

Tom and I jumped in the back with the hounds and the lion. We sat one on each side of the cage, trying to prevent the throngs from putting their hands in the cage. We were inching along, with the hounds baying and trying to get at the lion, and people were trying to reach in and touch a very frightened lion! Some even tried to get in the pickup.

After transferring everything to my old Jeep station wagon, we found ourselves boxed in by several abandoned vehicles. Tom and I kept the windows rolled up while the deputies tried to locate the owners and get the cars moved. Remarkably, we all had come through the ordeal unscathed. It was two more hours before we were headed north on Sheridan Boulevard. I dropped Tom off, drove to my parents' home, left the lion in her cage in the Jeep, tied my hounds up and fell asleep.

At breakfast the next morning everybody was talking at once. They had watched the news accounts, but now they wanted juicy details. I told the story and, as I feared, someone asked about the lion. Without looking up from my plate, I said she was outside in my Jeep. I knew what my mother's reaction to this would be, and I wasn't to be disappointed. She launched into a tirade about me bringing the cat home, at the same time trying to prevent the stampede of my three younger brothers rushing out the door to see the lion. Calming her down, I assured her that the lion, the hounds and I were headed to my camp the next day. I had enough city to last me a lifetime.

We fixed a place in the yard for the lion and I began getting my supplies together. The *Rocky Mountain News* and the *Denver Post* carried front-page pictures of me, the hounds and the lady holding Andre the poodle. Television news also carried the story, showing yours truly up the elm tree. The Jefferson County Sheriff's Department estimated that more than 3,000 people had been at the scene.

Being publicity shy, I had avoided the media. But my brief notoriety wasn't over. I received a phone call that afternoon from the director of the Oklahoma City Zoo. The zoo's snow leopard had escaped and the city was faced with the same chaotic situation. The director wanted me to come to Oklahoma City and recapture the animal. I politely told him that I didn't know anything about leopards and that I'd had a belly-full of city hunting and crazy people.

The next morning, much to my mother's relief, I headed back to my beloved mountains. That trip cured me of cities and, for the past 23 years, I have managed to live a life far from them. Being in the hunting business, it is impossible to sever the cord completely, because cities are where airports are located. However, whenever I must pick up a client, I drive straight in and right back out. I seldom stay overnight. Whenever possible, I send someone else.

I named the lion "Sally" and she remained with me for a year. She was pretty gentle, well-fed and enjoyed a good life. I would take her somewhere and turn her loose. Two hours later, I would return with one old trained hound and some pups, trail and tree her. I used areas with easy terrain and lots of Jeep trails, so most of the time I could get my old Jeep right up to the tree. Sally knew that the cage represented protection from the hounds and, if I took them around the hill and out of sight, she would come down on her own and go back into her cage. I doubt that she ever knew she had a name, but I became quite attached to her.

The next year I was guiding and hunting out of Gunnison when Colorado passed the law that made the mountain lion a game animal and prohibited keeping one in captivity. The Game and Fish supervisor for the area was Howard Kendall. I had helped Howard's agency trap elk and pack fingerling trout into the back country, and I considered him a friend. When I went to him to find out about my lion, he told me that I had three choices: kill her, turn her loose or obtain a park permit to keep her. To get the permit you had to own property and have proper facilities to house the lion. Living out of hunting camps, I was left with the other two choices.

I agonized for a week over what to do with Sally. I sure as hell didn't think I could kill her. On the other hand, I was concerned about her surviving on her own in the wild. Captured young, she hadn't learned the survival skills large land predators require. She had been with me for a year and her meals had been hand carried to her. Wouldn't it be better to shoot her and save her from possible starvation? After much thought, I decided to set her free. Perhaps she could survive on small game until she learned to kill larger game.

Dawn broke clear and crisp over the Gunnison valley as I loaded

Sally into the old Jeep for her trip to freedom. I drove north through the little spot in the road called Sargents, then up over Monarch Pass and down the mountain to Salida. From there, I drove east along the two-lane highway that winds through the canyons bend-for-bend with the Arkansas River. I wanted Sally to start her free life far from familiar country,

and I wanted her to be where I knew there were lots of other lions. At Cotopaxi, I crossed the bridge and drove deep into the boulder strewn mountains on a gravel road. As I had done hundreds of times, I opened the cage, Sally hopped out and trotted up a sandy wash to play the game again.

After she was out of sight, I stood there for a long while and finally saw her once more on a boulder pile, jumping from rock to rock. I'm sure that she expected that she would be back in her cage awaiting her meal that evening. She didn't know she would be entering forever one of the harshest and unfeeling of worlds, that of Mother Nature's. I climbed back in the old Jeep with a feeling of emptiness, drove off and never looked back.

Move That Moose

by Charlie Stricker
as told to Tony Caligiuri

C anada moose are big boys measured against any standard. For that reason, the recurring thought on the minds of most guides who hunt them is just how far the moose will fall from the nearest trail or road, because a good guide has to lead his hunter to game as well as pack it out. With that in mind, I was fairly elated when we began seeing a big buster on a regular basis near my hunting camp on Alberta's Smoky River during the fall of 1974. The bull looked to be record-book class, with a tremendous spread of 60 inches, and I figured he wouldn't be too tough to knock off within easy packing distance of camp. The only problem was the fact that our next two hunters were interested in elk and, as the seasons ran concurrently, a non-resident could only buy a tag for one or the other.

The hunters arrived at the airport and I explained about the big bull in such an excited tone that one hunter put off his elk hunt and agreed to buy a moose tag. Back at camp, moose sign was plentiful and I assigned my hunter to an Indian guide named Roddy Moberly. The next morning I rode out in the new snow with my elk hunter, reflecting all the way down the trail what an easy moose hunt the boys should have.

Eight days later, coming back toward camp with an elated elk hunter and a 6x6 rack atop a pack horse, my happy mood soured when I saw the moose hunter and guide riding through the poplars along the river. One depressed hunter and guide proceeded to tell me how the moose had all but disappeared on the first morning of the hunt. Fortunately, back at camp sat Roddy's brother Malcolm, one of the best trackers that has ever guided in the north country. After a quick conference, Malcolm speculated that the big bull had picked up some company and headed up to a game lick in the high country to get in some mineral time before the big snows came. With only one full day left to hunt, and a depressed, would-have-been-happy-elk-hunter-if-I'd-just-let-him-buy-an-elk-tag moose hunter, I was ready to try anything.

The next morning was the last day of the season. We saddled up the horses, packed enough groceries for two days and brought along two pack horses, just in case luck smiled upon us. The lick was in high country on the north side of the Big Smoky and with chunky, thick ice half way out to the middle on both sides, getting horses across would be a problem. Malcolm remembered that, years before, his dad used a good winter crossing up the river about a mile.

After crossing, even though he hadn't been there since a boy and the snow was more than a foot deep, Malcolm found his dad's old trail just by looking at a cut-off willow branch. The trail needed to be cleared of its new growth, and Malcolm and I took turns with the ax. Every once in a while, Malcolm would take the ax away from me, widen out a spot and say with a laugh, "Trail not 60 inches wide, moose is, make it plenty wide, Charlie." Malcolm had a rare sense of humor.

It took most of the morning to work our way up to the lick and we tied up our horses at about 1:00 in the afternoon. We had not walked a quarter-mile when we spotted the big bull and his buddies across a big willow canyon. Counting our luck would hold, we trudged into as nasty and rough a canyon as I had ever come across. With the canyon full of dead-falls, blown-down trees and three feet of snow, we only made 50 yards in an hour's time.

Soaked to the skin and nearly worn out, the hunter, Malcolm and I sat down for a powwow. Malcolm was the first to speak. "Shoot damn moose in the foot, slow him down and we'll herd him all the way back to the horses." We all got a good laugh over that, but my thoughts were on the more serious side of actually shooting the bull and getting him out of the canyon.

I started to build a good rest, but before I could even get out of my backpack, the hunter touched off a 400-yard plus shot. Malcolm and I just looked at each other. "Maybe him hit in foot and we can herd back to horses," Malcolm joked again. I wasn't quite so amused as I contemplated what to do.

We built a big fire, and dried ourselves out while we talked the situation over. We decided that Malcolm would go back for the horses while we still had plenty of daylight, and the hunter and I would work our way over to see if the bull had been hit. When we got there, the story in the tracks was plain as print. The moose was hit in the foot. Now an all-day joke had turned into the grim reality of tracking a wounded game animal through a jungle of deadfalls.

I picked up his track, and we found where he had laid down five times. There was a younger bull with him, and he kept getting the wounded animal up each time we got closer. For the next quarter-mile,

we saw him four times, and often we were so close we could hear his antlers banging in the willows. The going was rough and we never got a shot, but the last time we saw him, the unbelievable happened. The moose cut down a heavily-wooded side canyon straight to where we had tied the horses. Pumped up that Malcolm's prophecy was coming true, we cut out fast as we could. I figured the bull would come out of the canyon and cross over a knoll that had only a few jack pines for cover. The hunter got into position, the bull came out and one shot ended our moose hunt from hell. Malcolm and the horses were just a few yards away.

Laughing in disbelief at what had happened, we had the moose caped, quartered and packed by dark. The bull scored 210 Boone & Crockett points, and had a 60-inch spread, 40-inch palms, 13 points to a side and is still in the top 29 bulls ever killed in Alberta.

Like the man says, "I love it when a plan comes together."

Antelope Can Ruin Your Day

by Judd Cooney

B owhunters like to be close to their quarry, but this was too good to be true. The big buck antelope was standing less than 10 feet from where Victor, my bowhunting client, crouched in the bottom of the pit blind trying to become invisible. I had two other pits on this good-sized tank dam but several wise, trophy-sized bucks had been sneaking into the far corner to water, where my hunters couldn't get a good shot.

Late one evening, after the antelope were bedded for the night, I went back to the water hole and dug a new pit blind in the face of the dam, 15 yards from each corner. With prevailing wind, there was no way an antelope coming to water could wind the hidden hunter.

Victor is one of my favorite clients and has hunted with me for years, but on this hunt he was having a bit of trouble getting his arrow and one of the speedy pronghorns in the same place at the same time. I figured there was no way he could miss from the new pit, but I should have known better, having been subjected to Victor's brand of work before.

Shortly after daylight, a huge buck came trotting down off the ridge and walked onto the tank dam without giving the new blind a second glance. Vic watched him and when the buck finally stopped, Victor was on both knees in the bottom of the pit trying to hide in the shadows. The buck was only 10 feet from the top of the pit and, according to Victor, "He was lookin' right down my shirt collar! The only thing I could do so he wouldn't see me, was to *close both eyes!*"

Must have helped, 'cause the next thing Vic was aware of was the slurping sound of the buck drinking. The water was only *five yards* from the front of the blind and, when Victor opened his eyes, the buck was standing, head down, drinking between the blind and the water. That's close!

The shooting holes were set up for shooting into the corners and not for a three-yard shot in front of the blind. Vic had an arrow on the string but, every time he tried to move, the buck's head snapped up. As Vic said, "Those big ol' eyeballs pinned me right to the side of the pit."

This contest of wills went on for a full three minutes before Victor's patience snapped! He decided the only way he was going to get a shot was to jump up and take the shot on the run.

Ha! When the buck's head went to the water again Victor tensed and lunged up, trying to come to full draw. His broadhead hooked in the brush and pulled the arrow off the rest and nock. His bow quiver also caught on something and pulled the bow out of his hands so that, by the time he got to standing position for a shot, he not only didn't have an arrow on the string, he didn't have a bow in his hands. The buck took about three big leaps and then stopped 20 yards away to see just what all the commotion was about. Victor never would tell us just what he said at this point, but chances are it would have been unprintable anyhow. This buck may not have made Vic's day, but it sure made mine when I heard the story!

I have had the good fortune to bowhunt pronghorns with many of the best-known bowhunters in the field today and can assure you that antelope can ruin their day just as easily as for the neophyte pronghorn hunter.

Several years ago one of the best-known bowhunters in the country graced our humble camp with his presence for a week of bowhunting pronghorns. Since we are good friends and I do not want his sterling reputation as an excellent shot and world-renowned bowhunter to be smeared, and because I know he would try to get even for my making this story public, I will not use his real name. We'll just call this unfortunate fellow Jim.

I figured that I could take advantage of having such a dependable bowhunter with me and try to get some good photos of this bowhunter in action. I took Jim to a super-good water hole in the middle of nowhere that was being used by several real "boomer" bucks. There were two pit blinds on this tank. One on each side and it would be easy for me to sit in the one and photograph Jim shooting his buck from the other. Jim had recently purchased a new bow and was anxious to kill a good buck with it. He did admit, though, he hadn't had it long enough to shoot it as much as he would have liked before taking it hunting. I didn't anticipate any problem, 'cause on the range in camp he was putting all his arrows in the kill zone up to 30 yards. The shots from his pit blind would be a maximum of 25 yards. I figured for some good photos of trophy antelope being killed before the day was much older and some great trophy shots afterward.

We got to the blind about 3:00 p.m. for a late afternoon hunt under clear blue skies and warm temperatures. Ideal! Within a few minutes Jim and I were situated and I was engrossed in a lurid murder scene in one of the "pocket books" I always carry for such waits. Between every page I would look over the country behind Jim's blind and glance along my side of the water hole.

The first half hour passed uneventfully before I spotted a couple of does and fawns on the ridge behind Jim working their way to water. The tank itself was in the bottom of a gully and, when full of water, was 30 inches deep. Right now there was about four inches of water in the tank. The pronghorns coming from either side would pause on the ridge above the tank to check for danger and then trot rapidly down the steep, gravelly hillside to the water. Once finished, they scrambled back to the ridgetop and stood around surveying their domain.

The does and fawns came in and watered, seemingly oblivious to danger. While they were still sucking in the muddy water I spotted a good buck coming down the ridge and knew the does and fawns would act as decoys and bring him right in. Mamas and kids passed the buck on the way to the surrounding prairies and the buck never broke stride as he came over the ridgetop and headed for water.

I could see the tip of Jim's bow come up, so I prepared for action. The buck was totally unaware of danger until the broadhead-tipped shaft hummed over his back. He whirled and slowly trotted up the slope where he could get a good look around to see what had made the noise. He was still broadside to the blind at 20 yards when I saw the flicker of another antelope-bound arrow through my camera's viewfinder. I heard this arrow bounce through the rocks and saw the antelope put on a sudden spurt of speed as he topped the ridge. He still didn't know what was buzzing around him and there was no way he could wind Jim from his position, so he wasn't overly spooked. I was snickering to myself 'cause I knew Jim would be furious at his misses and doubly furious because I had seen them. He knew he was in for a rough bit of ribbing, and the day was still young.

The buck wandered back and forth on the ridge overlooking the tank for half an hour, trying to decide whether it was safe to attempt another drink. His mind was made up for him as he watched five does and fawns come down and drink on my side of the tank without the slightest sign of

danger. He moved down the slope in a flurry of gravel and, after checking the area once more for danger, lowered his muzzle into the water.

Almost immediately an arrow came flying out of the sagebrush blind and zipped under the buck's chest. Once more he started up the slope at a trot and, once again, an arrow came flying out of the bushes and zipped harmlessly over his back. This time he said to hell with it and headed for the open prairie at a run. I watched him for a quarter of a mile as he kept glancing back longingly at the water hole. Jim was down to two arrows in his bow quiver and there were still a couple of hours of shooting light left. Could be interesting!

The buck had stopped on a knoll 500 yards from the tank and stood

like a statue for the next hour, calmly surveying his surroundings. Suddenly, I heard the rush of hooves behind my blind as a herd of some 10 antelope came running down the gradual slope and proceeded to drink. There were a couple of yearling bucks and one P&Y buck in the bunch, but this buck was not nearly as good as the one Jim had missed. The distance was about 40 yards so I was sure Jim wouldn't try for a shot.

I had been trying to photograph the group in the golden, late afternoon light and had taken my eyes and thoughts off the other buck. The group finished drinking and, typical of pronghorns, whirled and ran up over the ridge out of my sight.

I turned to see where the other buck was and couldn't believe it when I saw him, once more standing on the ridge right above the tank. He edged to the lip of the ridge, took another look around and once more skidded down to the water's edge. He stood looking around to make sure there were no spooks around and then lowered his head for the third try at slaking his thirst.

I had the antelope framed in my viewfinder when he suddenly dropped and spun to head back up the bank. I just barely caught the movement of the arrow as it, once again, passed over the buck's back. For the third time the buck trotted up the steep slope and for the *sixth* time Jim's arrow came blurring out of the blind after him. This time Jim was a little anxious and shot in front of the retreating buck. Before the buck reached the top of the slope Jim jumped up in the blind and was shaking his new bow at the buck. "Get the ____ out of here, you no-good, four-legged ____ ____. I ain't got an arrow left and if you come back I'm going to wrap this brand new bow around your skinny neck!"

My eyes were in such bad shape from the tears of my laughter I couldn't even focus to get a picture of my staunch, unshakable, experienced companion showing what can happen when an antelope really wants to ruin *your* day.

I've Met Some Characters

by Tommy Thompson

W hen people think of hunting stories, they usually imagine hunters
as having the wildest and most incredible tales. This isn't always
the case. My career as an outfitter and guide has provided me with a host
of unforgettable experiences and bizarre characters, any of which could
stand up to even the weirdest hunter story.

For more than 10 years I was employed as a guide for the largest
hunting ranch in Texas. The ranch had a battery of 25 to 30 guides who
provided their own vehicles and, in turn, were boarded, fed and paid a
daily stipend. There was one hard and fast rule on the ranch: Pasture
assignment was on a first come, first serve basis. Each guide had to hunt
within the bounds of his assigned pasture. Immediate dismissal from the
ranch was the penalty for anyone caught disobeying this rule. Of course,
all the guides knew the system and how it worked. However, once in a
while a hunter didn't get the message.

On one particular morning in November, 1974, I had gotten a certain
pasture assignment since my hunter wanted a sika deer and two outstanding sika had recently been sighted in this particular pasture. Bill
Cowden, another guide, approached me about putting one of his turkey
hunters in a blind in my assigned pasture. I consented, as this particular
area had a good turkey population and the turkey hunter certainly
wouldn't bother our outing.

We were usually in our hunting area by daybreak. It was a beautiful
crisp morning and, about 9:30, I located one of the two big sika deer I

had seen earlier. The instant he spotted us, he broke and ran with my hunter and me in hot pursuit.

Meanwhile, Cowden's hunter was waiting patiently in the blind for the appearance of some turkey toms. Instead, a big sika came bounding toward the blind, followed closely by my hunter and me in my Scout! The first thing I knew, the turkey hunter came breaking out of the blind all wide-eyed. He threw his shotgun one way and he went the other, running for the trees!

We made a brief halt as I apologized to the turkey hunter. We all had a good laugh and both hunts resumed.

The funny part is, I knew he was there, but he sure didn't know I knew!

But of all the instances that have occurred during my guiding career, I do believe this one stands out the most in my mind. I was employed on a very large Texas hunting ranch and had met with people from all walks of life. This particular day I was to guide two clients from Los Angeles, California. They arrived on the ranch after lunch. I got them settled into their accommodations and then took them to the rifle range. It was customary to check all hunters' rifles for accuracy, as well to check the hunters. Everything went well.

After a lengthy discussion as to what they would hunt, it was decided they would each take an axis deer and a blackbuck antelope.

Their marksmanship in the field left a lot to be desired. After a day and a half of hunting and several complete misses, we had a grand total of one axis.

The morning of the third day, I spotted a blackbuck antelope feeding at a distance of 130 yards. I instructed the hunter in the front seat to open the door, very carefully, and use the vertical part of the inside of the door for a rest. The location of the blackbuck was slightly downhill from our position. I was seated behind the steering wheel of my Scout, observing through my binoculars. The first shot was fired with no results. I told the hunter to fire again, as the blackbuck threw up his head, and again the hunter wound up with the same results as the first shot. But this time, through my binoculars I could see smoke. Upon further checking, I noted the smoke was coming from under the hood of my Scout.

The blackbuck positioned slightly below us caused the hunter to see the image in his rifle scope, but the barrel was pointed at the curvature of the hood of my Scout. Both shots entered almost the same hole. Talk about accurate!

One shot got the battery (the heart), the other shot hit the shroud between the battery and the radiator. This shot broke the projectile, and my radiator (the lungs) looked as if it had been making love with a porcu-

pine! The blackbuck was safe and wondering what all the shooting was about.

I put the battery partially back together with strips of inner tube and we traveled from windmill to windmill, stopping at each one to fill the leaking radiator with water. Since we were several miles from headquarters, this took some time!

When the other guides heard of my plight they decided the hunter had gotten himself a trophy after all. As far as guide vehicles go, my Scout has a 108-inch CB antenna, which should put it way up there in the record book.

Throughout my career, I've come across a fair share of characters. One such individual, Earl Hyde, has lived on the same ranch for 79 of his 80 years. His folks owned the ranch when he came into this world and, in 1965 when Dale Priour purchased the ranch, Earl stayed on as foreman. To this day he still holds that position, and very well, I might add.

The Priour Ranch is known for its many species of exotic animals. I had made arrangements to take a couple of clients there to hunt aoudad and, having heard Mr. Hyde was a crusty individual, I decided I would do more listening than talking while on his turf.

In Edwards Plateau, Texas, we mainly hunt safari style, and that is the way we started our hunt, with Earl driving his old trusted white pickup, my hunters and me in the back. After dodging cedar and live oak limbs for some time, and bouncing over the rocky terrain, we spotted a good aoudad ram with a couple of ewes about 200 yards away. As any aoudad hunter knows, the aoudad isn't going to "pose" very long, so Earl hit the brakes. The pickup slid to a halt and he instructed the hunter to shoot the ram. At the same time the hunter took aim, the aoudads bolted and the hunter's shot was errant, hitting the ram too far back. The aoudads continued running into shinoak straight over the ridge. We watched the area without seeing any movement.

After a brief discussion, I told Earl I would sneak around, using a small draw for cover, and see if I could view the ram from the ridge above the shinoak motte, perhaps herding it back toward the hunters.

As I reached the ridge and peered over the edge, I saw the ram, which was sitting on his haunches, looking away from me, but toward the direction of the pickup. I decided, in that instant, the best course of action was to chase the aoudad and hope Earl and the hunters would come to my rescue. I ran from my cover and started after the ram, and let me tell you, all hell broke loose! I was astraddle him, holding both horns, and out through the shinoak motte we went! All I could see were rocks and cactus. I heard Earl holler, "Turn him loose, Thompson, before he hurts you!" About that time the aoudad had used up all his momentum. He fell beneath me and we rolled, head over heels, through the cactus and rocks, finally coming to a sliding halt.

Earl stood there and looked at me lying in the rocks beside a dead aoudad, cactus and shinoak limb scratches all over me, and said, "Son, you got more guts than brains."

That didn't sound like an acceptance speech to me, but I had to keep on trying because we still had one more aoudad ram to hunt.

We set out for another area to hunt and, in due time, spotted a herd of what seemed to be about 12 rams. Since aoudad love to bunch up, we spent a good bit of time carefully maneuvering to spread them out on a ridge about 180 yards from us. We instructed the hunter which one to shoot. As the rifle sounded, off the herd ran in a tight group, down a deep arroyo and up the other side. Earl drove off, driving hell bent for leather, after the herd. I yelled for him to stop, and stop he did, asking me why I wanted to stop. I said, "Earl, 12 rams went into that arroyo and only 11 came out!"

He replied, very matter-of-factly, "You had better be right, because we'll never see those rams again today!"

Sure enough, on closer inspection, at the bottom of the arroyo lay the aoudad the hunter had shot. Earl looked at me and said, "You might make a guide after all."

But Earl did manage to best me more than once.

One July morning, I had two clients from Saudi Arabia—actually one client and his manservant.

We arrived at the Priour Ranch shortly after lunch and went to check in with Earl. We found him very busy mowing hay, so we visited for a minute and then left Earl with his work to start our blackbuck antelope hunt.

We had been out about an hour when we spotted a blackbuck in the 21-inch category, at a distance of around 200 yards. I gave the okay for my client to shoot, but he shot too far back in the abdomen, and instantly the blackbuck was in flight. We immediately went to the spot where I had seen the animal hit and began searching for any signs to follow. We were able to find enough clues to keep us searching throughout the afternoon.

We gave up our search just before dark and headed for the ranch headquarters. When we arrived, Earl was just finishing up cutting hay. I related our story about the wounded blackbuck and told him we would be out early next morning to follow up our search, hopefully with his help.

The next morning, just after daybreak, we headed out. I showed Earl the area where the blackbuck took the hit and where I had marked the trail we had found the previous afternoon. Earl said, "Get in the pickup and let's go." Off we went, with me protesting we were headed in the wrong direction, my arguments falling on deaf ears. After about three-quarters of a mile, we came upon a ridge. At a distance of some 200 yards, Earl said, "What's that under that tree?"

I replied, "That's a rock."

Earl continued to drive toward that one particular oak tree and I kept protesting there was a rock under that tree! At a distance of 50 to 75 yards Earl said, "It's funny that rock has horns." There, facing us, was the white underbelly of a dead blackbuck antelope. I felt rather stupid.

After congratulating the hunter and field dressing the blackbuck, we headed back to the ranch headquarters. When I asked Earl how he knew that was a blackbuck antelope under that tree, he replied, "Because there never has been a big white rock under that tree!"

By God, Cap'n

by Duane Wiltse

"**B**y God, Cap'n, you gotta do somethin' about that damn she bear."

As I stepped down from my long-legged paint horse, I could plainly see that Don Juby, my trusty old camp cook, was as mad as hell. It's easy for me to tell when something is bothering Don, because he'll come striding across the Jones Creek Camp compound, to where I am tying my horse, red-faced and wiping his hands on his apron, beginning his loud sentence with "By God, Cap'n".

I'll bet old Don was hell on wheels in the South Pacific, where he served this great country with the 112 Signal Radio and Intelligence Company from 1942 to 1945. He told me last fall, as we were breaking camp in a blizzard, that he thought that the saltpeter that the army put in his food was finally beginning to take hold.

Don is 68 years old with a five-foot seven-inch robust build. A little burnt and crusty around the edges, he runs the camp with an iron hand, but has a heart like your mom's cherry pie: warm and cheery. Right now, though, he was splashing through the mud with rain bounding off his high forehead and fire in his eyes.

"As soon as I turn this horse loose and get in out of the rain, we'll figure it out," I said. "OK, Don?"

"Yah, right," he mumbled.

As I hung my yellow rain slicker behind the dining tent stove, I asked, "Isn't the fence working, Don?"

"I'll tell you exactly how that damn electric fence is working, Duane. Number 104 and her three cubs have been in here two nights in a row demanding something to eat. You can't expect them guides to hunt elk all day and fight griz all night. They gotta have some rest."

"But what about...," I tried to ask, but Don interrupted, anticipating my next question.

"I know, I know! The electric fence was supposed to be the answer to all our problems. When you and the Forest Service isolated the cook and dining tents with two strands of hot wire I figured I'd have some easy sleeping. Instead those cubs start to crawl through the fence, get a jolt, let out a bawl and come on through the fence. We end up being eyeball to eyeball with those furry little trash compactors while mean mamma bear huffs and pops her teeth at us just outside the wire."

"By God, Cap'n, I tell you it's enough to drive a man to drink. You gotta do somethin'," Don implored.

It takes some really special country for a grizzly bear to call it home. It must be as remote, wild and big as the bears themselves. We consider ourselves fortunate to have a permit to camp and hunt elk in such a pristine wilderness. You can drink from the streams, catch whatever native trout you want for the next meal and have fresh-picked strawberries or raspberries on the side.

The grizzlies teach us something new every year. One of the first lessons we learned years ago was to never leave a camp unattended overnight. Someone must sleep in the cook and dining tents, to prevent heavy losses and damage.

Grizzly bite everything, whether there is food in it or not, leaving holes about the size of a .38 slug in pots, pans, coffee pots, dutch ovens and the base of Coleman lanterns.

They very seldom enter a tent through the manufactured flaps, preferring instead to create their own private entrance just about anywhere else in the canvas. I think they dearly love to hear canvas being shredded by their long, sharp claws, because they never use their entrance as an exit. No sir-ee; an exit calls for a slash with the other paw and, just in case the griz may have overlooked a lantern or cast iron skillet, he'll go in and out until there are nothing but six-inch ribbons hanging from the ridge pole.

So, after a sleepless night of helping to counter number 104's endless forays on our larder, I saddled up and headed for a telephone to call in reinforcements. The U.S. Forest Service and Wyoming Game & Fish Department each sent two hands to help save us from the bear and the bear from us. They slept days, just like 104, and stayed up nights to entertain her by shooting off guns, firecrackers, Roman candles and nause-

ating scents. She must have really enjoyed the nightly shows because she came in about 9:00 p.m. for nine nights in a row.

The first thing that the battery of experts decided was that the electric fence had to come down. Being trapped inside the 20- by 40-foot fenced area with the griz was very hard on a body's nerves and disposition, they reasoned, so it was replaced by an eight-foot high chain-link fence.

That seemed to stymie old number 104, and the last two days of our hunt were uneventful. We all headed to town to pick up our next group of hunters, secure in the illusion that our camp was finally grizzly-proof and no one needed to stay in camp to guard it. Hunters and hands rode the four miles downstream to our end of the road trailhead where the vehicles were parked. We were all anticipating a hot shower and the reunion with our wives.

If I live to be 100, I'll never forget the sight that greeted us when we rode into the trailhead. A gaping hole, big enough to drive a pickup truck through had been clawed and splintered into the side of the wood plank barn. I had stored the extra grain in that area of the barn because there were no windows or doors on that side and, I figured, the grain would be safest there.

The signs revealed that a big, and I mean big, grizzly boar had ripped that hole, eaten what he wanted of the 100-pound sack of grain and had taken the rest with him. When something like that happens you think, "Oh my God, what are they going to do next?" I didn't have to wait long for the answer to that question.

We had just returned to camp and I was tending to some of the pack mules when I heard Don shout from the cook tent, "By God, Cap'n, you ain't gonna believe this."

And I wouldn't have believed it if I hadn't seen it with my own eyes. That old barn-wrecking boar had padded up the other side of the river and gotten back to the camp before we did. Finding our chain-link fortress locked up tight, he devised a way of unlocking it. He had brought his own set of keys; the same keys he had used on the locked barn—his six-inch claws. He reached up, got hold of the top of that chain link fence and, with unimaginable strength, smashed it down to size so he could crawl over and get inside the compound to raid the cook tent. Then it was just a simple backhand slash to remove the rear corner of the tent and begin the smorgasbord.

I won't bore you with an endless list of what he ate and how much he ate. Suffice it to say that the Wrangler and four pack mules were dispatched immediately for fresh supplies.

Over the years, I have found that it costs me an average of $1,500 for each successful bear attack.

Another lesson to remember is that a bear never forgets where he got a meal, so he comes back night after night. Even as long as a year after the meal, he will return just to be sociable.

By the next night, we had sewn the cook tent back together, braced up the fence and staked a dog on a short chain leash just inside the point of attack.

"I wish that damn dog would quit whinin' and whimperin'," one of the guides remarked during supper.

"I'll give him some elk roast gravy," Don volunteered as he ducked out of the dining tent to get our cherry pie dessert from the cook tent.

In a minute we heard, "By God, Cap'n, you better take a look at this sucker."

The scene that slowly came into focus as my eyes adjusted from the lantern-lit dining tent to the inky black night looked like something from a comic strip.

Backing away from his assigned guard area, the 20-pound dog had literally plowed a trench into the ground with his paws and his leash was stretched so taut you could have played a tune on it. The motivating force for all this digging, straining and whimpering was 600 pounds plus of grizzly boar sitting just outside the chain-link fence, with his nose thrust through one of the little openings in the fence.

That boar showed up for five more nights to sit outside our fence and panhandle. Needless to say, he sat wherever he wanted and we re-routed our midnight trips to the latrine.

I understand that if a person loses his sight somehow he can compensate for that loss by magnifying his other senses.

It has been my experience to enjoy a similar sharpening, quickening, magnifying of all my senses while living in griz country. I have become acutely aware of everything around me.

Early one crisp October morning, as I approached my Monaco Camp on horseback, I spotted the most beautiful grizzly I have ever seen. About 100 yards through the timber, in the upper end of our camp meadow, was a silvery blue grizzly grazing with eight of our horses. My saddle horse hadn't seen the bear yet and was impatient to get on into camp. But I wasn't about to ride mindlessly out into the open until I had checked things out. A little craning of my neck revealed that camp was intact and secure. The grazing horses were much more relaxed, even with the bear in their midst, than the nervous prancing paint I was on.

Cheryl, my daughter-in-law, who was substituting for my injured camp cook, Don McConnell, was sitting beside a small campfire, darning socks, with a rifle across her lap.

I rode gingerly out of the timber across the meadow and up to the hitching rail. Of course, the griz spotted me before I had cleared the timber and turned to face me, revealing a striking "V" of white hairs on his massive chest. His luxurious silver-tipped hair rippled in the slight early morning breeze. Our eyes locked as I passed within 40 yards of him. I will be eternally grateful for that moment of beauty, power and respect we shared as we looked deep into each other's being.

"Did you see 'Efrim'?" Cheryl asked, as I unsaddled my horse. Efrim is a respectful name for the grizzly bear used by mountain men.

"You bet," I replied. "Tell me about him."

"He has been up there for the last three mornings. He drifts up into the timber about 10:00 then returns about 4:00 every afternoon. "So far he hasn't bothered camp," she answered.

While splitting wood that morning, I watched my mule, Singer, with outstretched neck, flattened ears and bared teeth charge the griz three times. For reasons known only to Efrim and Singer, the bear dutifully ran up into the timber each time only to return a respectful 15 minutes later.

The hunters and hands nervously enjoyed the mule/bear exchange and took advantage of some rare photo opportunities, even cutting their daily elk hunts short to be back in camp before dark.

Efrim disappeared as quietly and mysteriously as he appeared.

Over the last 15 years, we have had lots and lots of black and grizzly bears check out our camps without doing any damage. In fact, it's not uncommon for hands to feign sleep when they hear a bear in camp, hoping someone else will leave their warm sleeping bag to brave the chill night air and spook off the intruder. But, the sound of pearly white bear teeth puncturing a six-pack and the accompanying gurgling of a chug-a-lugging bear will empty a guide's tent faster than a long-tailed cat leaving a room full of rocking chairs.

Don McConnell, my regular cook in Monaco Camp, is a salty character who I call "Bandit." He is about five-feet seven-inches tall, with a black droopy mustache and just the right looks, habits and attitudes to have played one of those lovable bandits in the B-Western movies of yesteryear.

Don is a stove-up cowboy, old beyond his 60 years from riding and shoeing too many snaky broncs. If it weren't for the plastic joints in each of his knees, I'd never be able to keep him in camp cooking. He'd be out guiding. No matter what happens, Don can always make do. He can make more good meals out of the fewest ingredients than anyone I have ever known.

Cheryl was subbing for Don because the fall before, as he was taking a hunter with his gear and elk to town, Don spent nearly an hour pinned under his downed saddle horse after a bad wreck. While he was twisting and straining to free himself and his horse, he pulled one of his plastic knee joints apart. He rode the remaining 10 miles to the trailhead, unsaddled the horses and then drove 50 miles to the nearest hospital with the equivalent of a broken leg. After many hours in the operating room, the doctor insisted that Don do absolutely no more horseback riding for at least one full year.

I've never known Don to get very excited about anything. He always seems to be calm and in control regardless of the wild goings-on around him. He is the kind of man with whom you feel comfortable riding the country.

Several years ago as I led my six excited elk hunters into Monaco Camp, Don walked around the cook tent to welcome us all. It was our first hunt together, and I had sent Don and a couple of guides into Monaco to set up the week before. The guides had come out a day earlier to help me pack up and get the hunters safely into camp, so Don was left alone in camp to finish up the details. I was anxious to see how everything was, and asked Don if things had gone well for him while he was in camp alone.

"No problems," was Don's reply to my concern.

Relieved, I rode over to the corrals.

Before I stepped off my horse, I spied a rolled up skin from a freshly killed black bear tucked up against the trunk of a big, shady spruce tree.

While the hunters were settling into their assigned sleeping tents, I eased back over to the cook tent where Don was busy preparing homemade soup and sandwiches for lunch.

"I thought you said there were no problems, Don. What about that black bear skin under the spruce tree behind the corrals?"

"Oh, you saw that, did you? Well, that bear wasn't any real problem. I just shot him before he became a problem," Don answered.

"So tell me about him," I urged impatiently.

"Well," Don began, "It was barely light yesterday morning and I was still in my sleeping bag when I heard what I thought were horses in the grain. I jumped up and ran outside in my long johns to run them off, but there weren't any horses in sight. It was just another calm, quiet mountain morning. I started back inside the cook tent, wondering if I was just hearing things when I heard the unmistakable sound of canvas being ripped by bear claws. I turned around in time to see that black bear coming out the side of the empty guide's tent. As he ambled up toward the tack shed, I went back to my cot for my rifle."

We stretch a large tarp over a ridge pole, leaving the ends and sides open for easy access. This is our tack shed where we store our riding saddles, bridles, pack saddles and assorted paraphernalia while we are in camp.

As Don rammed the 180-grain soft-nose home and closed the bolt on his ancient .30-06 the black bear was helping himself to his first mouthful of molasses-sweetened rolled oats.

Gingerly tiptoeing barefooted through the frosty pine needles, Don took a deep breath and rested on our wood splitting stump. He settled the cross hairs of the scope on the oat-augering culprit and touched off.

Don jumped up in surprised astonishment as the bear came roaring out of the tack shed right at him, as fast as a runaway freight train. By the time Don rammed another live round home, the 60 yards between man and bear had dwindled to 40 yards. By the time the .30-06 cracked the second time, the bear dropped, rolled and skidded to a stop only 30 yards away.

"I think I'll put one more slug in him from here for good measure," Don thought as he carefully squeezed the trigger on an empty chamber.

"Damn," Don said to himself as he high-stepped back to the tent for more bullets. "I only put two in this morning."

Shortly, he was sneaking around the other side of the tent for a better angle, he claimed later. But I say he just didn't want to go back to where the bear had seen him last. Good strategy too, I might add, when you are in a bear fight.

As Don sought to deliver the "one for good measure" he discovered, much to his dismay, that the return to the warm tent had fogged his scope and he couldn't see a thing through it.

Luckily, the second shot had finished the job. The first shot had just knicked the bear under the chin and gone on to destroy the brand new latigo on the only saddle in the entire tack shed—Don's!

Don and I lost several other latigos in a bear confrontation that resulted in the worst horse wreck either of us has ever had the misfortune to experience.

I think one of the most dangerous factors an outfitter has to cope with while hunting or riding in grizzly country is his saddle horse and pack stock. About half of the time the horses pay little or no attention to bears. It's the other half of the time that ages you so quickly and thoroughly, the half when just one horse believes with all his heart that the very demons of hell are about to latch onto his tail. When that happens it's "Katy bar the door," because stuff is going to get broken, your plunder is going to be scattered from hell to breakfast and your nerves will never be the same.

We were on a sheep trail, threading our way along a boulder-strewn hog's back ridge at about 9,000 feet elevation one beautiful September

afternoon. The ridge was so narrow at this spot that while on horseback you could easily see off both sides. To our right it was nearly straight down several hundred feet to a jagged rock outcropping. We looked down onto the lance-shaped tops of distant spruce trees. To the left of us was a tree-covered slope that was as steep as the one on our right.

Don was in the lead with three pack horses and I was following with another three pack horses. Behind me was our somewhat apprehensive sheep hunter.

The trail made a sharp right turn and Don clawed his way to the top of an especially steep and rocky portion of the trail. When his saddle horse reached a flat spot at the top, the lead ropes of all three pack horses were taut and strained nearly to the breaking point. The horses strained every muscle to make the grade, their massive lungs screaming for more oxygen as they gulped ragged breaths through foam-rimmed mouths.

I was resting my pack string at the base of the ascent, waiting for Don's string to top the ridge.

Suddenly, he yelled, "I can't hold them, Duane!"

Don's warning reached me just before the falling rocks and a heartbeat before the three rolling, plunging, crashing pack horses. With no room to maneuver my saddle horse, I quit him just as he was broadsided by a 1,200-pound horse-flesh bowling ball. I hit the ground running at a right angle to the cascading rocks, branches and horses. The second horse knocked me flat, but rolled over me so fast I was only bruised and scratched. I was on all fours and digging for the safety of a big pine tree as the third horse bounced over my legs.

From the tree that I was anchored to, I could see Don on the trail above me, still on horseback and peering into the cloud of dust.

He called to me.

"I'm all right, Don. But what the hell happened up there anyway?" I shouted.

"It was a griz. He stood up and popped his teeth about 20 yards in front of me," was his reply.

"Well, you may as well get comfortable up there because I'll be a while cutting these horses loose and getting back on the trail," I answered.

A few yards below me, all of the pack horses were hung up in the timber. Two of them were upside down against the trees and the third one was folded around a tree with all four feet off the ground.

When the pack horse Don was leading saw the upright bear, he just reared back and Don had to turn him loose or get himself pulled into the melee. After that, gravity took over and things got Western in a hurry.

Speaking of Western, it doesn't get any more Western than when you startle a grizzly sow with a cub. One of my elk guides, Richard Mason, and his brother, Dennis, experienced just such a close encounter of the worst kind.

We were between hunts so the boys went up above Jones Creek Camp for some personal hunting. It was a bright, crisp mid-October morning as they dismounted and tied their horses a couple of hundred yards below a springy aspen-lined meadow. They had just split up to begin their hunt. The gentle breeze was in their faces as they approached the lower end of the 20-acre meadow about 30 yards apart. The she-bear was in full charge, with her sights locked on Dennis, when the unsuspecting young man saw her. Richard's reaction and response was instant, aggressive and probably saved his brother's life, but greatly jeopardized his own. There was no time to think. No time to shout instructions. Barely time to do or die. Lunging a step toward the enraged grizzly, Richard shouted and fired his rifle in the air to spook her off.

Richard has survived several false charges by grizzlies with similar antics and has considered himself somewhat grizzly-proof. A very physically capable, macho young man in his mid-twenties, he is very good with his rifle, rope, horse, pack string and the six-gun that he wore. Richard was an accomplished boxer/slugger in high school. About five-feet ten-inches, built solid and strong as an ox, he grew up accompanying his father in this very drainage on numerous elk hunts.

But this was not a false charge!

In response to Richard's action the bear changed her angle of charge. In a heartbeat, the 500 pounds of anger bore into Richard at full attack speed.

Her piercing yellow eyes; her open, fang-filled mouth; her grunting and sick-smelling bad breath were in Richard's face before he could lever his Winchester and bring it into play. Richard went over backwards from the force of her impact, scattering pine cones and needles as they hit the ground solidly. When she struck him, Richard instinctively grabbed each of her laid-back ears using his strong hands and forearms for leverage. He was able to thrust his own face to the right and her bristling, snarling, wrinkled up nose to his left. The desperate maneuver saved his vital throat, but the pain was white hot as her massive jaw forced her teeth through his heavy down jacket and into his left shoulder. For what seemed like an eternity, Richard struggled to draw his six-gun, but the weight of the bear and the intensity of the attack prevented it. She was all over him, biting, shaking, swatting mostly his head, neck and shoulders. He was helpless. It was only seconds before Dennis ran over and excitedly fired two shots at the bear while she was mauling Richard. Luckily, the shots missed both Richard and the bear. Grizzly bears in

Wyoming are currently on the endangered species list and the federal bu-
reaucrats take a very dim view of anyone killing a griz.

With a parting swat and growl the sow left Richard bloody, bruised
and wiser.

The boys hustled down to their horses, rode the 10 miles to a phone
and reported the incident to the Wyoming Game and Fish Department.
Then they drove to the hospital in Cody for stitches to re-attach
Richard's left ear and a tetanus shot.

The one lesson the bears have taught us, and they reinforce it annu-
ally, is that they are absolutely unpredictable.

The old axiom of "an ounce of prevention is worth a pound of cure"
is never more true than when dealing with grizzlies. As Don Juby would
say, "By God, Cap'n, once you step in it with a griz, there is going to be
hell to pay."

Whiskey Canyon's Stock Killer

by Ron D. Moore

E xhausted, gasping for air, I struggled the last few feet to the narrow ledge and collapsed with my back against the face of the bluff. My legs were weak and trembling, my lungs felt as if they were going to burst and sweat burned my eyes. I stared down at the canyon, hoping to catch sight of my helper, Eddie Wisdom. Fifty feet from me, around a slight bend in the ledge, my pack of hounds had bayed a very large bear that was wounded—and very angry.

My gaze drifted from the bottom of the canyon to the Ruger .44 Rem. Mag. pistol in my sweaty hand and I shuddered. I was trapped on the ledge with a wounded bear and there were only two rounds left. Gathering all the courage I could, I started crawling around the ledge toward the bear.

It was late April in Young, Arizona, and the weather was beautiful. The trees along Cherry Creek were budding and spring was knocking at the door. I lived in Young where we operated a full-time hunting operation. Finishing up our lion hunts the first week in April, Eddie and I had spent the remainder of the month working on equipment in preparation for moving our spring bear camp to western New Mexico. We had spent this particular day bent under horses, nailing on horseshoes. It was a back-breaking chore.

Christie, my wife, finally had mercy on us and had brought some iced tea down to the corral. Sitting against the fence, letting the sweat dry on our bodies, we stared at the mountains surrounding the little valley.

Tomorrow, I told Eddie, we would get away from all this and take the hounds for an exercise ride.

When we unloaded our horses at the old Blumer Ranch the next morning, I was looking forward to an enjoyable day free from pressure. We had brought all the hounds, as this was to be an exercise day for the trained older dogs, and a discipline clinic for the younger hounds; all were fresh and rested. Soon after starting out, it became obvious that maintaining control was going to be a major problem until they settled down.

After climbing the trail to Catholic Peak, we spent most of our time not relaxing, but chucking rocks at the young hounds that wanted to trail everything from chipmunks to non-existent elephants.

I've always loved this spot as it seems that you can see the whole world from there. Directly below is Flying V Flat and far to the east are the rock walls of Canyon Creek on the White Mountain Apache Indian Reservation. Far to the south, Castle and Gunsight Buttes stand as lonely sentinels above Cherry Creek. When my work has worn me down, this place and others like it rejuvenate me and cause me to count my blessings.

Because of the number of hounds—and their zeal—I chose a route that would take us through the easiest country possible. Riding off on an old mining road to Flying V Flat, we turned north and stayed on the flat. Two miles up, we turned back west on a trail that led up a rugged small canyon and climbed out to where the trail hit Pine Springs Mesa on the north side of the peak. From there, we had a choice of two routes. We could go straight through Brushy Basin to the Blumer Ranch or we could go north across the mesa, take the trail at Pine Springs down to Crouch Creek, and down the creek to the ranch.

Brushy Basin is extremely rugged country and full of small varmints that might tempt the pups, so we elected to take the longer but easier way across the mesa.

The mesa stretches three miles north to the base of Gentry Mountain where Pine Springs bubbles up out of the rocks. It is the site of the old Brewer homestead, a once-thriving homestead where high hopes flourished. Only the rock chimney remains. On a small knoll lies the grave of a little three-year-old Brewer girl who died in 1910. A fence had been built around the grave, a granite headstone placed and irises planted. Long grown over, the only visitors now are the occasional cowboys who pass by. Each time I visit here, it saddens me to think how terrible it must have been to bury a three-year-old in this harsh land.

We had come within a half mile of the homestead when one of my trained dogs bawled in a shallow draw to our left. This had the same effect as pulling the pin on a grenade. The pent-up hounds started pouring into the draw in full bay with us close at their heels.

Our trek quickly lost any resemblance to an orderly hunt. We were a disorganized calvary. The hounds were running in circles around a dead, white-faced yearling steer in the bottom of the draw. The carcass and the sign around it clearly indicated that the steer had been killed and partially eaten by a very large bear. The bear sign was fresh and, by the time I mounted, the hounds were in full chase and heading toward Pine Springs.

With our horses in a long lope, we had little trouble keeping within hearing distance of the hounds as we headed down the gentle slope to the springs. I knew this would change when we reached the canyons above Crouch Creek. Most of that area is impassable by horseback, as the spring itself is located at the head of the roughest canyons. Reaching there, we could hear the hounds heading down to the bottom of the canyon. The tempo had picked up and it sounded as if they had jumped the bear off the water and were hot on its heels.

We held up at the spring to survey the situation and decided which way to go, because we couldn't follow the bear on our horses. The Pine Springs trail to our left led to the bottom of Crouch Creek, but far from where the bear had crossed. To the right was a rugged canyon that headed towards Gentry Mountain. To the west was the rim of Crouch Creek.

Crouch Creek's rim narrows to a point that overlooks the main canyon and separates the mouths of two canyons by only a hundred yards or so. A range boundary fence kept us from following the rim over the canyon the bear had taken. Another fence ran due north across the flat.

I knew from previous experience that the canyon was a favorite of bears in this area and that they chose this canyon when being pressured by the dogs. I guessed that the bear would continue down the canyon, round the point, and make its stand someplace in the other canyon. If we hurried across the flat we should be able to intercept it.

As we trotted and loped across the flat, a thought kept gnawing at me. What if the bear, full of cow meat and tanked up on water, decided not to go on to the bottom, but make a stand in the canyon to our left? Rather than heading to the other canyon to wait for the show to come to us, I decided we had better check the canyon to our left. We pulled up at the fence, tied our horses, climbed the fence and ran the 200 yards to the rim.

It was a good decision. The welcome sound of the hounds baying burst out of the bottom up to us when we reached the rim. The baying was frenzied, and it was not moving. The bear had made a stand and was fighting the dogs on the ground.

As we hurriedly jerked off our chaps and spurs, I became acutely aware for the first time that day of our firepower. The only weapon I had along was my .44 Rem. Mag. handgun with its 7^1/$_2$-inch barrel. Six rounds in the pistol and six in my pocket was all that I ever carried. Eddie had a semi-automatic .22 rimfire rifle on the back of his horse, which was still tied up at the fence. Running and sliding, we started off to the bottom of the canyon.

We reached the bottom, breathing heavily and drenched with sweat. The hounds and bear were in a patch of thick oak brush about 50 yards from us and barely 10 yards up from the bottom. Confident that the hunt would soon be over, we didn't take time to catch our breath. Instead, we quickly moved below to the fight. There was a deer trail leading through the brush to the bear, so we inched along, moving toward the animal.

But the bear heard us and broke for the bottom. I turned downhill on a run, beating the bear down, but puffing like a steam engine. As it bounded across the narrow opening 15 yards from me, I got off three quick shots before it disappeared in the brush. I was certain that all three shots had hit the bear, but it never broke stride. I covered those 15 yards in seconds as the dogs were coming into the bottom. The dark bulk of the bear was plowing through the brush so, trying to control my breathing, I fired the pistol's last three rounds.

I cursed as I fought to reload my gun with the last six cartridges. The hounds had caught up with the bear again and the fight was very slowly moving at an angle toward the top. The bear seemed to be getting sick, which meant I should be able to overtake it and finish the job. I instructed Eddie to return to the horses and bring them down to the fenceline that dropped off into the next canyon. At the angle the bear was moving, that was where it should top out if I didn't overtake it. Eddie was to yell for me if I didn't meet him there.

Moving up, I immediately spotted dark splotches of blood on the rocks and brush. But, pushing as fast as the brush allowed, I couldn't seem to gain on the hounds and bear. Soon the fight was pulling away from me. I finally collapsed and listened as the hounds faded out of hearing. Forcing myself to my feet, I headed up to where Eddie would be waiting.

I reached the fence 200 yards short of where I was to meet my helper, and grabbed a post, fighting to get my wind back. I couldn't hear a hound and there were no horse tracks on the other side of the fence. I wanted very badly to just lie down in the shade and wait for Eddie to get there, but I couldn't. I crossed the fence and began searching for where the bear and hounds had crossed. I found it just down the fenceline. The trail led straight toward the other canyon.

Following the tracks, I was sure that when I reached the rim I would hear the hounds and they would have the bear stopped again. There was only silence, however. They had to have turned down the canyon toward Crouch Creek. Where the devil was Eddie? I started along the rim, hoping to intercept my helper. Putting one foot in front of the other was now becoming a major effort.

Suddenly, I could hear the hounds loud and clear. They were all the way to the bottom and were really talking to that bear. I was just about completely given out—and torn between waiting for my helper and heading down to try to finish the bear. Anxious moments passed until I couldn't stand it any longer. I started down an old trail at a trot. I had forgotten how steep it was and my trot soon turned into a nearly out-of-control run.

Unfortunately, I rolled enough rocks to let the bear know I was coming, and when I staggered into the creek it had left.

I still could hear the hounds. They were in full chase and their voices were bouncing off the canyon sides, seeming to come from every direction at once. Finally, their voices faded completely away without my being able to get a direction of travel from them. In despair, I sank down into the cool pine needles and lay there for an hour until I heard Eddie calling down from the top.

While Eddie brought the horses, I tried to stretch out the stiffness that had set in while I rested. My old black horse was sure enough a welcome sight. Not knowing what direction the hounds had gone left us with one alternative: scour the creek bottom for their tracks. When we found them, the trail headed west up the other side of the canyon. We lost it when the ground gave way to red shale rock. The bear and the hounds had over an hour's head start on us and could be anywhere by now. But something kept telling me that the last one of my shots had hit that bear hard enough to make it too sick for a long run.

Once we reached the top, the country would turn to a flat mesa two or more miles across. In its condition, I was sure the bear would not attempt to outrun the dogs across that flat terrain. We now were across the canyon from where all of this started. To the south were three side canyons that cut into the mesa. Though short, they were extremely deep. It was called Whiskey Canyon because a moonshiner had a still there at the turn of the century. It seemed logical that we would find the bear and my hounds in one of those three canyons. But anyone having more than a passing experience with bears knows that, more often than not, they will do the illogical.

We pushed the horses to the top and pulled up to listen. I could hear nothing, but Eddie thought that he had heard a dog far away. We crossed the first two canyons with some difficulty, then Eddie suddenly pulled up and turned in the saddle, pointing his left ear towards Whiskey Canyon.

"I am sure I heard a dog this time," he said.

The sounds were faint, but they had to be close or we wouldn't have heard them due to the lay of this canyon. We fixed their position in our minds and pulled back. If we couldn't hear them, then the bear couldn't hear us. Being careful to stay at a distance from the rim, we rode along until we felt we were above the bear. Then we removed out chaps and spurs and hurried over to the rim.

Our guesswork had paid off. The hounds were directly below us, baying constantly. Eddie was cradling the .22 rifle in the crook of his arm. I started to tell him to leave it behind, but thought better of it. I had only six rounds left in my pistol.

This time we were careful to slip down the ledges as quietly as possible. With adrenalin flowing at full pumping capacity, it took a fair amount of self discipline to shake off the urge to barge ahead. We didn't want to spook the bear again for a couple of reasons. It was getting hot, the hounds were nearly spent and the canyon got extremely rough from this point down. From here, the pursuit would be on foot and I didn't have the reserves left for it.

The bear was not in the bottom, but on the opposite canyon wall. It would have been better if we could have come in above it. To make matters worse, the vegetation now opened up, meaning if we could see the bear, it would be able to see us. I froze in my tracks, motioning Eddie to stop. There, directly across the canyon, was the bear. It had its rear end backed into an oak bush, its ears laid back, and was swinging its head back and forth, trying to keep track of the hounds. There were hounds on both sides and a gutsy little female named Curly was right in front, just inches from the bear's muzzle.

We eased down behind a big rock to figure our next move. There was no way to cross without the bear hearing or seeing us, and it was a long shot with a pistol. There was also the risk of hitting a dog, but I couldn't see any other way. Gripping the pistol in both hands, I took a dead rest on a rock, held slightly above the bear, waited for Curly to move, then squeezed off a shot.

When I fired the bear flipped completely over backwards, sending rocks crashing to the bottom. In a heartbeat, it was on its feet and heading downhill. I hurriedly snapped off another shot which splattered on the rocks over its back. Forcing myself to settle down, I took deliberate aim and got off two more shots before the bear was gone.

I paused a few seconds, hoping I had inflicted mortal wounds. The hounds were aware now that I had caught up and were taking the bear back up the canyon with renewed zeal. Without waiting for my helper, I started down at a run, which quickly deteriorated into a struggling walk with my breath coming in short, gasping spurts. I had to force myself to go on.

The chase had now moved high up in the ledges, but my body would not obey my brain's command to keep going and I slumped against a pine tree. The dogs and bear were already about halfway up the stair-stepping ledges.

I grudgingly began climbing hand over hand, acutely aware that I would have to get very close to make my last two shots count. Every so often, I checked over my shoulder for Eddie. His .22 rifle was now taking on more importance in this hunt. At last, I pulled what was left of me onto the ledge with the dogs and bear.

I had been harboring a faint hope that the ledge would provide the bear with an option to retreat. But as I peered around the bend, I could see the bear 20 yards away and there was a sheer drop-off behind it. Its only way off the ledge would be right over the top of me. The bear was facing me. On its right was a large rock, on its left was the face of a large bluff and these formed a small V-shaped enclave. The bear had backed into it to protect its rear-end from the hounds.

On the plus side, a pinon pine's trunk obscured me from the bear's vision. A slight movement to either side and the bear would see me.

My legs were rubbery, but I began easing slowly toward the bear, being very careful to keep the tree between me and its head. A few of the dogs were aware of my presence and were lunging at the bear, causing it to swing its head in all directions. I wished silently that there was some way to communicate to the dogs that we had only two rounds left. I now was close enough to reach around the tree and slap the bear, but I still could not get a shot.

All the hounds, except one, had crowded into the space between the rock and the tree and were bawling only inches from the bear's face. One dog was in the narrow space between the tree and the bluff. Crouching, my heart pounding, I tried to come up with some sort of plan. The bear's attention was focused on the hounds on its right. If I leaped to that side I would be shooting head-on at the bear. A head shot is a must in this situation, but I would be shooting into the plane of its head and at this angle the bullet might glance upwards and not penetrate. There also was the possibility of being knocked off my feet by that mass of baying hounds before I could get off a good shot.

That only left one alternative. In one jump, I could be astraddle the hound between the tree and the bluff, and this move would bring the bear into full view. I would be so close that I would literally have to stick the barrel in the bear's left ear to shoot.

I cocked the hammer, took a deep breath—and my body would not move. I looked around for a place to escape if things did not go well, there was none. Where was Eddie? What I wouldn't give at this moment for his .22 rifle! I took another breath and leaped astraddle the dog, swung the pistol against the bear's ear and pulled the trigger.

When the pistol bucked, I instinctively jumped backwards, cocking the hammer as I went. I landed in a shooting crouch, fully expecting to see the bear hurling itself at me in a full charge. Instead, hounds were piling into the enclave with the bear. The welfare of my dogs snapped back into my mind and I charged in with the hounds. The bear was stone dead and I stepped back and collapsed in a heap. Drained from exhaustion and tension, I could not move. I knew I should be petting and prais-

ing my dogs, but I could not muster the strength to holster my gun, much less crawl back to the bear.

This was the position Eddie found me when he at last struggled onto the ledge, breathless, and wanting to know where the bear was.

"He's dead," I said. "Please get over there and pet the dogs."

Skinning the bear and getting back to the horse was a struggle in my condition. My muscles stiffened, making the seven-mile ride to the truck pure agony. Eddie, the youngster, had quite a chuckle at my expense as he watched the difficulty I had dismounting at the Blumer Ranch. My muscles seemed frozen in the riding position.

The bear was a huge old male with cracked canines worn almost to the gum line. This dental condition would have kept it in constant pain and done little to improve his disposition. Its weight was much below what it should have been and its pelt was in poor condition. I am sure its stock-killing practices would have escalated if I had not saved it from a lot of suffering and the possible slow death of starvation.

Of the 11 shots I had fired, eight of them had hit the bear—including the one behind the ear that had finally killed it. Four had struck the first time we caught up with it, yet it had covered some five miles after that. The old bear was tough, and it probably had reached much deeper into its reserves of strength to keep going than I had. The grit and tenacity with which bears cling to life always amazes me.

Eddie and I set to work moving my camp to New Mexico. I made sure he didn't forget the day the old man dusted him in the canyon. I have trouble these days keeping my britches hitched up, due to the extra weight of the pistol cartridges in my pockets, but it makes me feel more secure. Being down to one round was too close for comfort.

Assorted Commentary

by Mike Kraetsch

S omewhere out there must exist a large reference book of statements, comments, excuses and prerequisite sayings, that all hunters are required to read before going on any guided big game hunt. The statements seem to be universal no matter what the age, sex, social background, income or part of the country from which the hunter hails.

However, apparently not all hunters have spent the same amount of time studying the book and are not as well versed in the proper terminology and vocabulary for every given situation. Others have skipped a chapter or two and obviously haven't spent much time practicing their delivery and timing. Generally though, most hunters are naturals and can rattle off any one of the old standbys without the least bit of prompting.

At one time or another during any hunting season, most big game guides will be required to comment or answer a substantial number of these utterances, which must amount to at least the first half of the book, and occasionally they'll run into a hunter who specializes in the more obscure statements found only in the last chapters.

Here's a few of the more common hunter comments: "I can't believe I missed!"; "What's the elevation?"; "Hit him right behind the shoulder!"; "Boy, are they big!"; "My scope is fogged."; "What will that one score?"; "How much does he weigh?"; "I forgot my binoculars, or canteen, lunch, rain jacket, knife, etc."; "Are we lost?"; "My sights are off."; "Is he legal?"; "How old is he?"; "Which way to the truck, trailhead, camp, etc.?"

One of the most commonly used statements in the area of the country where I guide is the "Is he legal?" question. The preponderance of its use is probably due to our state's enactment of a mandatory four-point antler restriction for elk, and a three-point restriction for deer in some areas.

Actually, as a guide, I'd rather answer that question every time we spot a bull or buck then to have a hunter kill an illegal animal. Timing of the question is all important, however.

It was a beautiful Indian summer opening morning of the first rifle elk season a couple of years ago. My hunter Mark (name changed to protect my innocence) and I were hunting in an area that had several nice bull elk that were still bugling in the warm fall weather. We were working our way through some rolling aspen forest when we heard a bugle from a slope directly above us. Giving Mark some whispered instructions, we quickly moved toward the bull to close the distance and to locate a more suitable position before I would bugle a return challenge.

Upon reaching a better spot, I began to blow my bugle and had hardly finished when the bull bellowed an answer. He was coming in! I moved Mark about 30 yards up a rise ahead of me and motioned for him to take a rest for his .25-06 on an aspen tree. The bull would walk right past him if all went as planned.

As I bugled again and raked some brush with a stick, I could hear the bull breaking brush and horning trees as he worked his way up the opposite side of the rise. From my vantage (much lower than Mark's) the first thing I saw of the bull was his impressive 5x5 rack as he peered over the rise. Then his entire neck and chest came into view. I was tensed for the report of Mark's rifle and at just the moment I expected to hear the gun go off, Mark "whispered" in a volume that sounded shrill as a train whistle going off in the still woods, "Is he legal?" I answered "yes" as the bull broke brush about a quarter of a mile from where he had been standing broadside about two seconds earlier.

A day later, I placed Mark in a meadow that the elk were frequenting, for an evening stand. The meadow was one of a series of old beaver ponds that were being reclaimed by sediment and vegetation. At dusk the elk would come out from their heavy timber bedding areas to feed on the lush meadow grasses. I left Mark in a strategic spot so he could cover the entire meadow, and headed off to watch another pond in case the elk decided to come out there instead. I left Mark with instructions on when I would meet him at dark if I didn't hear any shooting.

I spent an uneventful evening watching hawks, tweety birds and squirrels at my beaver meadow, and was assuming Mark had done the same. I was waiting at our rendezvous site when I heard Mark's gun go off. My first thought was more of disbelief than concern. I thought

maybe he had tripped and shot himself, (Mark was a real *mover* in the woods). I cautiously made my way to the edge of Mark's meadow. By this time it was fairly dark, so I made a very deliberate display of waving my flashlight. I could see Mark's silhouette out in the middle of the meadow, so I made my way toward him.

This time it was my turn to ask, "Is it legal?" Marks' reply was a less than confident, "I think so."

Just what a guide wants to hear! After retrieving some help and some tracking lights, we located the bull a couple of hours later. I breathed a giant sigh of relief as our lights fell on the rack of a legal bull.

From the hunter's standpoint, one of the most utilitarian of all hunter commentary statements must be the utterance, "My scope is off." If it's bow season the statement can be modified to accommodate bow sights or string peeps, and still have the same versatility. Whatever the variation of the comment used, it has many applications. However, this statement must be used with extreme caution! If used improperly or delivered incorrectly, it comes across only as a terribly lame excuse.

Surprisingly enough, for some reason a great number of rifle hunters will decline to shoot their rifles to check their scope's alignment and accuracy before entering the field. They seem satisfied with the fact that they shot it about two months earlier in a 30 mile per hour crosswind back home and it proved "reasonably" accurate. It makes no difference to them that the three plane changes they made to get to camp also included three changes for their luggage. The fact that their gun cases were handled by a bunch of guys who somehow missed the audition for the part of the gorilla in the old luggage commercials has no effect on their decision not to shoot a couple of insurance rounds. These fellows are 180 degrees from the guys who must shoot a box a day to make sure they're still "on."

An example of poor delivery of the "Scope is off" statement invariably occurs after a hunter has missed...sometimes several shots at the same animal.

I was guiding for a well-known outfitter in New Mexico a fall or two back, and was sitting with a client overlooking a large meadow with a mineral seep and wallow in the middle of it. Like at the beaver ponds, the elk would move out of the surrounding timber to graze on the meadow grass and drink from the mineral seep every day at dusk. On this particular evening there were about 50 head of cows, calves and small bulls out in the meadow in front of us. We watched them feeding and playing for about 20 minutes, waiting for a large bull to move out from the timber. As we sat there watching some calves play tag, a nice 6x5 bull moved out into the clearing. We waited until the bull was about half way out from the timber before he was clear for a shot and the hunter could open up.

By this time my hunter was a nervous wreck. Four shots later the bull entered the trees about 250 yards away unscathed. Guess what the hunter's statement was? Yup. "My scope must be off." Bad timing, bad delivery!

If a guy is hunting along through some steep country and he loses his footing and falls down a sheer shale slope; if this guy tosses his rifle about half way down and watches it go skidding off a small cliff and land in some oak brush about 30 yards below him; and if upon retrieving his weapon he finds that his scope is at a right angle to his barrel; if this guy looks you right in the eye and, with no visible expression exclaims, "My scope must be off," now that's great timing and delivery! For some reason though, at about the time he retrieves his gun, the air usually gets a little blue. An experienced guide can usually pick out little excerpts

about $500 scopes and custom satin finished stocks. Most guys generally exhibit a great propensity for wanting to throw things as well. It's at times like these that most good guides will fall back on one of their old standbys like: "Shall we stop for a little lunch?"

Maybe one of these winters when I'm snowbound in my cabin and I've got nothing else to do but watch the water boil in the pot on top of the wood stove, I'll write a book of witty responses for guides. I'd probably have to include lots of pictures since most guides that I know only look at the pictures anyway. But then the guy who wrote the hunter's book would probably come out with a revised version and I'd have to update my book and we'd be in a vicious circle. Since I really don't want to get into that sort of thing, I'll probably just make some hot chocolate out of the boiling water and forget about the whole thing.

Two-For-One Bighorn

by Charlie Stricker
as told to Tony Caligiuri

Assuming that I've held what might be considered an official title, I guess it would be "sheep outfitter." For the past 30 years or so I've run some of the most consistent outfits in the north for Stone sheep, Dall sheep and Rocky Mountain bighorns. Now, Stones and Dalls are pretty predictable and, while hunts might take you on some steep climbs, success almost always comes to those who try. On the other hand, bighorns take a bit of luck thrown in with the normal skill and determination, even in the sheep-rich basins of my outfitting territory above Alberta's Smoky River.

Luck. That one magic word that often means the difference between a rough, cold, empty-handed walk off a mountain or a happy spike camp feasting on sheep ribs and admiring the horns of a full curl ram by the flickering light of a dying fire.

So on that August morning of 1978, I thought I had all the luck in the world as my hunter, Ken and I lay on our bellies and counted 42 bighorn rams in one bunch. One would go 40 inches and easily make the record book; there were 12 other respectable rams as well. In the 1970s it was fairly common to see big bunches of rams summered up like this in the high basins where they fatten up, unmolested in the mountain pastures. Since we were the first party of the year, I told Ken that I was fairly certain that the rams hadn't been worried about anything for the past three or four months. But the big boy didn't get to be as big as he was by being dumb. He and his buddies were in a basin that offered them good visibility and would be tough to approach from any direction.

Many times I had observed big rams lying 40 or 50 yards off the side of the main bunch hidden in some scrub willow, dwarf birch or shinoak tangle. They can detect the slightest movement, even from behind, and they have a highly acute, often underestimated sense of smell. I believe that bighorns in hunted areas further condition their sense of smell by associating shooting and dead rams with the smell of human beings. Keeping all this in mind, I planned our stalk, being careful not to move through any areas where we would run into sheep we hadn't seen.

We quietly bellied up over a saddle and there was the big boy right below us. Then our luck ran out. I felt a tiny wisp of wind against my neck and the ram was gone. No hesitation whatsoever! The instant the scent hit them, the rams looked like a music video of Hank Snow's "Movin' On." With all the rams up and running there was no chance to shoot. They slowed down about 600 yards out, and I watched them through my 10-power glasses, tongues lolling and sides heaving in the hot August heat. Though watching 42 rams move out in high gear was a grand experience, my hunter still had an empty spot on his trophy room wall.

I knew from past experience that when rams run that hard, they won't stop until there is a good stretch of Rocky Mountain real estate between them and the hunters.

Ken wasn't saying much. This was a short hunt and, as he didn't have much more time, he was a pretty disappointed sheep chaser as we climbed down to tree line. The advantage of a backpack sheep hunt becomes readily apparent when you're too tired to walk any farther. You just pull camp out of your pack and set up, which is exactly what we did. While Ken was busy being dejected, my mind was busy sorting out a hike for the next morning to another band of rams that I'd found on a preseason scouting trip.

Sleep in our little backpack tent came quickly after a dinner of freeze-dried food and Snicker bars. The next morning as we broke down camp, I could tell Ken was anxious, but I kept my plan to myself. Finally, he asked if I thought we would get a sheep today. I calmly said yes. Being both a sporting and drinking man, Ken bet me a bottle of whiskey that we would not get a sheep. I took the bet.

Spike camp banter being what it is, pretty soon the bet was one case of his whiskey to one bottle of mine that we would not get a ram. The deal sounded good to me, so I shouldered my pack and we pushed out to the area where I had first found the rams.

After four hours of hard walking, I saw the white rump of a ram bounce over a short knoll about 500 yards away. We worked our way up the knoll and bellied over the top, only to stare eye-to-eye with a young ram about 15 feet away. I backed up quickly, but for the second time in the same hunt, we had rams in high gear. We ran 150 yards to the head of the canyon and stopped to catch our breath. Ken was badly winded, and I was concerned how his shooting would be. The rams were bunched up just 30 yards over the edge.

The biggest ram was half-covered by a smaller ram. I didn't think Ken would have trouble at 30 yards, so I told him to take the ram when he was ready. The sheep were pretty nervous and were milling around, but

they didn't know we were there. I heard the safety click off, then heard the .300 Win. Mag. bark in my ear. I had my glasses on the big ram, and saw blood on his flank, so I told Ken to hit him again. Ken replied that he had hit him well and didn't need to shoot again.

I was thinking to myself, "This ram's walking away and the guy thinks he's hit good." Though it takes a while to recount, it all happened in a few seconds. Finally, the big ram walked over a ridge and I heard Ken shoot again. Now I was really confused, the ram wasn't even in sight and Ken was shooting. Then I got more confused when I saw that he was shooting at a ram that was already dead in the bottom of the canyon. We hustled down the canyon and found the big ram was crumpled up about 40 yards away from another, smaller ram. We looked closely at both rams and figured out what had happened in just a few minutes.

The smaller ram had bucked ahead as Ken shot, and the bullet passed through his neck, splitting into two pieces. The two bullet fragments entered the big ram's flank about three-quarters of an inch apart doing enough damage to kill him. Ken's other shots at the smaller, dead ram had fortunately missed altogether.

I told my nervous hunter we had to pack both rams out and hope that the Fish and Game Department would see the evidence as we did. After everything was off the mountain and at base camp, we delivered both rams and a signed statement to Fish and Game. They listened intently to our stories and informed us that an investigation would be conducted; most likely, charges would follow.

Ken flew home and I went back to base-camp thoroughly convinced I would be charged and feeling terrible about killing the smaller ram. After my next hunt was over, I checked with the game warden in charge of the case to see what the damage would be. Much to my surprise, we had been completely cleared of any wrongdoing and he even commended us on bringing in both sheep.

I called home to relay the good news and got another surprise. That day not one, but two, cases of whiskey had been delivered to the house!

The Get-Even Bear

by Al Pletzke

Gusting winds shoved ugly black clouds over our hide-out. Elm trees snapped in half, crashing to the river bottom below us, and I was worried. Barb O'Brian and I sat near a small clearing surrounded by poplar trees. Lightning flashed across the sky. Thunder roared down around us. As if held by flood gates, the clouds opened, drenching us with a violent downpour.

I made up my mind. "Barb, follow me. We're getting out of here, now!" I yelled over the sound of crashing trees.

We worked our way out of the poplar trees into the spruce for more protection. Within 15 minutes we were in the Jeep and on our way out of the woods.

It was opening day of Michigan's bear season and Barb was hunting bear, for the first time, in the Upper Peninsula. Her husband, Bob, had hunted with me the previous year, taking a nice boar bruin. This year he and Barb had returned to the small town of Bruce Crossing to hunt black bears.

Dropping Barb off at the ranch, I headed back for Bob. As suddenly as it began, the storm blew over and the wind died down. Bob was quite comfortable in a thick stand of heavy spruce; the storm hadn't affected him at all. After a quick discussion, we decided to stay on the bear bait until dark.

A half hour later, I noticed movement on the edge of the small clearing we were watching.

"Bob, get ready," I whispered. "Something's moving our way."

"You sure?" Bob asked as he followed my gaze. "I don't see a thing."

After 20 minutes, I was beginning to doubt my own eyes. Too much bear on the brain and too much rain on the noggin, I thought, just as a big bear stood up and cautiously looked around. As he shuffled silently into the clearing, I could see his big shoulder muscles rippling under sleek black fur.

Bob was ready. Raising the .300 Win. Mag., he gently squeezed the trigger, shattering the evening stillness with the rifle's report. The bear spun around and stumbled, almost falling. As he turned, he tried to locate the source of his trouble. Bone chilling fury flashed from his eyes as he glared in our direction. An instant later, he turned and crashed into the alders. Then, no noise—no brush snapping—just silence.

The shot was good. Sitting directly behind Bob, I had seen the bullet's impact. After a few minutes, we eased out of the blind and cautiously worked our way to where the bear had been standing. A wide trail of blood led into the woods. Forty yards later, in heavy alders and grass, Bob's bear was draped over a tangle of stumps.

"Bob, take the Jeep back to the house and have someone bring the tractor and trailer out here," I said. I'll field dress this fellow while you're gone."

By the time we arrived at the house it was dark. Bob was really happy, but Barb was disappointed.

"We shouldn't have come in so early," she said.

"Maybe you're right," I countered. "But I just didn't consider it safe out there. Don't worry. Today is your first day of hunting. Your chance will come," I said.

The next day Barb and I were back in the blind near the small clearing. I was glad we had left early the night before. A large poplar had blown down, smashing part of our blind. We could have been killed—or at least scared to death!

As we settled down in what was left of the blind the wind picked up, blowing steadily harder as the sun sank toward the horizon. An hour after we entered the blind, a movement near some old apple trees caught my attention. Barb had already noticed the coyote as it slowly worked its way toward the bear bait. Something, perhaps hunger, pulled the coyote toward the bait. He walked within two feet of the blind and never noticed our presence.

"Barb, there's something about that critter I don't like. Take him," I whispered.

She had to wait for the coyote to actually move away from the blind before shooting. At six feet, she fired. The coyote did a back flip and never moved. It was unusual for a keenly sensed animal, such as a coyote, to approach that close to a blind without scenting the hunters. Cautiously checking him for signs of rabies, we found none.

"We've created enough noise tonight. Let's leave. We'll try again tomorrow," I said.

The next afternoon, we were back in the blind playing the waiting game. Calm winds and an overcast sky made bear hunting conditions perfect.

"This is the night, Barb," I said, settling in for the evening hunt.

"I hope so. That coyote made last night interesting, but it's time for a bear!" she replied with the type of enthusiasm reserved for new bear hunters.

Three hours later a bear crept into my side of the clearing. He had approached from the deep brush of the nearby river valley. Cautiously, he meandered 20 yards into the clearing and lay down in the tall grass. Barb hadn't seen him yet.

"Get ready, Barb," I whispered, as I tapped her on the shoulder.

"Stop kidding," she replied, in a voice too loud for bear hunting.

The bear stood up and ambled toward the bait. Spotting him, Barb jerked the rifle to her shoulder, anxious for a shot. By then, the bear had walked into the clearing far enough for me to see his size.

"Hold that shot, Barb," I said. "I think you can do better than this fellow." We still had a few more nights to hunt, and I had a feeling a larger bruin would show up.

The next morning dawned calm, with an overcast sky that promised rain again. Barb had decided that if the same bear returned, she would take him.

Early in the evening, the bear walked out of the brushy ravine into the clearing. Without hesitation, he tramped to the bait and lay down to feed. Barb's excitement was electrifying! Nervous energy lit up her bright eyes as the .30-30 Win. flashed to her shoulder. The click of the Winchester's hammer sounded like a clap of thunder. The forest sounds fell to a deadly silence as Barb settled into what seemed like 30 minutes of trigger squeeze. As I waited for the shot, a movement out of the corner of my eye caught my attention. There, at the edge of the clearing, stood a monster bear. He was looking around, sniffing the air.

"Don't shoot," I hissed, pointing toward the large bear. "We've got a bruiser coming in."

The big bear charged into the clearing like a locomotive. Catching the feeding bear by surprise, he grabbed him by the scruff of the neck and, with a growl, shook him like a rag doll. Dropping to the ground, the smaller bear broke free and rolled away. Jumping to his feet, he raced for the safety of the woods. The intruder reared up and glared after the retreating figure as if to say, "Take that!"

The whole scene unfolded in a matter of seconds. Barb still had her gun raised with her finger on the trigger. The big bruin sat on his haunches, neck hair standing straight up as he glared toward the river bottom, where the smaller bear had disappeared.

"Take him in the chest, hit the white patch. Just relax and squeeze," I whispered, as my palms began to sweat, and my hammering heart threatened to bruise my ribs!

Barb took a deep breath and shook herself, trying to free her tension. The crack of the .30-30 Win. echoed through the woods. Time stopped as the big bear sat there, showing no signs of being hit. Then he simply crumpled to the ground. She had hit the spot! The bullet went through the heart and into the spine. The bear never knew what hit him.

I was the first to approach the big bear. One glance told me he wasn't going anywhere. Rooted to the ground like a statue, Barb stared unbelievably at the big bruin. Undeniable pleasure radiated from her smile. The excitement of shooting the bear had Barb talking a mile a minute as I sat my gun down and began field dressing the animal.

Bob had been hunting with his camera on another bait a mile away. We were sure the shot would pique his curiosity and that he would show up shortly. As I worked on her bear, Barb kept up a steady banter, bubbling with excitement.

Suddenly, she let out a terrified scream! Looking to my left I saw another bear break into the clearing. The snap of his teeth was audible from 50 yards. The bruin, the same animal chased off earlier, was now raging

mad. It was obvious he intended on settling the score for the rough treatment he had received.

The hair on the back of my neck stood up as I grabbed the .30-30 Win. from Barb and snapped a shot at the bear from waist level. The 25-yard shot hit the ground in front of him. Spinning around, he crashed back into the brush. Barb was really scared now, but I convinced her the bear wouldn't be back.

As I turned around to hand Barb the rifle, sounds of breaking brush again caught my attention. The terrified look on Barb's face told me the bear was back.

"I'll give that bear one more chance," I thought to myself, as I fired into the ground in front of him. Changing directions, he charged to the edge of the clearing and stood up, venting his rage by ripping at a tree with his front paws. Taking careful aim, I fired a shot into the tree above his paws, and tree bark exploded into his face. Letting out a loud growl, he dropped down, and thundered off through the trees. This time, I figured he was gone for good.

"If he comes back, I'll tag him myself," I told Barb.

A few moments later, Bob entered the clearing. We could hear the bear tearing at the trees and brush in the woods, but he never showed himself again. That was one mad bruin!

I finished field dressing Barb's bear while Bob congratulated her. It was a big bear, one of which she would be proud.

It was raining when we arrived at the ranch, but nothing could dampen Barb's delight. She was one happy woman! Her first bear, and a double charge to boot!

Just Another Day
On The Mountain

by Patrick Meitin

F rom the beginning I knew it was going to be a long hunt. Bobby Finhouser was a weird duck—the oddest person I have ever taken on a hunt. I walked into the house after being out bear hunting all day and met Bobby for the first time, without any warning from the hired help who met him at the airport.

"How tall are you?" Bobby asked me bluntly, "How much do you weigh?"

"Awh...six-four, 170," I answered puzzled, offering my hand for a shake.

Matter-of-factly Bobby announced, "I could whip you." Then he walked away, leaving me standing with my outstretched hand untouched. My number-one guide explained the man was some sort of fight promoter and fancied himself as a boxer.

After dinner, I took Bobby to the hunter's lodge to get him settled and carry part of the mountain of luggage extracted from his rented car. He wore his 12-inch barreled .44 Rem. Mag. in a shoulder holster which, I was told later, he had refused to remove when at the grocery store in town. Walking across the threshold of the lodge's log framework, the nimrod dropped his load of gear and drew his piece. I was about to drop to the floor when Bobby began to click off his unloaded pistol at each of the mounted animals that adorned the corners and shelves of the log cabin.

"Bang! I got that elk. Boom! I got the coyote. Bang! The lion's dead.

Bang! The turkey is dead. Click, I got the other elk...!"

"Oh my God," I whispered to myself. "See you in the morning."

This was going to be a long week! I would be lying if I said the thought of giving the man his money back and sending him home did not cross my mind. But as usual there were bills to be paid—always.

I stopped the Landcruiser, killing the engine with the same motion, at the end of a sandy wash that spilled from the rugged, cliffy terrain. The sun pierced the low, fog-like clouds, setting the mist afire. The fire burnt red then orange then yellow as Bobby and I trekked up the southern face of the Northern Needles of the Florida Mountains in southwest New Mexico. The Floridas are home to free-roaming Persian ibex, courtesy of the late Shah of Iran. Once only a force of 36 animals in 1965, the herd now numbers an estimated 1,500 animals in an area of no more than 150 square miles. Bobby had put in an application early in the summer and drew one of the coveted licenses. Because of the large number of animals, picking and choosing is routine. This I drilled into Bobby's head as we climbed high up the 8,000 foot mountain, racing the rising sun and fighting cactus and cliff. Nonetheless, the first hapless ibex that appeared on the skyline was gunned down by the hunter, his .300 Win. Mag. semi-auto spitting forth its 200-grain pills with thunderous percussion. The 100-pound animal fell victim to one of the five bullets— luckily, law allows two ibex per tag.

I shook my head as the giddy hunter leaped and bounded toward his downed trophy, looking like an excited mule deer jumped from its bed. I asked why my urging to pass the animal went unheeded, pointing out that the specimen he had just taken was barely legal, and stated that next time I asked him not to shoot, he might be wise to listen. Bobby watched as I skinned, caped and quartered the animal, excitedly relating each point of the triumphant kill and noting how he might choose a bigger gun next year. I wondered who he might hunt with next year. The boned-out meat was stuffed into my daypack, the cape and horns tied to the outside, and we continued hunting.

Later that afternoon, we were returning to the Jeep in daylight to avoid a nasty hike in the dark where cactus spines have an easy time finding their way into shins and knees. Near the bottom, I found three very nice billies through the binoculars. The billies walked on the seemingly vertical cliffs overlooking the vehicle, fearless in the dizzy heights. A hurried stalk brought us below the threesome, but daylight was fading fast and shooting hours would soon be past. A single pebble bounced from above our heads and into the broken rock at our feet. I cautiously peered above, sneaking away from the vertical wall so that I might see farther up the cliff face. One-hundred yards straight above my hunter's

head, the group was perched like ants on a wall, their bulging eyes staring blankly down on me. I hissed and waved my hunter over, pointing
inconspicuously toward the ibex.

The billies alternately hopped to another foothold and stopped to
glare down on the foreign blobs below. Bobby's gun roared against the
rock wall, causing sparks well below one of the ibex and sending down a
shower of shattered granite. Bobby's gun belched an evenly spaced volley of five deafening blasts, all to no avail on the frightened ibex who
disappeared into various crevasses and caves. The shower of rock splinters ceased and all was quiet in the darkening Florida mountains, then
Bobby's mouth went into motion. Each trigger pull was pondered and an
excuse for each missed shot was offered. Bobby's enthusiasm was unscathed by the failed aiming...no, far from it. He bounced from rock to
rock, relating each point of the encounter with the "rock goats," as he
called them. Funny, it seemed somehow we were on different hunts. At
least the food at the motel in Deming would be hot and the beds firm.

The next day, a 40 mile per hour wind threatened to blow me off the
razor-spined ridge where I sat glassing. Bobby was at my side, asking
questions of geologic formation or origin of species or some such non-
sense that a guide is expected to know. The first ibex to come through the
binoculars were a good mile away and across a deep cut in the landscape.
It would take us two hours of hard climbing over mean country to reach
the area. In the time lapse, the animals had disappeared. We stalked the
rock spires, criss-cross cliffs and wind-sculptured archways seeking our
quarry. As we crawled to the crest of yet another cliff, we found an exceptional specimen of an ibex perched on a pinnacle of pointed rock only
80 yards away. Bobby threw up his rifle and fired three rapid shots over
the billies spine and into space. The entire herd melted into the countryside ducking into out-of-the-way hiding holes.

While eating lunch on the leeward end on a rock column, protected
from the relentless wind, I continued glassing. Bobby quizzed me of the
species of grasses growing at our feet, the cause of the bad weather and
such. I answered as best I could, not wanting him to loose faith in the
great white hunters of the world. He asked for a canteen from the pack I
had been asked to carry earlier in the morning while climbing a steep
hillside. I found the quart canteen, filled to the brim, beside three boxes
of .300 Win. Mag. ammo, 100 feet of half-inch rope, a full bottle of
cough syrup, an entire roll of toilet paper, a U.S. Army compass, an
extra pair of socks, a small stuff sack of knick-knacks, 25 books of
matches and the most recent copy of *Outdoor Life*. Bobby reassured me
that every item was necessary.

The 10x40s continued nibbling away at the cliff and rock. Bobby

flipped through the pages of the magazine, stopping occasionally to ask my advice on one paragraph or another to check the validity of the author, I assumed. I found another group of ibex crawling on a rock face, looking like insects from such a long distance. Bobby's incidentals were carefully packed back into the bag and the long-winded stalk began. The land between the ibex and us was a maze of interconnected rock ridges, interspersed with cliff, loose rock and cactus, always the cactus. We walked hard until we were out of breath, but kept pushing as the ibex were moving into a sheltered box canyon and I worried about loosing them. A high, jagged cliff overlooked the area the ibex had gone into, 500 vertical feet with steep hogbacks running off and falling into the flats, creating thousands of small pockets around its base. The ibex were in one of these holes.

After a little footwork and a lot of peering through the binoculars, we found the group. The number of animals had grown considerably since last sighting. This had its good points and its bad. Seventy animals presented quite an opportunity to pick over and find a trophy, it also meant 140 eyeballs watching for danger. As the shadow of South Peak shrouded the area we slipped into one of the box-like heads, following a stair-step trail down the steep side. Bobby asked why he didn't shoot from where we stood, and assured me it would be a piece of cake. I hardly considered 500 yards across windblown space easy. I explained that it would be much more sporting to draw closer. Hitting the bottom of the cliff wall that shallowed as it crossed each ridge and grew deeper

crossing the many cuts in the hillside, we headed in the direction of a low saddle in a razor-back ridge, and toward the herd.

The footing was treacherous as loose rock clung to the near-vertical hillside, waiting for an excuse to inch ever closer to its ultimate destination, the bottom. Bobby fell once as we crossed a narrow chute and slid on hands and posterior 100 yards below. I was glad I had stripped him of his burdens to make better time, and now his gun would still be sighted in. I retrieved him to the trail, palms skinned and rear end bruised. "Now that's the romance of the hunt," Bobby said smiling. We approached the low spot in the hogback easing into sight. The ibex were still feeding peacefully, unaware of the dangers floating in from the north. Bobby again assured me it would be nothing for him to take any of the animals from were we sat, but his pining went unacknowledged. I carefully studied a deep gash in the one ridge separating us from the herd and worried that the 30-foot cliff might be a little much for the intrepid hunter in tow. We slipped out of sight and continued toward the herd, jumping cactus and dancing on loose shale.

Reaching the cliff leading into the cut, Bobby whined at the proposition of rock climbing. I reminded him that if I could do it with two packs and a rifle slung over my shoulders, he might be able to manage. The cliff was not especially tough as there were ample hand- and foot-holds to aid in the climb. We reached the cliff crest, finding a water-smoothed chute with vertical bumps in the bottom. Bobby reveled at his newly-found talent of rock climbing and actually began to look forward to finding another steep place to crawl up. In several instances, I would boost Bobby over a slick face and then hand packs and the unloaded gun up after him. Then I would be left to climb, tooth and nail on my own. We reached the flat crest of the ridge and belly-crawled to the edge to take a look at the ibex. I grabbed Bobby and jerked him away from the ledge after seeing the entire herd at only 150 yards. We crab-crawled to one side, drawing up behind a benchrest rock. Again I pushed Bobby's blonde head back behind cover.

The ibex crawled on the hillside like maggots, another nanny or smaller billy appearing from a fold or from behind a bush every time I looked again. Three huge animals immediately caught my naked eye, three sword-swinging billies surrounded by the throng of smaller animals. My binoculars grabbed one of the billies from the hill and brought him to my eyes. I almost spit out my tongue! The current world record, beating the Iranian record and coming from these mountains, sported 56-inch horns. The billy I was gawking at now had thick horns, sweeping rearward to his flanks and hooking back toward his shoulders. He was 65 inches if he was an inch! "It looks like we've got a world record down there," I said as calmly as was possible under the consequences. I expected to have to tackle Bobby to harness his exuberance.

"A world record, wow! That would be neat. Which one is it?" Bobby asked, as if not at all concerned.

"See the whitish ibex feeding off the darkest bush? The white billy standing below those two red rocks—next to the dead yucca. There, the one whipping on the bush there in the middle! See the head of the red shale wash, the two red rocks—go below that—the dark bush."

"No, I'm not sure—there are several of them that look good enough to shoot. I don't care which one I take—I will just shoot the closest." Bobby said smugly.

"Wait a minute—don't shoot a thing. Give me that gun!" I ordered, having an idea. I whipped off my Gore-Tex jacket, wadded it in a ball and put it atop our hiding rock and bench rest. I cradled the rifle in the jacket and propped it with two heavy rocks, putting the crosshairs on the billy. "There, the crosshairs are on the best one—*that* is the one you want."

Bobby grappled the rifle, losing the chosen billy. "It moved, I lost him. Hey, look at that one. He looks good. I'm going to shoot that one!" Bobby exclaimed, still looking through the scope.

"Whoa!" I pushed Bobby from behind the rifle and again found the largest billy. I nestled the crosshairs snugly in the lower part of the billy's shoulder. I let go of the rifle to see if it would stay sighted. "There, I've got him again, that's the one you want—don't bump the gun this time."

"Sure enough, that is the best one!" Bobby related. "Wow, he sure is nice, I'm going to take him. Okay, I'm taking the safety off now, the "X" is on him. Okay, I'm going to shoot now. Are you ready? I've got him, he's a dead son-of-a-gun, I'm squeezing the trigger. Okay, I'm squeezing the trigger, are you ready..."

"For God's sake, pull the damned trigger, man!" a voice screamed in my head, so loud I could feel a migraine coming on. My hair grew noticeably grayer as Bobby related each action and thought. I crawled to my binoculars and watched the billy, nerves tensed in anticipation of the muzzle blast, praying to see the ibex reach for the sky as he rolled over, dead as the Sphinx. Turning to see what in the world was taking the man so long to shoot, his rifle blasted, spitting a brass into my chest. I quickly turned the binoculars back onto the billy, finding him standing, head flung first one way then another attempting to locate the sound, as the canyon box filled with the echo of .300 Magnum. Bobby looked over the top of his scope, I over the binoculars, all of the herd was unscathed. "You missed, shoot again!" I ordered.

Watching through the binoculars a visible flume of smoke drifted from a rock behind the billy at the blast of the canon, then it was carried away by a lost wind current. "You shot over him, aim lower!" The herd came to the conclusion that these were not the safest parts and took flight. The herd of 70 moved as one, three more blasts from Bobby's auto canon went wide of one billy, then over another, low of another, then the gun was empty. I tore open Bobby's pack, grabbed a box of ammunition and tore at the packaging. I dumped the contents into my lap, demanding the clip from the gun, reaching over to get it myself in the same movement. I fed the shiny shells into the clip, jammed it into the gun's receiver and released the bolt onto the live ammo. I watched through binoculars attempting to direct Bobby's shots at the ibex that were now over 300 yards away and spreading up a vertical cliff. At each evenly paced report rocks would shatter close to one of the billies, the ibex paying little heed, merely going up. The gun would soon be emptied again.

Bobby handed me the rifle. I hurriedly loaded the clip again, knowing the animals were in little danger now, bouncing up the shear rock at 500 yards. Loaded and ready to fire, I handed him the gun. He took his position at the bench rest and fired away. Then it happened. One of the billies teetered, fell to his knees, regained his footing and then fell again, kicking. "You got one! Quit shooting—you hit one!" Another blast from the gun caused me to grab the rifle from Bobby. "You hit one—quit shooting. You're going to hit another and get us both in hot water!"

"Are you sure? I didn't see anything get hit. Which one did I hit? Are you sure? I really don't think I hit one, you must be pulling..."

"Give me my jacket back, I'm freezing to death—Yes, you got one. I am very sure, I saw him go down through my binoculars. Let's get over there, it's getting dark, there's gonna be hell to pay if we don't get off this mountain before dark."

Then I noticed for the first time that an angry storm was rolling in from the west, and I hoped it would give us time to escape the mountain. "Looks like we have to go over the way the ibex did, and it just so happens the road where Sonny is picking us up is that way."

Bobby thought that was I fine idea, as he had taken a liking to rock climbing. I gave him my lighter daypack, shouldered his well-stocked pack and rifle and started off the steep, rocky face into the bottom. When we reached the area where the ibex had stood, Bobby stepped into the escaped billy's hoof prints and reenacted the entire episode, holding his arms up to serve as ibex horns.

"Yeah, then he turned like this and, boom, then he ran over here and, boom, then they all..."

I couldn't help but laugh aloud. As much as I had thought of pushing Bobby off a cliff the last couple of days, I thought I liked him now. How could one not help but like such a comic. Bobby was serious, of course, but in his own strange way, very entertaining now that the pressures and seriousness of the hunt had eased. I chuckled, urging him on, as we had little time to waste and we still hadn't taken care of the trophy. The climb started leisurely, with plenty of crevasses and cracks in the cliff face for a climber to stick his fingers and toes into while climbing. I let Bobby climb ahead, suggesting possible holds and occasionally directing his foot into a hole. We reached the first resting ledge, the toughest third of the climb behind us now. Catching our breath, we resumed the climb and I took the lead. I hoped the search for the downed ibex would not be time consuming and looked forward to getting the first up-close look at the animal.

"The billy was right up there when you hit him!" I said, pointing to a

stunted cedar which clung to the rocky ground. Bobby looked up toward the tree while still walking, then lost his footing. His feet went out from under him as if an unseen force had swept them from beneath him, his boots rolling off the ball bearing-like pebbles on the solid rock. He rolled down a chute, fell off a short ledge, hit the shale and slid out of sight at the edge of the 100-foot cliff we had recently climbed. I stood in shock, but did not hear anything further after the shale came to rest. I scampered down the chute in panic, bumped into the shale and nearly slid off the edge myself.

"Help me, help me, I'm going to die! Your trying to kill me! I'm going to fall!" Bobby was screaming at the top of his lungs somewhere from the edge of the high ledge. I cautiously crept to the edge and found Bobby clinging to the crest, one hand grasping onto rock, the other holding several branches of a stunted desert oak. He hung above a wide ledge only three feet below his feet and was relatively safe, considering the situation.

"Are you hurt? Give me your hand, let go of the tree and give me your hand. Don't worry, your not going anywhere, there's a bench below you. Let me help you up," I said calmly, not wanting Bobby to die of fright while I reached for his hand.

"Don't touch me! I'm gonna fall! Get away from me! I can't move or I'll fall—get away!" Bobby screamed, almost crying.

"Your going to have to let me pull you up. Give me your hand," I said calmly, reaching down at him. "Bobby, Bobby! Can you hear me Bobby, give me your gawddamn hand!" I angrily grabbed Bobby's wrist and pulled him up the face, screaming and kicking, cussing at the top of his lungs about how I was going to kill him. Minutes later the whole episode was forgotten, and we went up to find his trophy.

The ibex lay dead on its side near the lone cedar. It was not the world record, but it was nice—nice enough to be ranked number four in the record book. Bobby walked around his trophy, not touching it, but admiring it from a distance. While I quickly field dressed the animal, Bobby handled the ibex by its horn tip, tipping it one way then another, saying nothing—which was a change. He finally spoke, complaining of the "goatty" smell, but said little else. It started raining as I dragged the 200-pound ibex to the cedar where it would hang for the night, using Bobby's 100 feet of rope. We hurried off the mountain, racing against the remaining daylight and a nasty storm.

It wasn't long before woolly clouds enveloped the mountain. It was dark. I had the foresight to stash two disposable flashlights in my small pack. Bobby's pack contained C-sized batteries but no flashlight—it was in the rented car. We clamored down the now wet mountain, rain coming down in sheets. Despite the Gore-Tex I was soaked to the bone, as was Bobby. From past scouting, I hoped to stay on the safest track and avoid high cliffs or extra thick cactus patches. We would go straight down the big slide, hit the bottom and walk down the middle of a narrow but clear sandy wash. The rock slide would be treacherous, but more desirable than stabbing cactus and grabbing brush, as everything growing near the Mexican border bites, scratches or stabs. It seemed a good plan. Then Bobby's flashlight faded out. The sealed disposable could not be recharged with new batteries, and it was a goner. We shared the one light—for 100 yards, when it too quit. The darkness surrounded us, thick enough to drown any spark of light. Camping was discussed briefly, but icy precipitation, high winds, wet matches and no available cover promised a miserable night—if we even survived. Besides, we were nearly there anyhow, I consoled myself.

In the overwhelming darkness, it didn't take long to lose our course. As the first prickly pear spine drove home, this became all too clear. We would stop to remove the spines at first, but soon found it a vain attempt, since they would be replaced soon enough. We scooted along, one careful step at a time, until I walked off a ledge. I can still remember floating, wondering where the ground and I would meet. It didn't take long, thank God, and I fell chest-down into a stiff blue oak. I was thankful for the oak—a cholla, yucca or prickly pear could have greeted me instead. Bobby yelled down at me, two steps from walking off the same ledge, curious as to why my footsteps had become inaudible.

"Don't move, I just fell off a cliff!" I yelled up.

The next eight hours seem a fevered dream now. The long, monotonous dreams one has when ill, when one thinks the night will never end, when one can see the space between cells and the plot is never resolved. I had removed my belt, hooking one end to a belt loop and the other to Bobby so he would not duplicate the mistakes made by me—the teeth-jarring walks off three-foot drops, walking into prickly pear clumps, chollas slapping into knees. Occasionally one of the strings would fall, adding another scratch, scrape or bruise to the collection. My shins felt like raw meat, Bobby's I think slightly better, as I was the mine sweeper. I kept a constant hand full of rock, to be thrown ahead to detect air. If a reassuring click was heard we would ease on, many times there would be no sound. We would walk sideways and continue throwing pebbles until there was a sound again. We talked of what we would eat when we reached the motel, talked of women we had known... Deep down inside I wanted to scream at the top of my lungs, but knew I couldn't.

"Say, have you heard the one about the..."

The road at the bottom of the mountain was empty. I hadn't really expected our ride to be there. My guides and I have an agreement with one another. We are all big boys and can take care of ourselves in the wild—if there was ever a real emergency we would die. Sonny wouldn't be back until daybreak. He certainly expected me to be sitting in a cave, aside a fire waiting out the storm. The rain quit. So we walked. At least the road was void of cactus and the like. The porch light at the ranch house on the highway grew larger in the following hour until we were standing on pavement. The nightmare was close to its end, we would soon wake up, shower in hot water, eat warm food and wear dry clothes. It seemed so close at hand now but still out of reach—town was 40 miles away. We found no one home at the ranch so we pushed on, walking down the middle of Highway 40. The lights from the border town of Columbus looked closer at hand but that would only put us farther from our ultimate destination, so we walked away from them.

The headlights coming up the shiny pavement ribbon were welcome relief. Perhaps we could hitch a ride, but I wondered who would pick up someone with a gun at 3:00 in the morning. The vehicle screeched to a stop, the doors swung open and a spotlight blinded me. I caught the glint of something shiny pointing our way.

"¿Quien va ya¿ ¡Pon las monos arriva!" the voice boomed from behind the darkness. Bobby, confused, walked toward the truck, beginning to talk but was cut short. "¡Alto donde euste estai ¿Como se llamos¿ ¡Alto, pon las monos arriva!" the voice barked again.

"Bobby hold still, put your hands on your head, your gonna get shot!" I ordered.

"Don't shoot, don't shoot, we didn't do anything!" Bobby pleaded.

"What the hell are you guys doing out here at this hour of the night? We thought you were illegals. Quite a few wets come up this way, and it isn't a good place to be late at night," the huge, black-haired man in the green uniform said, the edge gone from his voice. We explained our predicament, and received a ride to town, courtesy of the U.S. Border Patrol. The inside of the vehicle was warm and the radio played a nice tune. I apologized for getting the seat wet, but was assured by the big man it was no trouble at all.

"Hell of a time, huh?"

"We lived. It wasn't that tough after all," I said grinning like a madman.

"Yeah right—you probably thought it was a grand time. You seemed to enjoy the whole affair! Probably no big deal for you, but it about killed me," Bobby said, punching me in the arm.

"Just another day at the office. We do this every week out here you know!"

Monarch Of Divide Creek

by Ron D. Moore

Wobbling on legs that would no longer support my body, I sank down on the wet grass and tried in gasps to catch my breath. I had reached the limits of my endurance. I leaned back against a quakie tree and listened to the hounds barking treed across a small creek. It was morning and the hounds had fought the bear on the ground most of the night, finally putting him in a tree. The pitch of their voices told me that the bear was barely out of their reach and probably wouldn't remain treed for long. Somewhere back in the rugged mountains were my client and three hunting companions. Desperate, I decided to ease over to the tree and see if my presence would help keep the bear in one place until my hunter arrived. If he came down and ran again, I wasn't sure if I would be able to keep up the chase. As a young guide, I didn't want to lose the bear for my client if there was anything I could do to prevent it.

Regaining my feet, I felt helpless. I simply didn't have much left in me. Armed with only my Smith & Wesson light-framed .38 Spec., I slowly made my way across the creek toward the tree. The brush around the area of the tree was thick, and I used up any reserve I might have had pushing through it. I was close enough to touch the tree he was in before I could see the bear clearly. A few feet above the dogs, his hindquarters were all that was visible to me.

During the time this story takes place, most folks still considered the black bear a varmint; hunting them at night was legal.

Fighting hard to control my labored breathing, I tried to regain my composure and began what I hoped wouldn't be a long wait. Suddenly, without warning, the limb on which he was perched shattered near the trunk of the tree and gave way.

The bear's hindquarters dropped, and he fell out of the tree flat on his back in the middle of the baying hounds. Quickly circling him, the hounds got themselves a mouth full of bear and, for a few seconds, he seemed not to move. I cursed myself for getting myself and my dogs into this predicament. Now I was afriad that the whole nightmare had been for nothing. Suddenly, the bear threw the hounds off, rolled to his feet and was standing facing me 10 yards away. With a loud woof, he charged...

It was mid-May, 1968 and the Colorado Rockies were drowsily awakening from their long winter sleep. I was 25 years old, my new wife Christie was pregnant and we were living and operating our hunting business, such as it was, out of Rifle, Colorado. We were a young couple, full of hope and lofty goals, and dead broke. My new wife, a Texas school teacher, was making a valiant effort to adjust to life married to a big game guide and cowboy. Living on little more than love, we were eagerly awaiting the arrival of our first bear-hunting client of the new spring.

The mountains surrounding Rifle were high and cold; spring was always tardy in its arrival and the bears came out of their winter quarters late. For these reasons, I had placed a camp in the lower, warmer Brookcliff Mountains of eastern Utah, a five-hour drive from my home. There was an abundance of bear and they were moving around by the middle of May.

Felix Harper and his wife, Jewell, arrived by car in the middle of a beautiful spring afternoon. Expecting the average big game hunter we were a little surprised by this couple. Felix owned a small grocery store in the not-so-good-part-of-town in Florence, Alabama. He wore old work britches, had a sizable belly which hung over his pants, exposing a strip of bare belly. Jewell wore a one-piece cotton print dress with a pair of mens' britches underneath it and chewed Day's Work tobacco. Pure country from head to foot. We immediately liked this unusual couple.

Felix was raring to go, and was disappointed when I told them that we wouldn't be hunting here. Due to their late arrival, we wouldn't be going to camp the next day. Instead, we made ourselves comfortable on the front porch, got some iced tea and set about getting acquainted, telling some hunting stories. In a short while, we were joined by two friends, local guides Larry Gurr and Walt McCart, and they contributed to the hunting stories being told. Shortly after, another friend, Brian Deeter, showed up and soon we were beginning to run out of chairs and tea. As the main topic of conversation was hunting, I could see the fever to go hunting steadily rising in everyone.

Caught up in the fever myself, I mentioned that a local cowboy, John Bowles, had stopped by yesterday and mentioned there was a dead horse up East Divide Creek. The conversation soon centered around the horse carcass and the fact that, if there did happen to be an early bear season, there was a good chance a bear would be on the carcass. By the time the sun set, we had decided that we would go up Divide Creek about 9:00 p.m. to check the carcass. The story circle broke up with everybody going to gather up lights and thermoses of hot coffee.

The meeting back at my house that evening resembled an Arkansas coon hunt more than a bear hunt, as we loaded flashlights and hounds. Larry, Walt and I were bringing only our best dogs, totaling 15 seasoned hounds: a match for any bear. Felix was armed with a Winchester lever-action .308 Win., Larry had his .22 Mag. pistol, and I brought my .38 Spec. Walt and Brian were unarmed.

There wasn't a trace of moon that night and the blackness was total as we entered the timber and slowly wound our way up the rough road. I was driving with Larry and Felix in the front of the pickup, Walt and Brian keeping the dogs company in the back. As the headlights sliced into the blackness, the country had an eerie look about it with everything mashed down and wet from only recently departed snow. In another two weeks, it would change its face to one of full spring with everything coming to life.

Arriving at the horse carcass, which had become quite ripe, the hounds gave no indication that there had been a bear. Closer inspection indicated that it was being visited by magpies, crows and a coyote, but no bear. Disappointed, full of coffee and wide awake, nobody was ready to give up. Back down the road a short ways was another road that wound its way back in three miles, and dead ended in a high saddle. We put two old dogs out in front of the truck and headed out to the dead end without them showing any interest in bear tracks. Returning to the junction of the main Divide Creek road, I stopped the truck and we got out to stretch before the trip home. Larry suggested that we go check the horse carcass before we headed home. Thinking about the long trip to camp the next day, I was less than enthusiastic, but relented under pressure from the rest of the party. It was midnight as we headed back up the creek.

Pulling up across the creek from the carcass for the second time, the hounds exploded into frenzied baying, and Walt and Brian were having a hard time containing them. Leaving Larry and Felix to keep the hounds in the truck, I quickly crossed the creek to the carcass. A very large bear had been on it in our two-hour absence and, judging from the hounds reaction, we had chased him off on our return. I yelled back to turn the hounds loose and they clamored across the creek, heading up the steep ridge in full bay. The intense baying shattered the still night as we hurried to get our lights together. Telling Walt and Brian to stay with Felix, Larry and I sprinted across the creek and began the steep climb up the ridge after the hounds.

My adrenalin was pumping hard now and I tore at the hillside with a fast-climbing fury. Soon realizing that Larry had fallen behind, I hesitated a moment to better listen to the hounds. The bear had stopped and the hounds were fighting him on the ground near the top of the high ridge. Not waiting for Larry, I began climbing again with a renewed fury. Due to Felix's physical condition and age, and with the slope becoming steeper, I felt that if I could beat the bear and hounds to the top, I could turn the bear back downhill. That would keep him in the main Divide Creek drainage and out of the steeper, rougher canyons that he was headed for, and would give us a better chance of getting Felix to the bear.

I pushed on, my breath coming now in labored gasps, my body already crying for rest. The hillside had become so steep that I had to climb hand-over-hand. The 9,000-foot elevation was taxing my lungs to the bursting point. Soaked with sweat, I gritted my teeth and forced myself not to stop as my body was demanding. As I rallied my strength for a last ditch effort, the bear broke and ran, the hounds soon fading out of hearing range over the ridgetop. I collapsed in despair into the wet leaves, fighting hard to get enough oxygen into my lungs to satisfy their craving.

Soaked with sweat, I was soon overcome with the chills, unable to control the shaking and chattering of my teeth. Peering into the blackness back down the slope, I tried in vain to pick out the flicker of a flashlight. I was alone and a heavy silence hung over the dark slope as I dragged myself back to my feet and made my way toward the top. The chills and shaking quickly subsided when I began to climb, but upon reaching the top, my legs were like rubber and my wind was gone.

I could hear the hounds clearly now. They were in the bottom of the next canyon and had stopped the bear, fighting him on the ground again. I switched my light off and sank to the ground with my back against a tree to rest my legs and regain my wind. I stared back down the dark slope in hopes of seeing a glimmer of flashlight, but there was only inky blackness and loneliness enveloping me. With the darkness surrounding me, and the hounds' voices floating up from the canyon bottom, fatigue set in and I dropped off to sleep.

I had no idea how long I had slept when I was awakened by the chills and shaking again. I could still hear the hounds, only louder now. Shak-

ing off the drowsiness, I realized that they now were about halfway up the next ridge, not moving, still baying the bear. I looked again back down my trail, but still saw no lights. Where the hell were these guys? Stiff from the dampness, I started down the steep hill into the next canyon. Crossing the creek in the bottom, I began another steep climb with the intention of again trying to get above the bear. It had grown noticeably colder, but with the exertion of the steep climb I was soon drenched in sweat again.

As I climbed methodically toward the bear, my light was becoming very dim and thoughts flashed through my mind about confronting the bear with little or no light. I pushed the thoughts out of my mind and plodded up the slope.

The hounds and bear again began moving toward the top, and I once more had to start climbing fast in an effort to beat them to the top. Finally reduced to crawling on my hands and knees up the slope, they slowly faded out of hearing over the top. Three-fourths of the way to the top, I had lost the race again. My gasps for air now had a coarse, rattling sound in them. In the blackness behind me, I heard what I thought were human sounds and rolled on my side to look back down the slope. I was hearing chuckling sounds, and soon I could make out Larry's large bulk struggling toward me up the hill.

I felt like a helpless child laying there on my side, wheezing as Larry came up, laughing, and asked what I was doing crawling. "I have had it," I said. "Where the hell have you been?"

"Trying to catch up with you," he replied. Larry's light had given out on him soon after starting and he had been steadily following me in the dark.

"Where are the dogs?" he asked.

"They went over the top," I said, pulling myself to my feet. The gray ghost of dawn was filtering through the trees as we began climbing on to the top.

"Have you seen the rest of the crew?" I asked.

Larry had not heard or seen anything of the rest of our party. By the time we reached the top, the morning sun was beginning to peek over the mountains to the east.

We could hear sounds clearly to our left and down country. The ridge we were on ran down in a northeastern direction, forming a point which dropped off into a small basin that was broken up with small draws and covered in a carpet of thick oak brush and scattered stands of timber. The baying of the hounds was coming from this basin and the pitch had changed to a tree-bark. Larry and I sat down on a big windfall to catch our breath and assess the situation. Larry is a big man, six-foot, four-inches and weighing 260 pounds, and though he was mountain tough, he was a slow walker. We decided that I, being the fastest, would make one more try at reaching the bear and keeping him up the tree until we could figure out when and how we could get Felix there.

Leaving Larry, I started down the ridge at a trot. The point of the ridge became very steep and I slowed to a fast walk, the steepness taking a toll on my legs. Reaching a point directly across a creek from the hounds, I sank down in the grass to collect my thoughts and formulate some sort of plan. I fought the impulse to charge in across the creek, and made myself stay put until I got my wind back. Catching my breath, I got back up and, on weak legs, slowly and carefully began working my way across to my ill-fated rendezvous with the charging bruin.

I could see the anger and frustration in the bear's eyes as he crashed through the brush toward me, intent on venting his rage. Turning to run, I found myself hopelessly tangled in the brush and unable to move. My God, he's got me, I thought, as I turned back toward the bear. He had covered half the distance to me and was still coming in a determined charge.

Grabbing some brush with my left hand to steady myself, I took aim at the bear's head. At this angle, I had little chance of killing him but, if I let him get close to the muzzle blast, the sudden shock might stop him or turn him, giving me a chance to better my precarious position. At any rate, I would go down swinging with my remaining five shots. The bear was almost on me when I started squeezing the trigger.

From out of nowhere, a spotted hound I had named Bing broke through the brush, grabbed a mouthful of the bear's right flank and hung on. As this is a very tender spot, the bear's reaction was instantaneous and he whirled back in the direction of the pain. Bing released his hold on the bear and turned to run, but the bear had him, pulling the dog underneath him. As Bing fought desperately, he and the bear skidded back down the hill, with the other hounds piling on as they went. I could see the bear tearing at Bing as I fought hard to free myself from the brush. I began yelling at the bear in hopes of distracting his attention from my dog. The other hounds were tearing furiously at the bear, driven wild by Bing's cries of pain. By the time I got free of the brush, the bear had turned Bing loose, shook off the other hounds and was headed across the creek in the direction I had just come, with the hounds in hot pursuit.

Bing lay where the bear had left him and I hurried to him, forgetting about the bruin for the moment. I dropped down and cradled him in my arms, rubbing his old head. His eyes were glazed with pain, but he managed to wag his tail. He was bitten in several places and the skin under his belly was quickly filling with liquid. "I owe you one, old son," I told him.

"We'll get you out of here to some help." Looking across the creek, I could see the bear headed uphill and, above him, Larry headed downhill on a collision course. They couldn't see each other. I yelled for all I was worth at Larry, but I couldn't make myself heard above the din of the baying hounds.

Larry, realizing that the hounds were coming in his direction, stopped and was looking intently down the slope. The bear burst through a patch of brush 20 yards below Larry, and they saw each other at the same instant. The bear veered left and zeroed in on Larry, and Larry jumped behind the nearest tree, a little quakie about eight inches in diameter. If the situation had not been what it was, I would have been moved to uncontrollable laughter, watching a man of Larry's size attempt to hide behind that little tree. Fifteen yards from Larry, several hounds grabbed hold of the bear's hindquarters, and the bear turned and chased them down into the creek.

The bear and the dogs were getting hot and tired. Reaching the creek, the bear slowed to a plodding walk with the hounds strung out in single file behind him. Larry and I followed at a safe distance, trying to keep the bear in sight and encouraging the dogs. Bing had gotten up and was limping along with us.

We had to use a lot of caution now in order to avoid another charge. We might not be able to count on the dogs to save our bacon again. The bear went down the creek for 20 yards, turned up a grassy slope to a lone spruce tree and plopped down on his haunches in the shade. This left the hounds in the sun. They were getting hotter and soon had all but quit baying, some were even laying down.

To the left of the bear and slightly downhill was a big windfall and Larry and I, guns drawn, made our way to it. Flopping down, we presented a sorry sight—exhausted, under-armed, and no client in sight. Assessing the situation left us pretty gloomy. I doubted Felix had made it far in the steep country, and was most likely back at the truck with Walt and Brian, wondering where we were. If we decided to kill the bear ourselves, we were under-armed for a bear with his dander up. We weren't even sure we could accomplish this task without just wounding him. The attempt would present a great risk to ourselves and the hounds. We already had a mad bear on our hands, and wounding him would inflame an already volatile situation.

Peering over the windfall, the bear gave us some hope as he looked up the tree as if deciding to climb it. Our hopes were dashed when he lay down on his stomach. It looked as if we had reached a stalemate, and one of us was going to have to walk out and see if we could get Felix back here. Our train of thought was interrupted as the bear got to his feet, headed back to the creek and immediately lay down under another tree. The creek bank was timbered and at least gave shade and water to the hot, tired dogs. A definite lack of enthusiasm by the dogs became painfully evident as they began searching for places to lay down, periodically glancing at the bear and barking. Giving the bear the west side of the creek, Larry and I settled down at a safe distance on the east side.

Fatigue and despair setting in, we agonized over what to do. It was obvious that the bear was not going to stay put for any length of time. In our current physical condition, it would no doubt take most of the day to get the rest of the party into this canyon, and there was still no guarantee that the bear would be here when they did arrive. The hounds were at the point of quitting, and I wasn't sure how much longer I could get them to stay with the bear. We would have to try to kill the bear or leave him. A fine kettle of fish.

As we sat weighing the consequences of each action, we were startled by what we thought was a human voice hailing us from up the creek. Not wanting to yell and arouse the bear again, I whispered for Larry to stay put and slipped off up the creek. I had gone 300 yards when I clearly heard Walt call my name, so I called back and sat down to wait for him. My excitement waned quickly as I realized Walt was probably by himself and Felix would still be back at the truck. I lay on the ground, absorbing its coolness when, to my amazement, Walt came into sight followed by Felix and Brian.

Felix looked none the worse for the wear and, brimming over with excitement, wanted to know where the bear was. They had hiked all night, stopping often to rest. Although they had lost the sound of the hounds shortly after leaving the truck, they had continued in the direction they last heard them, hoping against hope to hear them again. As night passed into day, they became discouraged and decided to head back when they heard a gunshot far below them. Concluding that the shot could only have come from us, they hiked in the direction of the sound until they could hear the hounds. I led them off down the creek, my spirits high.

Larry's face registered a look of surprise when he saw Felix with us, just as mine probably had. I was about to deliver my speech to Felix regarding the importance of getting his wind, taking his time and to being sure and not hit a dog when Felix spotted the bear. Before I could say anything he jerked the .308 to his shoulder and fired. The bear jerked, then relaxed, not moving a muscle. The bullet struck the bear behind the ear, breaking his neck and killing him instantly. Drained from exhaustion and tension, we flopped to the ground in unison, too tired to indulge in the back-slapping that generally follows success.

As the rest of us lay in the grass like hard-ridden horses, Felix chattered away about how great this country was and how lucky he was to have gotten a bear so quickly. I decided that it could wait another day before I told him of all the trouble it had been to get this mean old bear. I marveled at the stamina and self-determination of this highly unlikely candidate for a mountain man, while dragging myself up to skin the bear.

The bear was a magnificent specimen, with a rich, brown spring coat and weighing in the neighborhood of 500 pounds. He was an old bear and his teeth were worn down almost to the gum line. He had lived a long life, managing to elude the bear hunters until today. Heading for the road, we took turns carrying the hide and went to great pains to not look tired to Felix. We were two miles downhill from the truck and, after a brief rest, Walt and I hiked up to get the truck. Upon arriving at my place, everybody headed for home and bed, but Felix kept me up until 9:00 that evening talking about the hunt.

I awoke at 7:00 a.m., with a night of sleep gone forever from my life and a heap more respect for my elders. We all loaded up and went to camp to enjoy some horseback riding and nature's never ending splendors. I learned some valuable lessons from the robust Southerner whose enthusiasm for life never seemed to wane. I had to evaluate my dedication and determination to my chosen profession, among other things. In later years, I came to realize that, at the age I was, one tends to take nature, life and the realization of your dreams for granted.

Felix and Jewell loaded up and headed back to their life in Alabama, clinging to their memories of bear and the Rocky Mountains. I bought a bigger pistol and Christie and I settled back to await the birth of our first child. A little of life's pressures were lifted and we could buy groceries, though there would be no money for small extras. Young and new to the hunting business, we didn't have all that many clients, and all too soon we would be back to living on love.

Just One More Arrow

by Judd Cooney

T here are few things I enjoy more than guiding and outfitting for
hunters. The challenge of getting a good trophy for a hunter many
times exceeds the challenge of getting a trophy for myself. The smile on
a successful client's face can't help but give an outfitter a sense of ac-
complishment. To be honest, though, I've got to admit there is one thing
I do not like about the job: the fact that it cuts down on the amount of time
I can hunt each fall. I have a standing rule that neither myself nor my
guides carry a bow or gun or do any hunting when we have clients in
camp. Each fall, I try to set aside a few days when we have no clients so
that we can try to get our game for the winter. Since these days are few
and far between, I value them highly and don't relinquish them lightly.

Several years ago I was booked solid for elk and deer bowhunters
except for the last four days of the season. I figured I owed it to myself to
spend at least four whole days trying to get a good bull after all my clients
had their chances.

I had just taken the last hunters to the airport; on the way home, I
stopped at the local sporting goods store to chat with the owner. While
standing there, a couple of bowhunters came in, all decked out in camo,
and asked if I was Judd Cooney. I hated to admit it in public, but finally
confessed that I was. They said they wanted to book an elk hunt. Assuming they were talking about the next season, I started giving information
on next year's hunts. They really stopped me short when they said they
wanted to bowhunt the last four days of *this* season. I tried my best to

explain why I couldn't take them, but ended up agreeing to take this father and son team for the last four days. They said I was more than welcome to bowhunt with them, but rules are rules! I told my wife we could use the money to buy beef. They had booked a 10-day bowhunt with another outfitter but, after five days of riding mountain trails on horseback and seeing only one doe mulie, they canceled the rest of the hunt.

I asked them if they had a bear license and they both laughed, saying they had bowhunted in Colorado for five years and had never seen a bear, so why waste the money? It was a dry fall and my hunters had recently seen a dozen or more bears in the springs and seeps we were bowhunting; they had even managed to take several nice ones. My new clients said with their luck, they would be tickled to see a deer or an elk.

Within half an hour after leaving the truck that first morning, I got Marvin, the father, within 30 yards of a cow elk, but he couldn't get a shot. This got them all fired up, so that evening I put Marvin and his son Randy on two water holes. When I picked them up that evening, they could hardly talk coherently. They had both seen elk on the hillside above their blinds and both of them had bears come within 40 yards of their blinds. They wanted to head for the nearest sporting goods store and get bear licenses for the next three days. That night around the fireplace, all they could talk about were bears and their hopes of getting one. I don't know what happened to their enthusiasm for elk and deer!

The following morning we got into elk again, but neither Marvin nor Randy got a shot. That evening Randy had a nice spike bull come into his water hole, and he centered the animal with an arrow and ended his elk hunt. Marvin saw a couple of elk on the hillside above his water hole, but neither the elk nor any bear made an appearance within bow range. We spent the following morning getting Randy's elk out and home.

That evening, both returned to their water holes with high anticipation. I could hear them coming through the dark long before they got to the truck and, by the feverish excitement in Marvin's voice, I knew he had an encounter with some type of four-legged critter. He was so excited he could hardly tell me what had happened.

He said he had been sitting on the ground in a blind of sorts made by clearing out some oak brush and building up the cover. The blind was about 10 yards back from the edge of the water hole, but was invisible in the shadows. He had a good 20-yard shot from where most of the sign indicated game had been watering. Marvin had been sitting comfortably for about an hour when a big, dark brown bear came bounding out of the oak brush and ran to the edge of the water hole. The bear was only 15 yards from where Marvin sat and his sudden appearance didn't give Marvin much time to get nervous, at least not then. The bear immedi-

ately stuck his nose in the water and started drinking. Without another thought Marvin drew his 60-pound compound and sent his arrow bearward. The arrow hit a little too far back and the peace and tranquility of the area came to a bawling, growling halt. According to Marvin, the bear went berserk and whirled around, biting and snarling at the wound site. He kept spinning, snarling and biting at anything he could reach, throwing mud and water everywhere.

At this point in his story, I innocently asked Marv why he didn't get another arrow into the bear.

"I didn't want that damn bear to know I was anywhere around!" he said. "If I could have gotten my arrow back and called the whole thing off, I would have! I've never been so scared in all my life and I don't ever want to be that close to a bear again, especially one that is looking for the thing that has caused its problem."

According to Marvin, the bear finally turned and went roaring off into the heavy oak brush. He could hear the bear for a few seconds, then nothing. He got out of the blind and stayed in the open, where an angry bear couldn't sneak up on him.

We went back and blood-trailed the bear in the dark, much to Marvin's and Randy's uneasiness. For the first 100 yards there was a good blood trail, but then it started to thin out and finally disappeared altogether–typical for a bear hit too far back. I think Marvin and Randy were relieved when I told them I couldn't find any more blood. But when I told them the next step in the hunt, they both looked at me like I was crazy.

We drove 40 miles home, picked up my four best Plott hounds and stopped in town to pick up a couple of my guides to go along for the excitement. By the time we got the dogs to the blood trail it was past midnight. The hounds hit the trail in full voice and took off through the dense oak brush, hot after the bear. We struggled through the thickets in the dark and could hear the dogs working the track far up the canyon. Within a mile the dogs started telling the world they had the bear treed and weren't about to let him get any farther.

Their baying and bawling added adrenaline to our fight with the oak brush, and it wasn't long before we were standing around the base of a huge fir, looking up at the bear some 60 feet above us. We could see that he was badly hit, but a long way from dead, and the only way he was going to come down was with the help of another arrow or two.

Marvin had a full bow quiver with six arrows so I didn't feel there was a problem; that is, until he sent the first two arrows smack into the middle of the night. What he thought was the bear happened to be a big black hole in the tree limbs above the bear. Marvin wore bifocal glasses, and when he had to look up he couldn't focus very well. His third arrow grazed the bear's leg and his fourth was another sky shot.

The excitement was getting to Randy and he had an urgent call from Mother Nature. He was relieving himself on the downhill side of the tree about the time the bear decided that he might be better off on the ground. A bear can come out of a tree as fast as a falling limb, and when this bear hit the ground in a shower of limbs and branches, Randy quickly lost all interest in his relief and darn near amputated a vital part of his anatomy with his zipper, diving headlong down the hillside.

The dogs sensed the bear's descent and were on him about the time he hit the ground. It took a few minutes to get our crew back together, but the dogs already had the thoroughly angry bear backed up against a downed tree, giving him a hard time.

I wanted to get this over with, so I moved Marvin into position for a sure shot with one of his last two arrows. My two guides kept the bear-dog fight well-lit while I moved to within five yards of the melee with my

unwilling bowhunter. I told Marvin I would holler at the dogs and they would back off the bear for a few seconds and give him time to get a shot. All went well except Marvin's arrow didn't go where it was intended and ended up in the bear's shoulder instead of behind it. What happens when you make a bad shot with a bow? Naturally, you put the next arrow in the same place and Marvin did just that! Now we had a really, *really* angry bear with two arrows pricking his shoulder and a bowhunter with no arrows to shoot.

Marvin needed another arrow to finish the job and the only place I could think of to get one was from the bear. I had my guides keep their lights on the fighting bear while I eased up behind the log. I knew my dogs would be on the bear immediately if he took his attention off them for a second, so there wasn't much of a chance of the bear getting over the log at me if I was quick. There are two things that keep me out of trouble: my cowardliness and great speed; and I can assure you my great speed was in overdrive when I grabbed that arrow and yanked it loose.

The bear didn't much like it, but by the time he realized what was happening I was well on my way out of there with the arrow. When I gave the arrow to Marvin, I told him to put this one behind the shoulder or he was going after it himself. He just nodded, dumbfounded, and did as I told him to end his bear hunt.

He and Randy came back the following year, but wouldn't buy a bear license, and one of the guides that was with us won't go on any more night bear chases. Guess they just don't like the dark!

Knife Fight With A Bear

by Billy Stockton
as told to Dennis Phillips

After more than 25 years of guiding clients on bear hunts, one of the most successful techniques I've found for putting hunters on really big bears is the use of a diaphragm call to mimic the sound of a calf elk in distress. While this trick won't work all the time—maybe just four times out of 10—when it does, the bear that comes to the call is usually a big old boar who's looking for an easy meal.

I believe the reason is that only mature bears, or ones that have been around for a few seasons, recognize the sound of a sick elk calf. I've called to young bears feeding on grass in the meadows in the spring, and all they do is look up and go back to feeding.

Older bears react differently. I've had them come meandering in slowly and cautiously, while others rush in so fast they leave little time for a hunter to react. I use this calling method mostly during spring bear hunts, but I first discovered that it would work several years ago during the fall bowhunting season for elk.

We had two bowhunters in camp from Florida. We were camped on Ten Mile Creek, on the other side of the divide from Wise River in late September. The weather had been unsettled that fall and the elk were late going into the rut. They were just starting to whistle and bugle.

Late one afternoon, we found ourselves in an area that I knew was holding elk. We set up on a hillside above a canyon overgrown with alder bushes. Higher up the hillside, there was a little blade knob. Above the knob was dark timber. I knew elk regularly fed up through the alder bushes and melted back into the timber, so I set up my hunter between two bulls in hopes of getting something fired up. I started to squall like two different bulls in a fight and was breaking tree limbs and raising all kinds of hell in hopes of stirring something up. Pretty soon, I saw some movement down in the brush, but the elk were coming from a different direction than I anticipated they would.

I quickly positioned myself between the elk and my hunter. Although I could see my hunter I didn't have a good view of his shooting lanes. To keep the action hot, I kept right on calling. Before long my hunter got into a shooting position, nocked an arrow and came to full draw.

Moments later he shot and immediately seven cow elk came trotting past me. I just knew he had ambushed a nice bull. He had a big smile on his face as I walked up to him.

"Boy! I just shot a bear," he said, shaking my hand and patting me on the back.

"You mean you shot a 'bear of an elk,'" I said, seeing how excited he was.

"No, I shot a bear, I tell you!"

For several minutes I tried to convince him that he shot an elk and he tried to convince me that he had shot a bear. Before long we were both starting to get half mad. Finally I threw my arms into the air and walked downhill about 30 yards to find an elk track that would settle this argument once and for all.

"I'll be damned." I said as I looked at a good blood trail and a nice sized bear track. "He really did shoot a bear!" All I could do was climb back up the hill and apologize to my hunter.

We figured that this bear was coming in to see how the elk fight was going to turn out in hopes that the loser might make an easy meal. He hadn't counted on a hunter laying in wait.

My client claimed that he got a good shot on the bear just behind the front shoulder. The blood trail led down through the brush toward the bottom of the canyon. It was getting later in the afternoon and, during the last few days, the weather was bringing in snow or rain during the evening. I knew that if we didn't track this bear before dark we would lose the blood trail by next morning. We might lose him completely.

There wasn't enough time to go back to camp for a rifle, and I didn't look forward to tracking a wounded bear in thick brush with only a grunt tube and a call. I gave that bear half an hour to 45 minutes, as much time as I could before I was afraid it would get dark on us.

In all my years as a guide, I've had seven bears on top of me and knew that this wasn't going to be easy. Looking into the alders below, I

also knew it was no place to take a hunter. Since all I had to protect myself was my knife, I thought about taking one of his arrows along as well, but knowing my luck, I figured I would probably stick the arrow into the bear, break off the shaft and end up fighting him off with a handful of feathers.

"Let me have your knife instead," I told my hunter. With a knife in each hand, I headed into the brush and down the canyon following the blood trail, which turned out to be a good one.

As I eased down through the alders there were bear trails everywhere. It was pretty steep and at times I was on my hands and knees. At others I had to crawl on my stomach. With the rain and snow during the last week, the ground was covered with wet, slippery leaves. I was inching my way through the brush being as careful as I could. I couldn't see much more than three or four feet in any direction and daylight was starting to slip away.

The blood trail was easy to follow and I wasn't sure if I would find the bear dead or alive. About halfway down the canyon I jumped him from his bed. He woofed at me and ran farther downhill.

"So far so good," I thought to myself and continued on. It wasn't much longer before the same thing happened. With a woof, he sprang from his bed, spun around and left. With the hope of bleeding him out and knowing that he wasn't willing to stand and fight, I thought this bear might be about spent.

By this time the hillside was really steep. It was all I could do to keep my footing. What I didn't know was that the bear had decided to run down the canyon and then double back on his blood trail and wait for me to follow. I got to where I could stand up because the hillside leveled out to a small bench about five feet wide. I thought that if he was going to bed down again this would be the place to find him. It was, but he found me first.

Suddenly the bear growled and reared up just three feet in front of me. Even though I was taking my time and being careful, this bear had hidden himself unbelievably well.

When he stood up, I dropped my hunter's knife from my left hand, grabbed a handful of bear and took a swipe at him with my own knife. In less time than it takes to tell, the bear hit me with a right cross on the left side of my head. I'm not sure to this day if he knocked me out, but the first thing to hit the ground was the back of my head. The next thing I can remember is rolling over on all fours and scrambling back up the canyon, dreading that the enraged bruin would grab me by the legs and pull me back down.

I managed to climb about 40 yards the way I came and stopped at a lone pine tree in the alder bushes. Only then did I realize that the bear wasn't following me. Either he was hit hard enough that he couldn't come uphill or he didn't want me bad enough. It took me a while to calm down and get my wits about me.

"Billy, you're one lucky fellow," I said to myself as I replayed the last few minutes in the mind. The one thing that probably saved my life was that just as I swung the knife at the bear, my feet slipped out from under me on the wet leaves.

As I slipped I moved into the bear, so when he hit me with his paw, he connected with just the heel of his pad instead of his claws. He could have easily taken my head off. He almost had!

Now I was left with other more immediate problems about which to worry.

I faced a major dilemma. I realized that I left my hunter's knife back down on the bench. If it had been just a regular knife I would have left it and bought him another, but this particular knife was custom-made with

fancy scrollwork and the guy's name etched on the blade. It was irreplaceable. With our guide/client relationship under stress because I doubted his word about what he had shot, I had no choice. I headed back down into that hole after the knife.

My left eye was swollen shut. Blood ran down my face and I was as edgy as a man could be. It was also pretty dark. I really didn't want to get into another knife fight with a bear.

I lowered myself slowly back down to the bench. The bear was gone. I kicked around in the leaves, managed to find the knife and got the hell out of there as quickly as I could.

Back on top of the ridge I gathered up my hunter. Until he saw my face, he had no idea what transpired down in the canyon. Without much talk, we headed back to camp.

The next day we went back into the canyon with a rifle. I picked up the blood trail again and tracked him another 200 yards down the canyon before the wound must have plugged up with fat and hair. We never did find the bear, even though we hunted that country and kept our eyes open for another week. I'm sure the bear's wounds were superficial and that he lived to tell his kin about the knife fight he was in with that crazy outfitter.

Start A Fire
To Stay Alive

by Walt Earl

B efore early January of 1972, I thought I had seen 'most everything go wrong that could on a hunt; but what took place on those cold days was a real classic.

It started out like most mountain lion hunts: we found a good tom track after several days, turned the three hounds loose, strapped on the backpacks and took off in pursuit. My client, a nonresident, had lots of gear and I gave him a hand. Most of it was photographic equipment, including a large telephoto lens, light meter, a couple of cameras, film and other large bulky pieces of equipment. I tried to suggest he leave some items in the truck, but he reported that all pieces were a must or none would work.

Our luck for this cat was destined not to be good. As we left the truck, I showed my man where I put the truck keys so, if we got split up, he could start the truck and stay warm.

After about an hour and a half of walking uphill and sliding along ridges, my man was starting to tire. I told him to take five and just follow my tracks in the day-old snow when he was ready, taking his time catching up to me and the dogs. My dogs would stay treed for over 24 hours, so he shouldn't sweat it too much if he couldn't keep up. Soon he was out of sight, still sitting on a rock taking pictures.

The sun was shining when we started out, but within three hours the sky had become cloudy and the temperature started to drop. I stopped on top of a ridge and dug in my pack for some bright pink surveyor's tape. I tied long strips to a small fir tree which was right alongside the trail. To one long streamer I attached a note which told my client to head back and not chance the bad cold and storm I could see building in the northwest. After I caught the dogs, I wrote, we would go home for the night, then start out fresh in the morning. He was to wait in the truck until I got back. Both gas tanks were almost full and I had several packages of dehydrated food behind the seat. I figured he would make out okay.

The lion tracks headed up to the divide ridge between Anderson and Three Mile Creeks which, at the top, was at an elevation of 8,500 feet. I thought I would catch the lion before then. But this was not to be so.

The temperature had dropped to 10 degrees or so and the clouds were quickly moving in; already they almost touched the top of the ridge. The wind started to blow like nothing I had ever experienced. The wind did not start out gusting, it started strong and never let up. It was kind of spooky, and I had a cold chill run down my back. I should have turned back myself, I thought, but since I never had before, I figured, why should I now? This storm was one which would leave me to wonder about my own sanity.

As I kept following the dogs and lion tracks it started to snow and the temperature kept dropping. Soon it was a real blizzard, snowing so hard that I couldn't see more than a few feet in front of me. I stopped just short of the divide top and got my wind. My gloves were wet and frozen so I changed into a dry pair. As I changed my gloves, I noticed that my fingers were so stiff I almost couldn't bend them. I decided that, if things were worse when I got over the top, I could find a cave and hold up until the storm blew over. I didn't realize just how cold it was until I topped the ridge. The snow was about waist deep and I had to half-crawl or "snow swim" my way to the top. Once I got down into the timber, somewhat out of the wind, I noticed that my cheeks and face were rather hard. I tried to pull off my left glove, but it was frozen to my hand. I tried to make a fist but found that my hands were almost useless. I knew that I had to find some shelter immediately or I soon would not be worrying about much of anything.

I walked down the side of the ridge until I got to some rock outcroppings which had some small caves in them. I knew I was in deep trouble when, as I knelt down to try and make my way into the cave, I put my left hand down to stabilize myself and felt nothing. I looked down at my hand and could see it was on the rocks, but I didn't feel anything. I looked around inside the small cave and my heart missed a few beats. Most of these caves contain small pack rat nests made of small branches, pine-cones and most anything a pack rat can find. This cave had not one loose pinecone or even a twig. I backed out and headed down the rock ledge,

looking for another possibility. After 100 yards, I came to another cave which I had to bend over to enter. Inside, it was approximately 10 feet wide and 15 feet long. There was a small pack rat nest to my left and an even larger nest to my right which had been built over several years.

My mind came back to hard reality when I tried to get my right glove off and could not. I managed to shake off my left glove. Near panic came over me as I saw that my fingers were snow-white and that the whiteness went up to the main knuckles on my hand. Trying to keep my cool, I stuck my hand under my right arm. It felt like a block of ice, but I knew if I was to be able to strike a match, I would need to feel with my fingers. I decided to put my hand down the front of my pants and hope for more warmth. I could feel my body temperature change after I had my hand inside my pants for a while and I started to feel a burning sensation in some of my fingers, so I had hope of being able to get a match lit.

I slid my backpack off and tried to unzip the pocket holding the matches. My fingers would not hold onto the zipper tab. I bent down and grasped the tab in my teeth, but my wet lips stuck to the frozen metal. I pulled my pack open and, as I let go, the skin peeled off my bottom lip. I rolled my pack around until the plastic pill bottle containing matches fell out. I was able to pop off the soft cap with my left thumb and shake the matches onto the cave floor. I got four or five matches squeezed between my thumb and index finger, and placed them at the bottom of the large pack rat nest.

Since I couldn't hold a match in my fingers, I placed a few more matches in a small pile at the base of the nest. Placing my frozen hand upon the small pile of matches, I tried to slowly roll them together. After the third attempt, they burst into a small flame. I watched in pain as the flame flickered and slowly started to burn. In my panic and hurry, I tried to roll some more twigs and pinecones down to get the fire going, but, before I knew it, the small fire went out. Again, I painfully and awkwardly piled more matches under the nest and they exploded into a flare-up which kept burning. Soon the smoke started to choke me and I hunkered down near the floor of the cave.

I don't know whether I dozed off or passed out, but, when I next knew what was going on, the heat inside the cave was hot enough to make my face start to burn and sting. I feel that this is what brought me around. I held my right hand up to the fire and rotated it until I was able to pull my glove off. In the dancing light of the flames, I could see that my fingers were pure white. There was no way I could move them. As the cave warmed, I finally stopped trembling. My left hand started to throb and burn, and I almost couldn't stand the pain, but as I shook and swung it, I found I could move my fingers and almost make a fist. I don't know how long I had been in the cave before I could grasp things in my left hand. I could not feel much, but if I watched what I was doing, I could make my left hand do what I wanted it to do. I took a large burning stick from the fire and lit the other nest. The warmth was too much and I started to become sleepy. I didn't want to go to sleep for fear of never waking again.

As the fires burned, I could feel a draft of cold air from outside being drawn into the cave. I pulled out my 10- by 10-foot plastic sheet to block off part of the entrance. It was already dark. I hadn't realized so much time had passed during my half-dazed hours in the cave. I was able to block off most of the opening and could now bend my fingers enough to make a very swollen fist. My right hand was still almost useless, with no feeling or movement at all. My cheeks had all but quit stinging and burning.

My eyelids were very heavy and I needed some sleep. I sat on my pack between the two fires and dozed off. I don't know how long I slept, but I must have had my right hand resting on my lap. As I moved, my hand must have slid off and slapped against a rock. The pain, which shot up my right arm, was the most unreal thing I have ever experienced and something which I hope to never go through again. No matter what I did, the pain would not ease. I had some aspirin in my pack and I took four of them, but that didn't help. The pain was so bad that I started to sweat and I passed out a time or two. I would hold my hand above my head and swing it back and forth as hard as I could. Nothing seemed to help.

I felt hungry, so I dug out some trail mix and munched on it. For a while, I began to feel a little better but, all of a sudden, my gut started doing flip-flops and out of the cave I went. I upchucked and felt very light-headed; I barely made it back to the cave before my legs turned to rubber.

I'm not sure how long I laid there but, when I came back to my senses, I felt better and the pain in my hands had eased noticeably. But they were so swollen now that I was unable to close them into a fist. The fires were down to solid red coals and I knew they were good for only a few short hours. I looked out the cave opening, noticing that the wind was down and the snow had stopped. It was still a cold bear out. When that fresh air hit my face, I felt it.

I dug out a pair of heavy wool socks from my pack and pulled these on my swollen hands. I slid into my pack straps and made my mind up that I'd make it back to the pickup before dark. At that time, I didn't realize I had lost 24 hours.

The best thing to happen was that my legs and feet were not hurt. I had no trouble walking, but certainly had felt stronger on better days.

I made the ridge top and was about to drop off toward the truck when I heard a dog bark. I looked up and saw my three dogs coming down the ridge. I whooped and hollered, and they came straight to me. They were glad to see me, but not as glad as I was to see them. I knew that with them I had renewed strength to make it down to the rig.

I slid off the top and made sure my hands stayed dry. I bumped my right hand once, and nearly lost it all again. As I came around the last ridge point above the pickup, I just about came unglued at the seams. My truck was gone! I hit the road with renewed energy. You just don't take a man's rig and leave him in a lurch in the mountains!

The dogs and I struck out down the road and, even though it was more than 30 miles to the closest house, I was so damn mad I felt as if I could have run the whole distance. I felt certain I would make it with no problems. Being unable to see the sun made it impossible to know what time it was.

I could tell that my client had left during the storm because the pickup tracks were all snowed in. There was maybe four or five inches of snow on the road and you couldn't see a fresh tire track.

We had walked for quite a spell when I noticed my old female hound looking and listening down the road. I could not see nor hear a thing. But I knew those dogs could hear better than me and soon they were wagging their tails. I knew a rig was coming. Sure enough, a fellow cat hunter, who was out on his own, came down the road. When I showed him my hands, he loaded my dogs with his and headed down river to my home. About 20 miles down the road we met my hunter coming back to look for me. He had gone down to a cafe to eat.

My client was innocent. He didn't know what he had done and didn't realize what could have happened by his taking that pickup. Upon explaining the situation, and showing him my hands, he felt very bad, but as he drove me the rest of the way home, I thanked him for being there.

It was three weeks before I could use my hands to grab something without the pain causing me to wet my pants. I had had frostbite before, but not to this extreme, and I hope it never has a chance to happen ever again.

Ma Nature is truly no one to try to outguess, and, had I not had the proper items in my pack, I probably would not be here to tell this story.

To this day, I always carry that pack with me. Whenever I'm out in the woods, I load it with a 10- by 10-foot plastic sheet, waterproof matches, and food. Remember, don't go out hunting for anything without having a small pack containing such life-saving items—you never know what is around the next corner.

The Elk With The Lady's Name On It

by L.C. Trimber
as told to Brook Elliott

Years ago, I guided for an outfitter in Idaho. We had just finished packing about 150 bales of hay into our early season camp, when George the outfitter, said to me, "LC, I've got this man, and I'd like you to take his wife hunting. They're both very experienced sportspeople. In fact, they just came back from a 21-day African safari."

Now when old George would start trying to sell you on hunters you hadn't even met yet, a young guide like me had cause for concern. I was a bit more than apprehensive.

George was the boss and he certainly could tell me what to do, but his softsoap continued. He went on to tell me that this fine filly was so good looking she could stand in for Marilyn Monroe in *Bus Stop*.

Despite my leeriness of George's approach, I said to myself, this has got to be a pretty sharp gal, right? I mean, good looking *and* an accomplished hunter to boot?! Who better than me to lead her to a trophy elk? Right?

I told George I'd be happy to take 'em. Then the clients showed up. My Marilyn Monroe double was in tough shape. *Really* tough shape. I mean this gal was two mules wide and about 12 hands high. Must have gone 240 on the hoof, standing about five feet, three inches. She was blonde, I'll give her that, but that was the only similarity to Marilyn.

Their first night in camp, I talked the couple through the various procedures for the hunt. I stressed that we would use the horses instead of just walking. This gal was all for that, although I had my doubts about her ability to even get on a horse, let alone keep it under control.

"One thing," she said to me. "I don't care how big a bull we get, as long as it's bigger than my husband's!"

Her husband, Jack, had killed his only bull the year before, and it scored about 180 at the most, so I didn't think there would be a problem. We'd get us a small 3x4, or something like that, and she would be happy. Little did I know.

Next morning we were up for breakfast at 4:30, and I started packing the horses. She said she'd fix lunches and get ready. Then she disappeared for about half an hour.

When she emerged from her tent, she was ready alright! She had put on all her makeup. I mean she wore this heavy duty stuff—powder, rouge, lipstick and who knows what all. And she had on her hunting outfit. Looked like she had come right out of Eddie Bauer. Had those britches on with the extra seat sewed in the back, for instance. And had on her riding boots, real fancy jobs. I thought she had a pair of hunting boots as well, but all she'd brought were these west Texas roach killers.

We took off on the horses and got into the country I wanted to hunt. Picketing the horses, we moved down maybe 150 yards. She wasn't going any farther. Just couldn't make it.

It was just breaking daylight and in this country, right when the sun comes up, it turns cold real quick. So, naturally, I had to build her a fire. And there we were, sitting under this tree with this fire going, right when we should have been out hunting.

Things weren't looking good. I told her we would have to get into some other country if we were going to get an elk. She said, "Fine. Why don't you get the horses and I'll wait here."

I was less than 50 yards away when she decided that being alone wasn't going to work for her. She started squealing and hollering for me to come back, not to leave her. She was scared to be alone!

So that took care of day one. We went back to camp, and spent the rest of the day drinking coffee, telling hunting stories and stuff. Had a grand old time of it, too.

The next day we went through the same process. I figured if I could keep her on horseback, we would be a whole lot better off. We even left a little later in the morning because she said she was so cold. So it was well after daylight when we actually got started.

We were pausing in some boulders, out of the wind, when she tells me again how important it is to get an elk bigger than Jack's. And just then I heard an elk busting through the brush, coming from the north side of the ridge.

I told her not to get excited, everything would be fine, but to get ready because an elk was coming through the woods. And there he came, a 6x6 bull that would score 360 easy.

So here's this experienced African hunter, with all those animals to her credit. And at 40 yards she put the crosshairs on his chest, pulled the trigger, and missed! That bullet went clear over his back.

But the bull didn't bolt! Instead, he turned down the hill and ambled off. Now maybe he was 60 yards out, and she threw the gun up again, pulled the trigger and missed again. This time she fired in front of him.

I told her to relax, and squeeze off the shot. Everything would be fine. She tossed that custom-built Mauser to her shoulder once more, sighted through that expensive scope once more, and fired once more, just as the bull turned around a point of rocks and went out of sight.

There was a crashing sound as he went down!

Before I could say anything she ran down to those rocks. And there was that bull, a whole lot bigger than Jack's, laying on the ground.

Before I could stop her, she was down there, and had her tag slapped on the bull. She was all excited, jumping up and down, and couldn't wait

to get some pictures. I was afraid she was going to have a heart attack or something, and I spent some time just calming her down. I got so busy with her, I didn't think to check for bullet holes, blood or anything.

She finally relaxed a bit and repaired her make-up (she carried a whole kit of the stuff in a saddle bag), and we got ready to take pictures.

I decided the angle was wrong, and lifted the bull's rack to move him. Just then he decided to wake up and make tracks elsewhere. Now, I rodeoed a lot when I was younger, and have grabbed ahold of horns before, but never like this!

The bull was shaking his head, while I hung on for dear life. She was yelling, "Hold him! Hold him, LC!" Meanwhile, I was yelling, "Don't shoot! Please, don't shoot!"

This went on for maybe a couple minutes, but it felt like five years. Finally, I let go where I could roll in a snowbank, out of the bull's way and he continued down the hill.

I had barely caught my breath, when we heard shots about a half mile off in the direction the bull had taken. Mounting up, we rode down there. Sure enough, there was our bull on the ground, with these boys just about finished field dressing him.

Now the fun really started. She had seen this bull fall in front of her rifle, and it was certainly bigger than Jack's. And she was not going through all of this again if she could help it.

"Thanks for stopping my elk," she told them fellers.

"Do what?" was the natural reply.

"I said, thanks for stopping my elk. I shot him up on the hill and he's mine."

Well these boys weren't buying any of that. They shot him. They knew they shot him. That was final, and they let her know it in no uncertain terms.

Finally she said, "I don't want to argue about it. That's my elk and that's all there is to it."

So one of them said, kind of sarcastic-like, "Waddaya mean your elk? You got your name on it?"

"As a matter of fact, I do," she replied. "Here, I'll show you."

You can imagine their reaction when she showed them her tag already attached. And, of course, the elk belonged to whoever tagged it.

But things worked out for those boys, too. For them, elk was really a side thing. They were from back East, and had come out for mule deer. So I told them I would be back the next day, and put them onto some mulies to make up for their trouble.

Everybody wound up happy.

It Takes All Kinds

by Billy Stockton
as told to Dennis Phillips

One of the things I enjoy most about guiding and outfitting is the chance to meet a lot of different people. If you talk to any outfitter, he'll tell you that eventually you'll get some bad apples, but I can honestly say that I've had very few people I couldn't get along with.

Most of the hunters we guide are good, experienced hunters, particularly the bowhunters. It's usually during the rifle season that we see a mixed bag with some fellows who have never hunted a day in their lives and others who have never even spent any time in the woods. But that's fine, because they hire us to make sure they have a safe, enjoyable experience and have an opportunity to see and take game.

Sometimes, though, you can't help but chuckle at the things clients do.

One year, during the late rifle season, we had a party of four from Atlanta who were hunting for both elk and mule deer. We split the group up with two hunters per guide. The two fellows I had were cousins. One was named Charles and the other Chuck, and for two guys with similar names, they were as different as night and day.

Chuck had never been big game hunting and wasn't quite prepared for the conditions he would be facing—like mountainous terrain and cold, snowy weather. But he was game for anything we suggested.

On the first day of the hunt, the three of us set off on foot. We headed up Whiskey Gulch, a drainage right behind our lodge and, as they say in my country, it was "steeper than a cow's face." There was about two feet of snow on the ground, and I was leading the way up the ridge with Charles behind me and Chuck bringing up the rear.

It always takes a few days to get used to the altitude and to learn how to pace yourself in these mountains. I always tell my clients that if they're running short on wind, just stop and we'll take it easy until they find a pace that's comfortable. Chuck was having trouble, but wasn't letting anyone know until he got a sharp pain in his ribs due to lack of air.

With no warning, Chuck started hollering and rolling around in the snow. Charles and I looked at each other with bewilderment.

"I've been shot with an arrow!" Chuck shouted as he twisted around, trying to pull an imaginary arrow from his ribs. Charles and I both got so tickled at the sight of him that it was several minutes before we could explain that there weren't any bowhunters in the woods, let alone any who would shoot at him.

Somehow, that set the tone for the rest of the week. A few days later, the three of us were hunting in another area called Seven Mile Creek. I set Chuck down at the junction of two well-used trails in hopes that he could spot some elk or deer moving. I took Charles with me to hunt another area.

There weren't any deer or elk moving that morning, but a big bull moose and two cows soon came by. At first, Chuck didn't really know what they were, but fortunately he knew they weren't elk because he had seen pictures of elk. It wasn't long before he figured out they were moose. Then he got worried. He had heard stories about moose, particularly bulls, attacking people, so he figured he'd better clear out before they spotted him.

How to leave without being seen was his biggest problem. He knew he couldn't just stand up and walk out or he might be run down by a charging moose. About the time he decided how and when to leave, Charles and I were headed back to pick him up.

At first we couldn't see Chuck, but knew he wouldn't leave without us. Then we saw a little bump moving in the snow. Chuck had figured out that if he got down on his belly and crawled out under the snow drifts, which were about three feet deep in this area, the moose wouldn't see him and attack.

To us it looked like a big mole burrowing his way through the snow, except every now and then Chuck would stick his head up and look around to see if he was still heading in the right direction. He didn't have to worry about the moose anymore because our laughing spooked them out of the meadow, and he escaped unharmed.

Because Chuck and Charles were from the South and hadn't spent much time in wet, cold weather, I was careful to tell them about hypothermia and how to stay warm and dry. It proved to be important advice because later that week a blast of cold air dropped into the state, and the temperatures were close to 30 degrees below zero during the early morning. I repeated my warning to Chuck about the early signs of hypothermia.

"If you get real cold hiking around this morning and start to shiver, let me know," I said. "Particularly if all of a sudden you start to warm up for no reason. That could be a sign of hypothermia. Let me know and we'll stop, build a fire and warm you up."

He had plenty of warm clothes and was dressed for the weather. Just to make sure he would be comfortable, I loaned him a goose down coat with an insulated hood that he cinched up so tight you could only see his eyes and nose.

We started off walking up a ridge that morning and I was breaking a trail in the snow with Chuck 10 to 12 feet behind me. He seemed to be making good progress, but he told me later that he'd been trying to catch up with me for 30 minutes before he could finally grab me by the shoulder.

When I turned around he said, "Bill, Bill! Hurry and get a fire started because I'm freezing to death."

I knew he was really concerned by the sound of his voice, but when I took a good look at him I noticed there was sweat dripping off the end of his nose. The hiking combined with the down jacket had him all heated up and he thought it was advanced hypothermia!

Back in my early days of guiding, I had a client who was rifle hunting for elk. We were hunting on horseback and my client was saddled with a pretty gentle horse. I was riding a bronc that needed a firmer hand to keep him under control.

One morning we were riding across a high ridge scanning the canyon below for sign of elk. Before long, we spotted a herd of elk about 300 yards away. They had started up the other side of the canyon, but hadn't seen us yet.

"Get off your horse, get a good rest and start shooting," I told my hunter. I had planned to spot his shots for him, but after the first round my horse exploded and started to buck. We jumped right over the hunter, who was still shooting, as we bucked and crow-hopped into the timber.

After a while I managed to get the horse's head up and calm him down enough to ride back. On the way back to the ridge I thought to myself, "This guy has got to think I'm the greatest guide he's ever seen. He's had a great hunt, got to shoot at a nice herd of elk and on top of that, he got to see what a great bronc rider I am. I don't imagine I can do anything wrong in his eyes."

Those thoughts didn't last long because the first thing my hunter did when I rode up was get up off the ground, throw his hat down in disgust and shout, "You're no guide. You're just a goddamn cowboy!"

He was mad because he thought he missed a nice 6x6 bull that was in that herd of elk and figured I was trying to show off my rodeo skills. As it turned out, we rode over to where he shot at the elk and found a blood trail and eventually the elk about 50 yards away.

One spring, during bear season, I had a hunter in camp who had never hunted bear, and I don't believe he'd ever done much hunting of any kind. One thing for sure, though, he had enough rifle to take a bear. He was carrying a .458 Wthby Mag. The only problem was that he was afraid to shoot it. He was small-framed and not too tall, and I guess the recoil was more than he could handle. He even told me that one of his buddies had sighted it in for him.

Even though this hunter didn't seem too experienced, it didn't matter to me. During bear season, the weather is usually beautiful and you don't have to head up into the real high country to find bear. All the moose, elk and deer are still on their winter range and I can show a client 100 to 150 head of elk a day. My bear hunts are a great way to get someone started on big game hunting without working them too hard.

One day, this hunter and I were walking along the side of a ridge and I happened to look up. Above us about 100 yards was a nice bear, standing up on his hind legs trying to figure out what we were. I knew he couldn't see us and he hadn't been able to wind us either.

"That's a good bear if you want him," I told my hunter. "But you'd better take him quick before he catches our scent."

The hillside we were standing on was pretty steep and I should have told my hunter to drop down on one knee for a better hold before shooting. Instead he threw up his gun and touched it off while he was standing flat-footed and looking uphill.

Both he and his gun went flying through the air past me. I grabbed him with one hand and his gun with the other and got them back together on the ground while trying to keep an eye on the bear. When I finally looked back up the hill, the bear was folded up like an accordion, rolling down the hill end over end toward us. Then he disappeared from sight.

Between us and the bear was an old prospector's hole that was probably dug in the late 1800s. That bear rolled down into that hole which was about 10 feet across and 10 feet deep. After the congratulations were over, I went down into the hole to skin the bear. For some reason, I took my rifle with me, which nine times out of ten I never do. It turned out to be a good decision.

I rolled the bear over and was about to set to him with the skinning

knife when that bear woke up! Neither of us liked the predicament; he less than I!

Things got exciting in a hurry. The bear was spinning around in that hole, snapping, biting and growling, and it was all I could do to keep out of his way. He really wasn't after me because he was still dazed, but his rolling and spinning around knocked me down a couple of times. I finally managed to get my rifle, stuck it in his ribs and finished him.

We later figured out that instead of hitting him in the chest, like I thought had happened, the bullet went through the base of his ear and exited behind, taking only a piece of hide and a little flesh off the skull. There was nothing wrong with that bear except that I was about to skin him alive.

I crawled up out of that hole and said, "Whew, that was a close one!"

But no one was there to answer. I looked around and my hunter was about a half mile down the canyon, running for all he was worth. It took me about a mile to catch up with him and let him know everything was okay.

That's when I figured out it's better to kill a bear before you try to skin it—at least when a client's around.

Hermit Of
The Beartooths

by Bill Butler

Apparition-like figures moved steadily onward, disappearing and then reappearing with equal suddenness, as the wind gusted powdery snow through the bitterly cold darkness.

The storm was raging wildly and the drifts on the trail were deepening rapidly. Across the icy trail ahead lay a deeper drift.

The small, gray-whiskered man stepped from the sled so the dog would have a better chance of pulling it through. Ice on the trail was covered with fine, wind-blown snow.

As the man started to push the sled, his feet slipped suddenly from beneath him, dropping him on his left hip under the force of his full weight. He tried to raise his body erect again, but he could not. He was still a mile from his cabin. It was 10:00 p.m., snowing and drifting heavily, with no other humans within miles.

The temperature stood at 12 degrees below zero. If he could not reach his camp soon he would die of exposure....

The man was James H. Ayling, better known as Jimmy Joe. Four days before New Years in December, 1964, he decided he needed more supplies for his larder in the cabin on East Rosebud Lake where he was the winter caretaker of several summer cabins.

He hitched up his young white Siberian husky, Chommie, and sledded into Roscoe, a distance of 12^1/$_2$ miles. He spent most of the day visiting and buying supplies in Roscoe and got a late start going back.

Some boys going cat hunting gave him a ride to the two-mile bridge above town, and he traveled on alone from there. He had food, tools and snowshoes on the sled. The well-trained husky pulled the sled easily at first but, as the storm got worse, Jimmy Joe helped push the load when they came to a big drift.

Jimmy Joe was 61.

He had left his native home in New Jersey when he was 20 and traveled to the Northwest Territories of Canada, where he trapped and learned how to train dogs. He once had a wolf for a lead dog on a team. "He was so mean I always had to handle him with a whip," Jimmy Joe said. He stayed in the north country a few years, then came to the Red Lodge, Montana area and decided to stay.

Jimmy Joe was alone in the storm, as he had been most of his adult life. He did not panic. Death had walked near him before. He had had his life spared three times previously. He had almost died as an infant, had diphtheria as a child and also had swallowed caustic while still young. ...He did not lie in the snow long. He wrestled himself onto the sled made of a wagon and skis and signaled the dog to go.

He pushed as much as he could with his good leg. Sensing the situation, the husky lunged into his harness with everything he had. He wildly clawed his way through the ever-deepening drifts. As the sled bounced over a rock in the trail, the tailgate flew out. Jimmy Joe stopped the dog, backed up and retrieved the lost part. His supplies would fall out without the tailgate.

There was a place about a quarter of a mile below the cabins where the road always drifted badly. That worried Jimmy Joe. He yelled encouragement to Chommie just before they hit the area and the dog poured on the speed. They went through it like a snowplow and never slowed down until they reached the cabin.

Ten years earlier, in 1954, the snow had been so deep that the old hermit could not open the cabin door from the inside, and had to crawl out a window. He was thankful that it was not that deep now. He would not have been able to pull himself up through a window.

Usually when he left the place for long, he would hide the key high overhead in a toilet some distance from the cabin. This time he had concealed it beneath a wash tub near the steps on the front porch. This was a fateful change in routine, as now he would not have been able to remove it from a high place.

Jimmy Joe put the end of the string from the key into his mouth. He kicked with his good leg and squirmed until he was up the steps, across the porch and in front of the cabin door. He gripped a porch railing near the door and tried twice to stand so he could get the key into the lock. Each time he fell, he bit tightly on the string.

On the third try he slid along the wall with the strength of his good leg until he was in a standing position. He unlocked the cabin door and fell back to the snowy porch.

The wind was now blowing 80- to 90-miles per hour, as it often did in the canyon of the East Rosebud River.

His clothes flopped wildly and the frozen snow stung his eyes and weatherbeaten face. Jimmy Joe reached inside the door and grabbed a block of wood to prop the door open.

He also found a shovel he could use to pull his useless foot when it would catch on the steps as he dragged the sacks of supplies into the cabin. After painfully moving the supplies into the cabin, he once more pulled his horizontal body out the door, across the porch and down the stairs. He lay on his back and unharnessed his dog.

The husky hauled Jimmy Joe up the stairs, but, as they were going through the door, the violent wind blew the block free. The door, driven by the wind, jammed to a halt with Jimmy Joe's left foot wedged between its bottom and the porch. He savagely kicked the door several times with his right foot until it swung free, thinking, "What if it had been my right foot? I wouldn't have been able to get loose." He pulled himself inside the cabin and the door slammed again. At least now the storm was shut out.

After getting the cabin lighted, he set about the business of making a fire. He shook the ashes in the wood stove, dragged the heavy coal bucket to the stove and soon had a crackling fire. He had just enough water left for tea and for a drink for Chommie.

Jimmy Joe's supper that night consisted of water, tea and bread, and Chommie had water and bread.

Jimmy Joe could not get into his bed so he slept on the floor with Chommie curled against him. At 4:00 in the morning the cold became too much to bear any longer. He looked at the thermometer. It showed five degrees below zero in the cabin. He again built a fire and waited until morning. Jimmy Joe had a radio, but no other means of communication with the outside world.

Luckily a local rancher came by to say hello that day and discovered the injured man. He took him to the Red Lodge hospital, getting there at 4:00 that afternoon, 18 hours after the accident. Jimmy Joe's hip was broken in three places.

The rancher kept Chommie through the long weeks that Jimmy Joe lay in the hospital with a metal pin in his hip socket.

Story of the accident soon got out and, on April 30, 1965, a citation for distinguished dog heroism and a medal were presented to Chommie from a dog food company. It read:

"This citation is awarded to Chommie, owned by James H. Ayling in recognition of distinguished dog heroism. This award is made with our congratulations to both dog and owner for outstanding service to humanity."

Jimmy Joe came out of the hospital with pain in his hip occasionally, and lived in a cabin 15 miles from Red Lodge in the Beartooth Mountains. The cabin stood on Forest Service land and was built in the early 1900s by a man named Martin who packed everything except the logs in on horseback before there were any roads.

The cabin is at the edge of a meadow a few yards from Rock Creek. There are trout in the creek and moose, elk and mule deer sometimes feed in the meadow. In front of the cabin hangs the sled, an axe, and some dog harnesses. There is a sawbuck out in front and a large woodpile that Jimmy Joe cut and split up after skidding the lodgepole pine poles to the cabin with Chommie. There is only one door in the cabin. The stovepipe comes up through the roof to one side of the ridgepole. A bed, stove, table, chair and bench furnish the cabin. The cabin smells of pine smoke, tea and sunlight. There are two windows.

One night in the fall, when there were no berries because of an early freeze, a large bear stuck his paw through one of the windows. He planned on coming in until Jimmy Joe hit him on the nose with a block of wood. The next morning the brazen bear strolled past the chained, barking dogs and on toward the cabin again. He stopped only when Jimmy Joe opened the cabin door. The bear did not run. When Jimmy Joe walked toward him, the bear stood up on his hind legs between two trees. Jimmy Joe raised the double barreled 12 gauge shotgun to his shoulder and both barrels of string buck put an end to the marauder at 10 yards.

Jimmy Joe carried a Ruger .357 Magnum pistol when out hiking in the mountains as a precaution against grizzlies and black bears. "Never throw a rock at a grizzly bear," Jimmy Joe once told me. "They believe that they own five square miles on all sides and will charge you if they think you dispute that ownership. Don't run, but back away slowly. This is true of the large males especially and also of large male black bears."

Jimmy Joe used to kill elk and deer almost every year. One autumn, when he first came to Montana, he was camped near Sawtooth Mountain hunting elk. One evening, a large six-point bull bugled from the timber and then trotted into the meadow full of fight. He started chasing the horses, so Jimmy Joe shot the cream-colored bull in the shoulder. The bull charged him immediately. He shot it again, this time in the brisket as it ran straight for him.

He had one bullet left in his .303 Ross English-made rifle, and he knelt down behind the granite rock and waited. When the bull was so

close that Jimmy Joe was sure that he would not miss, he fired, striking the bull right between the eyes. "I could have spit in his eye where he fell," Jimmy Joe told me later.

After I had come down from hunting bighorn sheep on the plateau in back of Jimmy Joe's cabin one day, I decided to stop and say hello. He invited me in for tea. While the water was warming, Jimmy Joe showed me his book collection. Some of the titles were *In Cold Blood, The First Battle of the Marne, The Jellico Papers, Documents Relating to the Civil War, The Naked Runner* and *Death of a Peer*. As he rolled a cigarette, he reflected, "I don't like the modern novel; this stuff I read is too dry for most people."

There were books about the British government and navy. There were many more about the sea and boat making. Jimmy Joe's interest in these things came naturally as his father had spent 55 years in the British navy.

Jimmy Joe had started work on a scale model of the ship the *Bon Homme Richard* of which John Paul Jones had been the captain. He did not buy a hobby-type model kit but started only with the blueprint from one of his books. He then carved the ship's hull, masts and rudder from white pine to exact scale. He used Irish linen for the sails. Ropes and riggings were made of thread, soft wire, copper wire and nylon rope. His tools were chisels, hand drills, saws, files, pliers, hammers and a small vise and anvil. It took him all winter to finish the ship, complete with working rudder and anchor that drops. "If it will not float when I finish work on it, I destroy it," he said. "If it floats, I sell it for $300."

Jimmy Joe had adopted a Cantonese orphan girl in Hong Kong, and was her legal guardian. He sent her $40 a month for three years. Her letters came with a translation into English.

A picture of her hung in Jimmy Joe's cabin.

As we drank our tea, I mentioned to Jimmy Joe that I had noticed two unfamiliar white dogs tied near the cabin. "They are Siberian huskies like Chommie," he said. "I bought them as pups. They work well with the old dog. We cover the 15 miles to Red Lodge in $2\frac{1}{2}$ hours. When they see a rabbit or deer cross the road ahead, they make the wind whistle around my ears."

Jimmy Joe lived most of his life in the wilds. Although there are many hazards to such, he was determined to be close to the solitude and beauty of nature as long as he was able.

And he was able for the better part of his 67 years, before death came in the form of cancer March 13, 1971, in Red Lodge.

The Pretty Canyon Bear

by Patrick Meitin

H owls from my hounds grew fainter falling into the bottom of Pretty
Canyon, or Flower Canyon, or Sid's Prong—one of those damn
hellish canyons that form the head of Animas Creek. It was darn hard to
tell in the jungle brush grown up after the '56 fire that had swept through
about 250,000 acres of the wilderness. The sapling aspens, young live
oaks and especially the locust bushes—one-inch-thorn-type-locust-
bushes—made travel in these parts extremely painful.

We wore heavy canvas jackets as we lunged and swung at the unyielding brush, although it was easily 80 degrees Fahrenheit in the shade
of the occasional spruce. We made bad time through the brush: my outfitter partner, Ross, the hunter, myself and...the hunter's girlfriend,
Crystal. She had insisted on coming despite our most eloquently embel-
lished persuasion to stay home. She had already torn her brand new tan
safari shirt and mussed the once-white Nikes.

The forest had grown quiet since the dogs had faded over a far ridge
and their howls were absorbed by the wilderness. We plodded on, staying with the clients, although I would rather have run ahead. Coming to a
creek, we fell to our knees and greedily drank the ice-cold water. Crystal
refilled her canteen to the brim, fell on her back, cussed for having not
quit smoking and the fact that dancing apparently had not conditioned
her fully for the task.

Wayne Riggs, our hunter, was very proud of his recent catch and
bragged that Crystal was the finest exotic dancer in Cincinnati. The

words flowing from Crystal's pretty mouth shocked me at first, but she had come to be one of the guys, talking freely, without the pretense that is so common with most women hunters bring to the camp.

Reaching the crest of the ridge at 10,000 feet, we could again hear the hounds over the labored breathing and the cussing of our clients. The dogs were still on the trail, carefully deciphering the scented code the bear had left behind as he walked about the forest in search of food or a mate. The pace slowed a bit, though we were still in a hurry, as the clients insisted they were going to die if we didn't take a breather. So we stopped. Wayne and Crystal fell to the ground in a heap, Ross clamped onto his knees with his hands, looking like he might bend double if his grip failed. I ran to the nearest edge to listen.

I could hear each dog individually now: Noon, Cleatus, Blue with deep male voices, booming with each found track; Wee-Two and Popcorn with high-pitched screams. The hounds continued up the adjacent ridge until the bear was jumped and the howls became more urgent and more incessant.

Now we had no time to rest! We must get there now! The bear was treed!

I roused the hunting party from their rest with the latest good news from the hounds. The sting of the thorns was forgotten as we fought through the jungle like people possessed. Our lungs would soon burn from the altitude and the pollen knocked from the thick vegetation, but we paid little notice and plodded on. Wayne's pack, which held his take-down recurve and protruding aluminum arrows, caught on every tree we passed. We joked about what would have happened if he had brought his cantankerous compound bow, which we had talked him out of in lieu of the take-down. Crystal fell on her face several times and cussed like a sailor. The saplings seem to come alive when one is in a hurry, grabbing at loose clothing and joining hands at shin-level to trip an out-of-balance hound chaser. Under the blanket of thick leaves waited branches, rocks and stumps that boot toes caught on, sending hunters tumbling headlong downhill. The sound of howling hounds grew louder as we ripped ever closer, although catching sight of them was still impossible in the dense brush.

Approaching the area where the hounds howled, the brush became thicker, if that was possible. The flat area was choked with small oaks and stunted spruce trees, bent and twisted from years of five- and six-foot blankets of snow and high winds.

I could hear hounds screaming just a few hundred yards away, but could not catch sight of them or bear. I clawed through the brush until I could go no more, then continued on hands and knees under the crushed canopy. As I drew closer I could hear the sounds of growling, popping teeth and snapping branches mixed with the barking and howling from fevered hounds. I drew my .45 Colt semi-auto, sliding the receiver back until it stopped and letting it slip from between my thumb and forefinger. The round slid into the receiver with final certainty.

I wiggled through the tight brush toward the sounds of the fight and finally saw one of my hounds howling into a dark clump. The bear rushed out of the bramble, close on the heals of Blue. The other dogs took advantage of the situation and bit at the bear's rear end, only for a second, until the bear whirled to swat them off.

Situations like these always made me nervous. In the tight quarters, it was much easier for a bear to get in a crushing swing or a crunching bite on a hound that turned to flee only to run smack into one of the restricting trees or bushes. I had lost very few hounds, and the few that were lost fell victim to lions in rock, but the chances are there when dogs and bear mingle in the thick stuff and the bear fights on the ground.

When mishaps do occur it usually takes the form of nasty gashes or sore ribs. In any case the confidence of the hound is the greatest loss, and your best hound can turn into a marshmallow in one hunt, quitting at the worst possible time on later hunts.

I laid on my belly now, no more than 20 yards away from the perimeter of the circle the hounds had made around the large black bear. The bear made another mad dash, this time at Wee-Two, nearly clamping down on her hind quarter! I had to do something!

The bright chartreuse post nestled into the black notch at the rear of the Colt pistol and this settled on the shoulder of the furry bear. The trigger was half squeezed when Cleatus jumped in front of the bear, so I eased off. Several more attempts to get a slug into the bear all resulted in a hound in the sights. Sometimes in front of the bear, sometimes behind, the risks were all the same. I shot my pistol on a regular basis for just these occasions and was confident I could shoot either of the bear's eyes out at this range, but I didn't take chances with the dogs, my children. I watched over the top of my Colt waiting for a clear shot, but one was not presented. The bear was now wheeling this way and that, and the hounds acted like kiddies in a jungle gym. As the bear darted after another hound I got my spilt-second chance. The pistol jumped, and the blast was soaked up by the vegetation, just as the bear turned to bite at another hound. The bullet grazed the bear's skull, nicked his ear and skipped into the thick brush behind him. The bear shook his head and roared at the burning of the crease across his head. The hounds attacked him from all sides, causing him to realize he was outnumbered and flee into the jungle, the dogs flowing slightly behind. The howls grew fainter again as the entourage fell deeper into the bowels of Pretty Canyon.

I remembered now I had lost my group. There was little hope of finding them in this tangle so I hoped to find them later at the tree, if this contrary bear did tree. I tore deeper into the bottom, the vegetation still thick. I was drawn on, by the siren song of the bellowing hounds, the thorns and brush doing little to slow progress in my possessed state of mind. I stopped suddenly, again listening to the hounds in the bottom. The dogs had quit receding into the distance, their chopping barks telling me they had bayed again, or perhaps treed the bear. I fought harder though the brush now, kicking and flailing, but making little better time. When I finally fell on my face and rolled to the bottom of a chute, knocking the breath out of my lungs, I decided I might make better time moving slower. At any rate, the sounds of the hounds were growing more audible now, bouncing through the trees.

Amidst the great burn was an island of ancient spruce that had survived the wrath of '56. From there the hounds' pleas to the hunters they expected to follow came clearly; only 300 yards straight across—half a mile the way I was forced to go. I fought into the island that opened slightly under the shading trees standing staunchly over the rest of the runtish forest.

There I found the hounds gathered under the largest of the trees. Noon was standing, front feet resting on the trunk of the great tree. Cleatus sat away from the tree, where the branches were thinner, and watched carefully, barking occasionally. Tardy sat beside him. Blue ran around the tree, crazy at not being able to get at the bear, barking wildly at one spot then running to another. Wee-Two's barks were piercing, high-pitched screams that pinpointed her location, as were Popcorn's. Up the old spruce sat a chubby bear, looking snug and comfortable in his lofty perch. The bear was growling slightly, slobbering a lot more, looking uphill. I presumed it was Ross and the fearless hunters that caught the bear's attention. "I hope the fools remember to play the wind and make some attempt at sneaking on the tree." I thought. "I don't need this bear jumping!"

My hunch was correct, the puffing group soon showed themselves. The thick brush and thin altitude had done little to curb Crystal's foul mouth—it had become worse if anything. Crystal had another rip in her safari shirt. Ross just smiled as Crystal rudely related the past two hours, fighting such-and-such brush the so-and-so stump that had tripped her, the cursed thorns, the sticks that had been damned by God.

Wayne paid little attention to the ranting of the finest exotic dancer in Cincinnati now, but looked into the tree searching for the record-book potential of the animal and wondering if the gunfire that he thought he had heard earlier had done any damage. Meanwhile Wayne assembled the bow he had dragged through the brush all morning and expressed concerns of making the straight-up, 40-yard shot through the tight branches of the spruce. I noticed for the first time, with a bit of concern, that Wayne had only four arrows in his carrying pouch. I wandered about the tree, looking up, locating a suitable hole to shoot through toward the bear. Ross and Crystal leashed dogs to be tied away from the tree and out from under foot. Wayne nocked his first arrow and flung it into the top of the tree.

"Wait a damn minute man!" I screamed, running over to look through the narrow hole Wayne was shooting through, the arrow sailing into space, or maybe Water Canyon. "What are you doing? Let us find a decent hole to shoot from first. Don't shoot any more arrows yet!"

We circled the tree, each peering up through the branches, squinting under the high sun. One hole was too small, another had just one twig in the wrong spot, still another didn't show the proper piece of bear hide. Finally a hole was found that satisfied all involved, and Wayne eagled himself for another shot. The next arrow bounced through the branches, flew in front of the bear's nose and into the sky, and the arrow following did much the same. The second arrow soon whistled back down to earth close to where the group was watching with anticipation as each arrow was launched. It was retrieved and a fresh broadhead was added. It, too, was soon wasted, shot into the spruce trunk under the bear's vitals. With one arrow we slowed the pace of the shooting again. It was hard to hear over the drone of the howling dogs who were used to something happening by now.

The bear shifted in the tree a bit, allowing a better shot. We found a log that had fallen, caught by some of the still-living trees, offering a stair step 20 feet closer to the bear and out of some of the underbrush. I calmed Wayne, telling him this shot would be closer and easier, but reminded him our supply of arrows had dwindled to the one he held, ruining any reassurance gained before.

Wayne studied the situation, weighed the bow in his hand, chose one small spot. He came to full draw, letting the arrow slip into the air. The arrow nicked a branch, diverting from its flight plan slightly and struck the bear in the paunch where it stayed impaled. The bear became understandably upset, biting the arrow and extracting it from the burning hole in his gut. The bent arrow fell to the ground where it was snatched up and hand-straightened, as best as a human is able. The last-chance arrow was handed to Wayne, with as much luck directed its way as possible. Crystal even gave the bloody, gutty shaft a kiss. All the luck imparted caused the shaft to fly high. We were out of missiles for the bow.

Wayne extracted his borrowed .41 Rem. Mag. from its shiny-new holster, opening the cylinder and giving it a spin to check for cartridges, or maybe just because that is what he had seen "The Duke" do on the late night cowboy shows. Wayne aimed carefully and shot the pistol for the first time ever. Bark below the bear shattered in a shower of splinters. Wayne looked at me with a puzzled look on his face. "Shoot again!" I urged. At the command, Wayne emptied the pistol into the tree, hitting the bear once with a nonfatal hit. I pulled the hammer back on my Colt, Ross looked over the top of his .357 Mag., Crystal sighted her baby .380 semi-auto as Wayne fought to reload his magnum. The bear then decided the tree was not such a safe place to rest and that he had been doing much better on the ground, thanks. The speed at which a bear can come out of a tree backwards, shimmying down the wide trunk like a badger shimmies over dry ground, has never ceased to amaze me. Wayne had just snapped the restocked cylinder back into the frame of the Smith and Wesson when the bear started down.

Wayne blasted at the bear as he slid down, his bullets knocking limbs and bark and splintered wood from the tree, but little from the bear. Then Ross, Crystal and I began our assault. The war did little apparent damage to the bear as he ducked between branches on his way out. Twenty feet from the ground the bear took flight, gliding through the air like a boulder. He hit the ground with a thud six feet before my blazing muzzle, other bullets whizzing past from my left into the thick brush. The bear melted into the edge of the jungle. I took chase, firing as I ran, Crystal's pistol occasionally notching the trees in front of me as she shot around me. The hounds that Ross and Wayne turned loose behind me ran through my legs and to my right and left as they dove into the brush where the bear had vanished. I fought at the brush following the dogs, my pistol leading the way. When I broke into a small clearing the bear had made a stand on a pile of rotten logs, the adrenaline keeping him alive more than anything now. Noon leaped on the bear, fevered by the smell of blood and the presence of a man that would save him from anything—he thought. Noon was batted off the bear and hit hard against a stump 20 feet from the fight, propelled by the awesome strength of the bruin. Noon did not move.

I charged to within spitting distance of the hackled bear, swinging my Colt. I jerked at the trigger, but nothing happened. The dogs mobbed the bear, Blue screaming out as the bear swatted his side. The Colt's receiver laid open, its gaping mouth empty of the shiny shells that the weapon fed on. I threw the gun to the ground and turned back to where the shooting had began. I ran into Wayne and demanded his weapon. He reached to his empty holster and looked back up at me in horror. "Damn,

I dropped my pistol. Man, I lost it!" Wayne said stupidly. I pushed him to the side and, finding Crystal, snatched her toy gun from her hands. I ran back to the pile of hound and bear and jumped into the middle of the throng. The hounds went crazy, biting at the bear from every direction, as I stuck the pistol into the bear's side and started pulling the trigger. The bear rolled over, breathing his last morbid gasp, falling onto my left foot and pinning me to the log. The hounds bit and tugged at the loose hide of the bear. Noon limped over and licked my face.

The gang of hunters broke through the brush now, their eyes widening at what they saw. I kicked the bear off me with my free foot and saw to Blue and Noon. They were sore, but basically in good shape. The other dogs still mauled at the dead bear, their reward for the long chase.

"Goddamn, you're bleeding, did the f____ bear get you? Crystal asked, wiping my cheek with the bandana taken from her head.

"Not that I know of, probably just a stick scratched me!" I laughed.

"Man, are you all right?!" Wayne and Ross asked at the same time, echoing one another. "Man, you're crazy!" Wayne continued.

"I'm not crazy, am I Noon?" I said, giving the hound a hug. "Wayne here's buying you a steak tonight, Noon!" I laughed, roughing the hound around a bit. "The fun's over now ladies and gents, let's get on with it!"

The red sun was crouching over the foothills when we reached the Continental Divide where the truck was parked. We stopped to soak in our last view of Pretty Canyon in the bronze evening light. The person that had named this canyon must have seen it in the evening light, I thought. It was indeed a pretty canyon, from here. Obviously the soul who named it had not ventured into its thorny interior to bring back one of its pretty bears.

"It is a pretty canyon, isn't it?" Crystal said as we walked down the trail toward the truck. "A very pretty canyon." The group just grunted, too tired to talk.

Singer And The Bear

by Duane Wiltse

"He's hit us again! If that damned bear has crapped in my sleeping bag this time, you boys can just get yourself another cook 'cause I'm going home!"

There was no love lost between Don Juby, my elk camp cook, and the renegade bear that had been raiding our camp on Jones Creek with maddening regularity, every time it was left unattended, in fact. This time it had only been overnight while we took our group of hunters back to town and picked up a new group for the second hunt.

In all my years of experience as a hunter, professional guide and outfitter, I had never run into a bear as cunning and bold as this one. He was big, very big, and even though we had survived two major attacks which had decimated our cook and dining tents, and several sneak attacks in which he stole supplies and scattered horses, we still didn't know for sure if he was a black bear or a grizzly bear. The Wyoming Game and Fish boys had him pegged as a griz. I had seen him once in the dark but still couldn't be sure.

Just a week earlier, in the cold, gray light of the false dawn, Don had a very close look at him. It was the first elk hunt of the 1981 season, and we were very busy. I had six elk hunters in my Cabin Creek camp on the Elk Fork drainage 35 miles west of Cody, Wyoming; two trophy bull hunters in Buffalo Hill's old camp, Camp Monaco up near the Yellowstone Park east boundary; and six more eager fellows here at the Jones Creek camp, a mere two hour horseback ride from the east en-

trance to Yellowstone Park. This country teems with wildlife—massive
bighorn rams, bugling bull elk, mountain lions, moose, coyotes, mooch-
ing black bear, and the incredible Ursus horibilus—grizzly. So, it was
impossible to guess our raiding bear's origin or ancestry. But the one
thing we did know was that he was rapidly becoming a real pain in more
ways than one. Ol' Don hobbling around on his crutches could testify to
that.

About midway through the hunt all the elk hunters had filled their
tags, so we were getting up late that morning. Don had built fires in the
dining and cook tents and was on his way over to the latrine, when suddenly he heard this startled "woof" to his left and what first appeared to
be a waist high bush grew into a seven-foot tall growling bear.

Now Don had been around these mountains some 60 odd years and
knew how to take care of himself. The bear experts will tell you there are
several courses of action that you can take in a confrontation like this,
and I am sure Don chose the same one most of us would choose. First, let
me remind you that he was on his way to the latrine, not coming from it.
The second thing he did was to say what he had already done, then drop
the lantern he was carrying and go crashing up a small pine tree he'd just
come around. Of course, all the commotion aroused the rest of the camp.
But, when the odd assortment of bearded, blurry-eyed, long-under-
weared, barefooted, scratching hunters and hands turned out, the only
thing left to see was a little pile of broken glass and green metal that used
to be the lantern blazing beside the path and Don wrapped around this
little six-inch pine tree about 12 feet off the ground, swaying back and
forth like the pendulum on my grandfather clock.

We all started laughing and Don started cussing and coming down
that tree madder than a wet hen. He was cussing us as bad as he was the
bear. He wasn't halfway down when he got tangled up, lost his balance
and fell heavily to the ground. He landed with a thud on his side and just
laid there. Nobody was laughing now. In fact, you could have heard a
pine needle drop. Directly, Don caught his breath and commenced cussing that bear in earnest. We checked him all over and the only damage we
could find was to his pride. But when he tried to walk back to the tents he
discovered a lot of pain in his hip. We fashioned a pair of crutches for
him out of a couple of crotched poles so he was able to get around reasonably well for the rest of the hunt. He reminded me of a boiled owl. He's
such a tough ol' bird.

After the first couple of attacks, Don was to stay in camp between
hunts to protect our larder from further destruction, but after that fall he
wasn't healing up and felt that a couple of hours soaking in a hot bath tub
at home would make him as good as new. While in town, he checked

with his doctor and found that he had cracked his pelvis. In time for the next day's trip into camp he had gotten a pair of good factory built crutches and had them secured under the diamond hitch of the pack horse he was leading. Don was leading the four new elk and bear hunters and I was bringing up the rear with the rest of the pack string, so he was the first to see the tatters of what used to be our cook tent fluttering in the fresh mountain breeze. That's what prompted his words about going home.

Our cooks always sleep in the cook tent, as their cantankerous presence is usually enough to deter scavenging hunters, hands and other critters of the night. There was only one other time that I can remember when the ploy didn't work. Years ago, before Don started cooking up here, a dad-burn grizzly big enough to shade a saddle horse, rider and all, came into camp early one morning, slashed open the back of the cook tent, stuck his bushel basket-sized head in and latched on to the sleeping bag, cook and all, and dragged the whole feature-flying-cussing-conglomeration into the middle of the meadow before the cook popped out of that cocoon and legged it for his rifle like the devil himself was shaking that sleeping bag. Until you've seen a grizzly in action you can't comprehend the power they exhibit or the fear they instill. When things settled down some, the cook informed me that I could stick this camp up...well it doesn't really matter where he told me I could stick it. Suffice it to say, his recommendation was an impossibility. As he rode off across the river he muttered something disparaging about endangered species.

And now Don was threatening us with a similar fate. Fortunately, the bear had not bothered Don's bed at all—just destroyed everything around it. The hunters were quick to pick up on the situation and hurriedly dismounted and began picking up, cleaning up and salvaging what they could of our food supplies.

Don and I fixed some sandwiches for everyone and sent the hunters out with one of the guides. We sent the other guide back to our cabin with the list of supplies we needed to replace and instructions to be back before breakfast. He returned about 10:00 p.m. with the eggs, bacon, and Crisco so necessary for breakfast. As I settled into my sleeping bag that night, I began to wonder if that bear could count too. He always came in when everyone was gone. I could just imagine him lying up there on the mountain somewhere, all comfortable and dry under a big spruce tree, keeping track of us with one big beefy paw and planning his next raid.

Well, I had a surprise for him. A big surprise named Bill Lambert. Bill was a tall, raw-boned southern boy living in Cape Canaveral, Florida. He was in his mid-fifties and still nearly as tough as his early twenties when he used to box and beat trained gorillas in old-time traveling amusement shows for Saturday night fun back in Alabama.

Bill and his hunting partners Del, Dave, and Ken had gotten wind of our bear problem, changed their original hunting plans and booked this second hunt of the season with us because Bill wanted a big black bear.

The five of us were sleeping in a big Indian teepee I had erected for our summer trips. We had a 30-gallon, barrelwood-burning heat stove in the middle with a four-inch stove pipe going up to the smoke hole in the top of the teepee, and five bunks with foam pads built around the circumference, so we had lots of room and were very comfortable.

We had about four inches of fresh snow and were looking forward to another successful elk hunt. Around midnight I got up to tend to nature. I was only a couple of steps away from the teepee flap, half naked, no rifle or anything, and there was Bruno, bigger than life! We both froze and were locked eyeball-to-eyeball long enough for all the good deeds I had ever done in my life to flash through my mind, so you know we were not there for long. It was only a second before he growled and I hollered and dove back into the teepee for my rifle. In the faint moonlight reflecting off the new fallen snow I saw him disappear into the timber beyond the latrine. I levered a shell into my grandfathers's old Winchester .32 Special that had been handed down to me and fired into the air hoping that would at least keep him out of camp for the rest of the night. With flashlights we discovered that he had indeed been back in the cook tent, but it had appeared at first that nothing had been touched, so we all went traipsing back to the teepee.

Don had moved his gear into one of the smaller sleeping tents and hadn't even bothered to get up this time. Some of the boys were debating the odds of the bear returning that night but Bill declared, with a twinkle in his eye, that there was no way that bear would return after what I had called him. "Didn't you guys hear Duane holler 'Get out of here, you pot-licking bear?' A pot licker he called him. Nothing can stand up to that kind of verbal abuse," he laughed. "Not even that big old bear."

But I could see Bill was secretly delighted that el-bear-o had changed his M.O. and was sneaking into camp while we were still here. That was certainly going to increase Bill's chances of bagging a big bear on this hunt. Around the supper table the next evening, after a long, hard unsuccessful day of elk hunting, the talk turned to devising some sort of alarm system to alert us to the bear's presence should he make another pass at us that night. Strings of tin cans around the camp perimeter, horse bells attached to the cook tent, aerosol cans dipped in bacon grease, were all discussed with enthusiasm and discarded as unpractical ideas.

Don allowed as how, by God, something had to be done, 'cause he couldn't keep up with the thievery, and if we wanted any pies with our

suppers somebody better damn well shoot that bear...and soon!

What's shooting the bear got to do with having pies, everyone wanted to know?

"It's plain to see you guys wouldn't make very good bear detectives," he snorted. "One of the things I had the wrangler bring back from the cabin the other night was a new can of Crisco, right?"

Everyone nodded in agreement.

"Well, I only used one spoonful from that can, and I've searched high and low for it and it is nowhere to be found!"

"That's the last straw, Duane. What the hell are you going to do about that rotten bear?" everyone exclaimed at once.

"Well I guess I'll have to resort to tying Singer behind the cook tent," I replied.

"Well, hell, we might as well forget about having any pie on this hunt," the hunters grumbled as they headed for the teepee.

"I admit Singer is good, Duane. In fact, I've never seen his equal anytime or anyplace, but I don't see how you figure he's any match for that bear, even if it is only a black bear. That critter is smart and biiiggg!" Bill said as he paused to light up a going-to-bed cigar.

By the time I had belled and double tied Singer in a little clump of pine behind the cook tent, the fellows were all in bed. Before I turned out the lantern I said, "If any of you guys shoot my riding mule tonight he's going to cost you $5,000.00 in cash. He's the best riding mule in the whole damn world, and we're not going to be arguing about it over a dead carcass in the morning, we are going to get it settled right here and now, before we go to sleep."

"I've tied him in that little patch of pine behind the cook tent so don't shoot him when the ruckus starts," I said.

"What good is that going to do?" someone asked.

"He has instructions to tell me when the bear is in camp," I replied.

"By golly Duane, you got a deal, Bill laughed. If any of us shoots your mule we'll pay you $5,000.00 on the spot. And I'll guaran-damn-tee-ya something else, I came all the way from Florida for that bear and if he comes back tonight he'll be leaving via pack horse!"

About midnight Singer's emphatic snort woke me.

"The bear's in camp, boys," I said without budging from my sleeping bag.

Dave came plumb across the teepee with his 7mm Rem. Mag. at the ready, shot out the tent like the flap on his longjohns was afire, hit that snow with his bare feet and froze right there, not 10 yards from Mr. Camp-Wrecker Supreme. Directly behind the bear was Singer. Dave's hesitation allowed Bill, who was sleeping right next to the tent flap, but who had stopped to put on some boots, to arrive on the scene. Bill had his .44 Rem. Mag. handgun at the ready. Even though Bill wanted that bear so bad he could taste it, his good sense and sportsman-like attitude required him to wisely defer the shot to his hunting partner with the rifle.

By this time Bruno had decided that being between Singer and two hungry hunters was as bad as being between a rock and a hard spot. As he started back his favorite escape route he presented Dave with a perfect broadside shot. With the snow, the moonlight and the 4-power scope he couldn't miss. Bill relaxed, Dave squeezed the trigger, and the firing pin struck an empty chamber with a resounding "click". Dave and Bill swore as the bear disappeared into the black timber beyond the latrine again. Singer shook his head and stomped his front foot in disgust. The three of us, still in our sleeping bags, laughed so hard our stomachs hurt.

A couple of hours later Dave's stumbling over the wood stove and knocking down the stove pipe jerked me from a deliciously erotic dream to full awake! I hadn't heard Singer snort, but Bill had. In fact, he told me later that he was only feigning sleep and was now convinced that Singer and I knew what we were doing and wasn't about to let Dave and his empty rifle come plumb across the teepee and beat him out the flap again. So, he was listening intently and when Singer snorted and stomped his foot, Bill was ready. Barefoot this time, his .300 Win. Mag. ready, one foot out of the teepee and the other one planted firmly on sand inside the teepee, he was braced for a good, clean shot. That's when Dave arrived amidst the smoke, soot and rattling stove pipes. Off balance and expecting to find the entrance empty, Dave was not prepared to apply his brakes so soon and crashed into Bill who was, at the moment, settling his cross hairs on Mr. Destruction's shoulder. The momentum of Dave's journey carried them both out of the teepee and into the snow on their hands and knees on a level with the somewhat startled and nervous bear. The two Magnum rifles roared as one, the flame from their barrels lighting up the night and singeing the hair on the big marauder as he went to the happy hunting grounds.

The next night, we gorged ourselves on bear steak and fresh apple pie for supper. Some of the apples were saved and everyone took his turn affectionately feeding Singer his favorite reward for jobs well done

The empty Crisco can and other litter from somewhat more successful raids were found some time later under a large, dense spruce tree with a perfect view of the camp below.

The bear turned out to be the biggest black bear taken in northwest Wyoming that year. He was 13 years old and his teeth were all worn down to nubs. His left canine tusk was completely hollow and abscessed. The poor old devil was in pain, hungry and at the end of his rope.

So Bill took home a beautiful trophy that wouldn't have lasted out the winter. With our camp gone, he would have died the long, slow death of starvation and may have hurt someone in the process.

The fellows all have personal reasons for wanting to return next year. Del claims he saw a bull elk with ivory plumb to his ass and wants to hunt him again, and Ken saw a mule deer buck he swears was big enough to bugle.

Even though we spent many hours hand-sewing our tents back together, the cook tent couldn't be saved and we burned it right there on the spot when we left.

There are plenty of marks on the dining tent, however, that will always remind us of Singer and the bear.

6x6s By The Dozen

by Billy Stockton
as told to Dennis Phillips

Mid-September is a great time to bowhunt for elk. I do most of my guiding in the east and west Pioneer Mountains of the Pender Wilderness area in Montana, and the weather this time of the year means warm days and crisp, cool nights—just the right conditions for getting the elk fired up during the rut.

There are plenty of elk in this country and I seldom have any trouble putting my clients onto game. However, some years are better than others and one fall I was guiding two hunters, Wade and Doug, out of an area that we call Swimming Women Creek. An hour before dawn, we had hiked out of a drainage and were heading into the next, just as the sun was starting to lighten the sky.

Not too far ahead we could hear horns clacking together and knew immediately what it was. Up to this point the elk were not fully into the rut, so this was an encouraging sign and we hurried through a small finger of timber to the edge of a long meadow about 150 yards across. I knew there was a wallow at the far end, so we set up and waited for more light. What we saw is something that I've seen a number of times, but I had never been able to show any clients.

In that meadow we counted 22 head of six-point bulls. Four or five nice bulls were sparring with each other—it was still too early for them to be fighting seriously—and three others were as big as elk get—they would make the record books with no problem. Not all these elk were great big six-pointers. There were some first-year sixes and several were second-year sixes, but there wasn't a bad one in the herd.

Bachelor herds of elk are common in late summer and early fall, but this was as many big elk as I've ever seen together. Finding this many bulls before the rut really got started was pure luck and we had stumbled onto them.

It was still early so we decided to watch and see what these elk were going to do. Before long the three biggest bulls wandered into the timber and disappeared like smoke. The younger bulls stayed around the meadow for the next hour sparring, marking and rubbing trees and wallowing in the mud.

At about 9:30 it was starting to warm up and we knew the elk would

soon be heading for the dark timber to bed down, so I hurried to set up my hunters. Now was the time to see if we could call one of the bulls to our end of the meadow. The terrain was ideal for an ambush. Nearby, just inside the meadow, was a bushy tree so I put Wade there and then located Doug below me in the timber. I set up between them and started to call.

Immediately, one of the better six-points threw his head in the air and started across the meadow toward us at a fast lope. I estimated this bull would easily score between 300 and 325 points, and I was sure he was going to cooperate. The bull ran straight for the bushy tree Wade was crouched behind. He never scented him because the wind was just right.

Not 10 feet from Wade, the bull stopped and bugled. I thought it was going to knock all the pinecones out of that tree and blow Wade's hat off, too. Wade was really getting excited, but he couldn't shoot yet. Down below in the timber, I whistled and called, trying to get the bull's attention to draw him out just far enough for a clear shot.

By this time Wade had convinced himself that the bull knew exactly where he was behind the tree and that the bull had every intention of hooking him with his horns. But the bull didn't know about Wade, and started to come around the tree toward me. It was now or never as Wade drew his bow and...the arrow fell off his bowstring.

He quickly bent over to pick up his arrow and when he looked up, he was staring right into the eyes of this big six-pointer. Wade was now about as excited as a man can be and I can't blame him. As much as I've been around elk in my life, I would have been excited, too.

I could tell he wasn't sure what to do. Being nervous about his arrow falling off a second time, he pinched the nock of the arrow between his teeth, got the arrow back on the bow and was almost to full draw before the bull figured out what was going on. In less than a second the bull spun around and was gone.

Hunting Alaska Brown Bear The Hard Way

by Jim Bailey
as told to Christopher Batin

G enerally speaking, brown bear hunting in Alaska is not dangerous if you use common sense and take the proper precautions. But there are times when bears are unpredictable; indeed, in many cases, the hunter becomes the hunted. Such an encounter happened to me several years ago while hunting in my guide area of the Talkeetna Mountains in southcentral Alaska.

The September moose and bear season was about half over. I had several clients in camp, one who wanted to take a grizzly bear. I took to the air that afternoon in my Piper Super Cub and aerially scouted for bear sign in the mountains near one of my outpost camps. The area hadn't been hunted that year, and there were several rows of bear tracks near the riverbank. The country looked good, and I returned to camp to pick up the hunter.

Because same-day-airborne hunting is illegal, we flew into camp late that afternoon, unloaded our gear and relaxed, choosing to talk about the next day's hunt. Little did we know it would be a hunt to remember for a lifetime.

After breakfast, we walked down a gravel bar that ran the length of the river. About 50 yards from camp, I looked across the river and spotted a large grizzly bear walking down the bank. I grabbed my client's arm and crouched down.

"Let's see what this bruin is up to," I said.

I pulled out my binoculars and sized up the bear. It was a blonde grizzly, one of the most coveted of Alaska's big bears. I judged the bear to be in the $8^1/_2$-foot range, a respectable trophy for my client. Yet, watching the bear, I had an intuition that something wasn't right. I continued to watch as the bear searched the area intently. Finally, about 15 yards up the bank, the bear clawed at a partially buried caribou carcass.

The bear had probably killed the caribou a day or two ago. I envisioned the scenario that probably took place: the bear hid in the dense spruce and ambushed the unsuspecting caribou as it walked by.

While the bear began to feed on the carcass, I motioned for my client to follow me back into the woods. We scurried back to the camp, took off our packs and planned our strategy. While discussing our plans I stopped talking when I caught a glimpse of the bear walking down the bank. The boar stopped directly across the river from us, and began scratching and pawing the ground.

My client felt certain he could make the 100 yard shot from where we sat. Normally, I don't allow my clients to shoot that far at grizzlies. But the field of fire was open, there was no wind, the bear was in the open and my client was a policeman from back East who was familiar with firearms. I gave him the benefit of the doubt, and nodded for him to go ahead and take the shot.

The bear remained in full view on the opposite bank. My client took plenty of time to position himself, and arrange a solid rest on an old spruce log.

He waited for the bear to stand sideways before firing. Through the binoculars, I watched the bullet hit the bear, albeit a bit too far back. Before I could grab my rifle and make a follow-up shot the bear had made a 50-yard dash for the woods. From the way it acted, I knew the bear was wounded. There was no other alternative. We would have to go after him.

I immediately untied the floatplane and, with the hunter onboard, taxied across the river. About 20 minutes passed before we reached the shore. Tensions were high as we entered the forest where the bear had disappeared.

I started stalking immediately. The more I stalked, the harder it was to find any sign of blood. The dew on the red blueberry leaves made it appear as though the ground was covered with droplets of blood. I had to touch each one to see if it was, in fact, blood or water.

After $4^1/_2$ hours, I found a faint blood trail going uphill. I knew we had trouble now. A seriously injured bear will almost always angle downhill, but bears with plenty of life will head uphill. The thick spruce and forest growth kept visibility down to a minimum. Whatever needed to be done we would do, but I hoped we would find the bear dead.

After 45 minutes of cautious, uphill stalking, we came to a depression in the forest understory. The bear had stopped there to rest momentarily. The overturned leaves, blood drops and tracks were very fresh. We were close. Perhaps too close.

I instructed the hunter to continue looking for sign while I remained alert and watched the forest openings around us. The scenario was perfect for a bear charge, and I didn't want to be caught with my head down in such close quarters. With my finger on the rifle's safety, I positioned my hunter about two feet to my right, and we slowly continued on.

Minutes later, all hell broke loose. About 35 yards away, on the other side of a small, winding creek, the bear jumped out of the brush. It charged straight toward us, growling in anger.

There was no time to think. I leveled on the bear with my .338 Win. Mag. and fired once, twice. The leaves were off the trees and I could see each bullet hit the bear. I fired a third time. Each shot knocked the bear

down, but immediately it would get up again. The bear kept coming. I emptied the fourth round, and the bear was still charging. The bear was 10 feet away and coming strong when I made my fifth and last shot.

I had no time to reload. The hunter was mesmerized by the charge, and held his rifle tightly. The bear was almost on us. I snatched the rifle from my client's hands and leveled on the bear, hitting him squarely between the eyes. The bear crumpled and laid still. I took two and a half steps, and my foot hit the bear's nose, a distance of about seven feet, a bit too close.

I don't blame the hunter for not shooting. Everything happened so fast, I barely had time to think myself. In fact, I didn't think; I just responded instinctively.

The bear was indeed an $8^1/2$-footer and, except for the seven bullet holes in the hide, the pelt was in excellent condition. The hunter was amazed at the holes my .338 drilled through the wrist-thick alders between me and the bear. Amazingly, all the bullets found their mark.

I believe the bear might have won the confrontation had this scenario taken place a few days into the hunting season when more leaves were on the trees and visibility was minimal.

While this charge was enough to last a lifetime, another one took place six days later. I was scouting bears for a hunter who had recently arrived in camp. Not seeing any bears during the first hour, I flew over the area of the bear charge I had experienced six days earlier. To my surprise, I observed a huge grizzly feeding on a moose within 100 yards of camp.

I immediately flew back to the main camp to inform the hunter. I then learned that he had been on five unsuccessful hunts here in Alaska with other guides, and he really wanted a big brownie. Although the hunter was excited about the bear, we had to wait. Once it started to get dark, we flew into camp. I kept the airplane's engine running as quietly as possible during the landing, to avoid spooking the bear. We eased into the tent, and I didn't build a campfire. We had a cup of coffee and crawled into our sleeping bags to wait for daylight. I didn't want to do anything to bother that bear.

The next morning, dew had covered the ground, which made stalking easier. I briefly discussed strategy with the hunter, advising him to take only his rifle. We started hunting right from the cabin, guns loaded and ready. The bear could be anywhere.

I didn't know exactly where the kill was located, but with a bit of dead reckoning, I found it about 70 yards ahead. Looking through the binoculars I noticed that, during the night, the bear had completely covered the moose carcass with brush and dirt.

We stayed put and remained silent for about 20 minutes, waiting for any sign to indicate the bear was still in the area. After seeing nothing but a few birds, we advanced toward the kill, rifles at ready. About 50 yards away, I caught a glimpse of the other side of the three-foot high mound and froze in my tracks. For a split-second, I saw the bear sleeping. Then it awoke with a start. Looking around, the bear saw us, and charged immediately.

Primed from the charge that took place a few days ago, both the hunter and I shot our .338s simultaneously. Both shots hit the bear, which then whirled and entered the brush before we could get off additional shots. We cautiously trailed the bear for about 100 yards before we found it dead.

At nine feet, two inches, the dark brown boar was impressive. Interestingly enough, both shots hit the bear within two inches of each other. They had entered just below the nose, hitting the heart.

Of all the bears I've hunted in Alaska, these were the only two times I've been charged, both occurring within six days of each other. The more I guide bear hunters, the more I am surprised. But that's Alaska bear hunting for you. It's exciting, and always unpredictable!

Stalking The Glacier Rams

by Ken Fanning
as told to Christopher Batin

Hunting stories about sheep often create the most excitement. Dall sheep offer some of the most rugged and aesthetically pleasing hunting available in North America today. It is excitement par excellence, especially when done in Alaska's rugged alpine glacier country, which offers some of the most beautiful and inherently dangerous hunting found anywhere. The largest sheep in the world are found and bagged in the state's glacial wastelands.

My hunting area is in the Alaska Range, a wilderness area surrounded by river-like glaciers. It's a remote area, accessible only by Piper Super Cub or Helio-Courier.

I enjoy father and son hunts, and glacier country is the perfect environment for this. Dr. Joel Callahan, 51, of Mississippi, wanted to book a sheep hunt for himself and his 20-year-old son Joel Jr. It was Joel Jr.'s high school graduation present, and a 15-year dream come true for Joel Sr.

Because his job didn't allow many opportunities for regular exercise, Joel Sr. stayed in shape by jogging regularly. He knew the rigors of a sheep hunt in mountain country. In fact, he was shopping specifically for a rugged, backpack-type hunt. After much conversation and reference checking, he contacted me about two years prior to the date he wanted to hunt. Finally, he booked a mid-August hunt for him and his son.

When the time came for the hunt, I was amazed. It appeared as if this hunt was made to happen. The weather was perfect. We quickly purchased our food supplies, and the bush planes were in time and ready for us. We departed in later afternoon, and enjoyed the hour-long flight to my camp.

The camp was already set up from a previous hunt. After dinner, we relaxed a bit and talked about the things hunters usually talk about: the area, trophies won and lost, and hunting gear. We couldn't hunt that evening, as same-day-airborne hunting is illegal in Alaska.

I roused my hunters and my assistant guide, Ron, at 3:00 a.m. Dawn comes early in the far north, requiring us to rise early and be in position prior to first light; that's about 4:00 a.m. in the summer. This is important strategy, because rams move down to the lower levels of the mountain to feed at first light. For me, it's the best time to scout for trophies and, if conditions are right, to make a stalk.

We first had to cross a glacial moraine, which consisted of black rock, glacier dust and ice. As foreboding as it appeared, it made a suitable highway to access parts of the various mountain peaks that bordered the glacier.

After hiking a short distance, we located nine rams about two miles away. They were down low, feeding in an open meadow. When the group moved behind a knoll, we scurried into position and managed to move directly below them at the base of the mountain. I set up the tripod and spotting scope, and waited patiently to see where the sheep would bed down. Of the nine rams, five were full curl, and two were record book material.

After a few minutes, the oldest rams moved 50 to 75 yards away from the group. That's when everything fell apart. The old rams saw or sensed us, and spooked. The group followed, bolting up the mountain to a place so rugged that access required technical climbing gear.

Even though we were discouraged, we spent the remainder of the day glassing to see if the rams would become accessible. Those boys spent the entire day on peaks so high they needed oxygen. We trudged back to camp at 10:00 p.m., discouraged over our bad luck, but optimistic about the next day.

At the moraine, right where the glacier split into three fingers, I stopped the group. On the opposite side of that winding river of ice, I saw five rams in one bunch, seven in another and three way up the glacial valley. In the first bunch, I could tell two of the five had heavy bases, but it was difficult to judge in the rapidly disappearing light. We scurried back to camp, elated and excited about the next morning.

Several hours later, we prepared a Siwash camp and equipment necessary to spend several days across the glacier. But first we scouted out the rams we stalked the day before. They were holding in the high peaks. Judging by their attitude and position, I surmised they wouldn't be down for three or four days. I sent Ron to investigate in case we needed to return at a later time. Meanwhile, I took both hunters across the glacier.

We wasted no time crossing the glacier, trying to cover the most ground before sunup, since sunlight quickly causes the glacial ice to melt and walking becomes slippery and treacherous. On hot, sunny days, the ice melt, which may be a trickle at night, becomes a running torrent by mid-afternoon. We would need to get across as quickly as possible.

We climbed out on the moraine and crossed the first two rivers of ice, avoiding the crevasses, vertical walls of fissures and additional moraines we encountered.

We didn't have much time before daylight. We had to get across the open ice before there was sufficient light for the rams to see us. About halfway across, we stopped at a huge boulder pile to rest, watch and wait for Ron.

Ron soon arrived and said the rams we had spooked the day before were staying high on the mountain. The sun just started to peak over the ridge, and we immediately located the rams about a half mile beyond the

end of the glacier. The rams were low on the mountain and, since there was no way we could move across the ice without spooking them, we spent the next six hours cramped in a rock pile. Finally, the last of the five rams walked out of sight into a remote drainage.

We scurried across the glacier, which was slippery from the warm sunshine. Climbing back onto the moraine was tough. We had to cut hand- and foot-holds into the ice, and even tried sliding down a 60-foot embankment. If we had crampons the matter would have been simple, but they were left in camp. However, it was only a matter of time before we were off the glacial ice and heading up toward the rams.

When we last saw of them, the rams were moving rapidly and we had to run to see if they were still in the drainage. We had already decided that Joel Jr. would take the first ram. I knew one of the rams we were stalking was a spectacular animal, but I didn't want to reveal that to the hunters, in case we couldn't get close enough for a shot.

We eased up the mountain. The next glimpse I had of the rams they were in an amphitheater about 500 yards above us. We continued up the slope. About 30 yards from the crest where Joel Jr. would take his shot, I had both hunters load up and rest. This is important to not only maximize accuracy on the first shot, but to minimize the hunter being winded, should he need to run before he can make the shot. Once we crawled up the last crest that hid us from the rams, we stopped. I told Joel Jr. the rams could be anywhere but, as far as I could tell, they were about 70 yards away.

When we reached the crest, I located two rams about 40 yards away, another a tad higher. There was another ram oblivious to our presence, feeding contentedly about 15 yards to the left of us. After careful searching, I became concerned. I couldn't locate the largest ram. After crawling up several more feet, I spotted him about 15 feet below the first two, and feeding upward.

I motioned Joel Jr. to ease up to the ridge. He knew which ram to take. He scurried up and, after what seemed like minutes, made a single shot. The ram that was 15 yards from us bolted to the right, and another that we had not seen bolted across us by a few yards. I don't know who was scared more, us or that ram.

Joel Jr.'s ram was dead with a single shot. Both hunters were ecstatic. The horns measured 40 inches on one side and $40\frac{1}{2}$ on the other. They were an unusual set of horns with an impressive flair.

After the usual skinning and photo taking, we raced down to set up camp next to a bubbly creek with plenty of alpine flowers.

The next morning was Joel Sr.'s turn. We hadn't walked a half mile before we located four different groups of rams. The only way we could

access those animals was to get above them, which required stripping down to bare basic gear and climbing uphill. About $3^1/2$ hours later, we crested the mountain ridge and were met by a cold, howling wind. I quickly found a rock pile that provided shelter from which to glass. Twenty minutes later, we located another batch of rams, but nothing large. I opted to walk down the crest of the ridge to scout for additional rams and especially to get out of the wind.

After several minutes of walking, I pinpointed a small knoll that would meet our immediate needs. I was aiming for that point, with Joe Jr., beside me when, 200 yards ahead, two large rams walked out in front of us, grazing downhill. We signaled Ron and Joel Sr. to hurry down. It was too late. The sheep saw us and walked, stiff-legged, around the corner of the hill. One sheep was a dandy, about an 11-year-old. Joel Sr. and I eased over to the ridge. The rams were down in a ravine about 175 yards away. Joel Sr. settled in, took a good rest and dumped the largest ram in two shots. The ram tumbled about 400 yards and stopped in a rock gully. The ram had heavily broomed horns that measured $35^3/4$ inches—a very handsome, respectable trophy.

After skinning out the meat and hide, we took a short, afternoon siesta before heading across the glacier. The going was rough: all of us were carrying our share of camp gear, sheep horns and meat, and the glacial ice melt was flowing heavily on the ice, creating an extremely slippery surface. We took a few tumbles and over five hours just to cross the glacier, but we finally made it in one piece with no broken bones. Two tired but excited hunters, and guides for that matter, stumbled into camp at 8:00 p.m. that evening, to complete a successful sheep hunt in Alaska's glacial wilderness.

The Apricot Ram

by Gary Peters
as told to Don Brestler

There were five of us guides, Malcolm "Stretch" Main, Paul Wesier, Larry Paxman, Bill Hanson, and myself, working for South Nahanni Outfitters in the Northwest Territories. It was the end of July, 1979, and we were trailing 24 head of saddle and pack horses on the North Canal Road to our base camp on Rainbow Mountain, one mile south of Little Dall Lake. This trip is 220 miles and takes seven days of long, hard riding to complete. The trail took us through brush, muskeg and tundra of this beautiful country. It rained lightly continuously. At night we hobbled the horses and set up a wall tent. Our boss flew into base camp ahead of us.

There were a lot of moose to be seen, cows with calves and huge bulls in velvet. The small bunches of mountain caribou would sometimes mingle right in with our horses, scaring them. Four grizzlies, a sow with a cub and two others, were also spotted at not too great a distance. We had to cross and recross the Red Stone River continuously. A few years ago a guide had drowned in this river. We stopped to read the small wooden sign erected in his honor. It struck home the seriousness and danger of guiding in this country.

We finally reached base camp, wet and trail weary. The next three days were spent shoeing horses, cutting firewood and fencing before the hunters arrived. All of our supplies were flown in every two weeks along with the change of hunters.

When the hunters arrived, the afternoon was spent getting acquainted, telling a few stories and discussing hunting plans. It was the hunters' idea that our names be put in a hat and drawn for by the hunters. Destiny definitely had its hand in choosing Charlie as my hunter. He was a robust, 200-pound farmer from Pennsylvania. Although in his early 50s, he had already suffered a heart attack, but it didn't seem to bother him much now. He was a gentle sort of man, and really latched onto me. Although having licenses for other game—moose, wolf, caribou and grizzly—he quietly informed me that he was only interested in getting a legal Dall ram. Having saved up for years, this would be his big once-in-a-lifetime hunt.

To spice up the guides' enthusiasm, each hunter put $50 into a kitty to go to the guide whose hunter took the largest ram.

The next day we kept busy sorting out equipment, packing horses and adjusting stirrups for the riders. We all left camp together, but split up after two days. Three of us guides and our hunters headed south to one of our spike camps 10 miles away on the Clearwater River. On the trail, we had a hard time keeping the hunters from shooting the dozens of caribou we saw. They had small antlers and were still in the process of shedding their velvet. We also discouraged the hunters from shooting the moose we encountered. A large supply of fresh meat so early in the hunt would burden us down.

Our spike camp consisted of one wall tent. We had no stove in the tent and did all our cooking over open fires. This far north there was no darkness, so we could choose our own hours for hunting. Shortly after we settled into camp, it started raining lightly and continued steadily for three days. The mountains were clouded in. This was certainly no hunting weather so we stayed in the tent. Without a fire, we were forced into a steady diet of peanut butter and jam sandwiches.

My hunter, Charlie, could fall asleep faster than any person I've ever seen in my life. Once he closed his eyes, he was gone. I was left talking to myself lots of times.

Once the weather broke we were all glad to get out of camp and go hunting. I was in top physical shape, a good thing because I had to pack all of Charlie's gear—his .300 Wthby Mag. rifle, shells, rain gear, lunch and even him later on!

One morning on our way up a mountain, Charlie and I stepped across a small stream not too far from camp. After a short, but steady climb, we stopped to rest. While I glassed for sheep, Charlie had an hour and a half nap, snoring continuously and loudly. I spotted three sheep which we pursued for four hours, but they were long gone.

Charlie was getting tired. On our way back down the mountain we stopped and had a late lunch and a half hour sleep. When it started raining, Charlie realized he had left his raincoat on the mountain, so I went back for it. Charlie woke up when I returned and I asked him how he felt. He said, "Fine, after my little snooze"—three hours! He was glad to get his raincoat because the rain was really coming down now. While scouting out another basin, we spotted the three sheep again which turned out to be a ewe and two young rams.

Returning to camp in a downpour, we discovered the little stream we had crossed that the morning was now a raging river! We were scared to cross it. We could see the distant spike camp, but couldn't make contact with anybody to bring horses over for us. I fired a couple of shots to no avail. With no alternative, we took refuge in a small grove of stunted pines.

I cut some boughs and laid them across each other, forming a mattress to keep us off the wet ground. Cutting two large plastic garbage bags to use as a ground sheet and a tarp, I made Charlie as comfortable as possible. He fell asleep immediately. Scrounging around, I found a little dry wood and got a fire going. I was starved, having shared most of my lunch with Charlie. Between having to continuously search for firewood, having ice cold water running down my neck from my hat and having to put up with Charlie's snoring, I didn't sleep all night!

It finally stopped raining that night so the next morning we decided to wade the river. Finding a suitable crossing I stepped into the water. Charlie, however, was reluctant. He couldn't swim a stroke and was afraid of the rushing water. Taking his hand, I offered to lead the way. He still hesitated. I was positioned a little under him, so with one quick move I pulled his heavy body over my shoulder fireman-style. He was quite a load for my five-foot, eight-inch, 130-pound frame as I headed into the river. The rushing water was halfway between my knees and hips. I had a hard time keeping my balance, but finally struggled to the opposite shore. Charlie never said a word.

Camp never looked so good! All I wanted to do was eat and sleep— which we certainly did! The following day the fellows in camp were talking about this big ram with a badly broomed horn. The other hunters didn't want him, but Charlie seemed interested.

The next day, with a good rest behind us we started out after the broomed-horn ram. This time we were taking horses and staying to our own side of the flooded stream.

Riding west up the valley, we kept stopping to glass the various side canyons. Two hours later we came to a large horseshoe basin where the ram was last seen. The area was about three miles across, with lots of grass. It was rocky, but very open. Glassing the basin, we spotted two interesting looking rams on a bluff, a long ways up the side of the moun-

tain. All I could see was their back ends. Finding some small bushes, we
tied the horses up onto the lower edge of one side of the rim. We started
hiking. The weather had turned sunny and hot, and we were both thirsty.

As we followed the rams, they went out of sight for a while and then
came back over the rim near the top. Glassing, I saw a larger ram come
out from behind a rock crown on the skyline. He walked between the two
smaller rams, not looking at either of them. He made a wide circle and
started grazing.

It was still a long way up to the rams, and it was going to take some

hard climbing to get there. After a few hours of hiking, Charlie became dehydrated and didn't want to go any farther. Fortunately, I spotted some wet rocks ahead of us and was able to lure Charlie a bit farther up the mountain. On his hands and knees, he sucked the rocks to get what precious moisture he could.

While he dozed I caught some dripping water in a small plastic bag. When the plastic bag was full, I woke Charlie up and he drank it all in a few gulps.

Showing him the ram, which was 460 yards away, Charlie had to look at it through his scope rifle. He promised not to shoot. "Now" he said, "at least I can say I had a big ram in my sights."

Content with that, Charlie was ready to quit and go back.

I remembered then that I still had this old can of apricots in the bottom of my backpack. I hate apricots, but carry them as a desperate last resort. Promising Charlie a drink if he would go farther, we started our stalk. A short distance later he stopped and questioned the source of his drink. I told him about my can of apricots, but said that he would not get them until he got within shooting distance.

"Look," Charlie said, "I'll give you $100 right now for those apricots." He was serious! I refused, telling him I wanted him to get that ram and I wanted to win the jackpot.

"Hell," he said, "I'll tip you more than that jackpot." Realizing that I was determined not to give up the apricots, he demanded to see the can. I dug it out. I believe it was "Pride of Okanogan" brand. Upon seeing the can, he agreed to go on, but made me carry the can in my hand, telling me not to leave his sight. He revealed his suspicion that I might get out of view and eat the apricots myself. I reassured him that I wouldn't.

After grazing a bit, the big ram returned to lay down upon his rocky crown once again. Charlie could not and would not go any farther until he got his apricots. I quickly opened the can with my hunting knife and handed them to him. He noisily downed the juicy fruits, while I looked through the spotting scope and planned our strategy. We only had one choice, and that was to slip out of sight over the top of the rim. Here we could sneak up closer and then crawl on our bellies through a shallow depression back into the basin.

Having done this, we were now level with and in full view of the ram. He was lying with his legs stretched out toward us. He was still a long ways away, but we were as close as we were going to get. After a short breather, I placed my backpack in front of Charlie as a rest. I told him to take all the shells out of his pocket and line them up in a row on a rock beside him, so he would know exactly how much ammunition he had. There were 12 shells. I would keep track of where the shots were hitting through the spotting scope. When Charlie took aim, I noticed the end of the rifle. It looked like he was conducting an orchestra with it! I placed my hand on the barrel and said, "Don't shoot—you're not ready yet." He had shot a lot of deer and I reassured him that this was no different. He admitted that he was a little excited. After a brief talk, he settled down and again took aim. This time the barrel was holding very steady.

After Charlie touched off the first shot, the ram stood up, but I couldn't tell where or if he was hit. As the ram came slowly down off the rock crown, Charlie's next two shots went wild. The ram appeared hurt as he slowly limped over the top of the rim. Before he was out of sight, Charlie fired a few more rounds. He told me to take his rifle and go get the ram, that he was in no condition to go any farther.

Refusing the rifle, I instructed him to stay where he was and went off to follow the ram. When I reached the rock crown there was quite a blood trail.

All of a sudden, Charlie was sending a volley of shots over my head. The ram had come back in sight on the crest of another ridge that abutted the rim. The ram was way out of range and I was afraid Charlie might shoot me! Frantically waving at him, he stopped shooting. The diminishing blood trail was still easy to follow. It went along the summit of the ridge and then abruptly out of sight over a steep rocky edge. Cautiously peering over the edge, I saw the ram. He was directly beneath me, a stone's throw away, standing on a small grassy slope. His head was hanging down near the ground and he looked as if he wasn't feeling well at all. I quickly retraced my steps back to Charlie. When I got there, he was lying on his back groaning and breathing hard. My first thought was that he was having a heart attack!

After talking to him, I learned that he was just dehydrated and tuckered out. All of his shells except those in the rifle had been fired. I worked the lever to find only one shell left. I said nothing. I handed his rifle back to him.

He still wanted me to take his gun and finish off the ram. I insisted that it was his ram and he would have to kill it. I told him that I would take his rifle and go back to the rocky ridge above the ram and wait for him. He would come at his own speed.

The ram had not moved a step. Soon, I heard Charlie bellowing out my name. The yelling didn't seem to bother the ram, he just lifted his head a little and dropped it again. I waved Charlie over to where he could see the ram. I told him that he was going to have to make his first shot count or the ram would be gone forever. The ram was standing away from us at a 45 degree angle. Placing Charlie in a comfortable sitting position, I instructed him that he would have to shoot low. He should hold his horizontal crosshair even with the black tip of the ram's tail. Charlie eased off his shot, and the ram fell forward, tumbling down the rocks. Charlie jumped up and started yelling that the horns would get busted! I reassured him that the ram would stop rolling and that the tough horns would not be damaged.

Picking our way down through the rocks, Charlie was exhilarated! When we got to the ram he proved to be a beautiful specimen—full-bodied with long, even, unblemished golden horns. After the handshaking and back slapping, I put my tape on his horns. They measured $13^1/2$ inches around the base and $36^1/2$ inches long—terrific! Examining him, we found that Charlie's final shot had broken the ram's neck.

Searching for the first shot we discovered that most of his left front foot was missing. Out of all the shots, it was only the first and last ones that had hit the animal. I didn't realize that a sheep would bleed so much through a foot wound.

Charlie levered his rifle and found that it was empty! He looked at me sideways, smiled and nodded his head. I smiled back, now we both knew about that last shell. There was a small waterfall where the ram lay so we both had a good long drink. Providence was now in our favor. While Charlie rested, I caped out the ram. Charlie seemed to come back to life and was feeling much better now. I instructed him to go back, get the horses and ride into camp. Shouldering my heavy load of horns, meat and cape, I headed down the rim on a shorter route to camp.

It was 8:00 p.m. when I got to the tent. The fellows were there and just itching to hear what happened. I told them that they would have to wait and hear it all from Charlie.

Twenty minutes later Charlie rode into camp, had a strong cup of coffee and related the whole story from start to finish. He even admitted to me packing him over the flooded creek the previous day. He said that he didn't have anything against the other guides, but that "this little guy is the best damn guide in North America! He coaxed me all the way up to the ram with a silly little can of apricots!" he exclaimed. "I still don't believe it!" Charlie then went on to say "You guys can hunt all you want, but Gary and I are going to stay in camp, relax, eat, sleep and enjoy life for the rest of the hunt."

I enjoyed it for a couple of days, but then got restless. I never cut so much firewood for one camp in all my life!

The other hunters connected with two nice rams to happily end a successful trip. The apricot ram won me the $150 jackpot. Riding back to base camp one afternoon, Charlie told me that his saddle was slipping. When I caught up to him, he got off and laid back in the grass. In the few moments that it took me to tighten the cinch, Charlie had fallen sound asleep. He was snoring so loudly that he was scaring the horses. This man amazed me as much as I amazed him.

On the last day at the dock after everything was packed up, we said our farewells and the hunters boarded the plane. From the window Charlie looked out and held up the empty apricot can. We both smiled.

A year later Charlie wrote to me, telling me that his mounted ram's head was now proudly hanging in his living room. Right beneath the head and mounted on the same specially made base board was the famous empty apricot can! Quite a trophy with memories of quite a hunt!

Men Of Adventure

I f there are any "men's men" left in the world today, they are the guides and outfitters who lead NAHC members on exciting, challenging hunts across North America. Seventeen guides and outfitters have shared their most exciting and unusual hunting adventures in this book. Here are the stories of how they came to be men of adventure:

Jim Bailey grew up in Arizona, where his family lived in a circus tent on a tract of land near the Mexican border. While his father worked for the border patrol, Jim remembers hauling water for horses and cattle, and raising chickens for the local Indians. When he wasn't in school, Jim ran a trapline and caught fox, bobcat, coyote, even a mountain lion. After he turned 18, he volunteered to serve as a paratrooper in the 101st Airborne Division. There he met a buddy, who had a flight school, and Jim soon learned how to  fly. After obtaining his commercial license, he helped his friend ferry airplanes across the United States.

One day, Jim saw the movie, *Hatari*, and talked with one of the stars of the film. He remembered the star saying, "If I was a young man like you, I'd learn to fly and head to Alaska." Jim listened to the man's advice, and journeyed north to find something more challenging.

Jim worked with guide Nick Botner for a few seasons during the fall months, acquired his assistant guide's license and became a registered guide in 1971.

Jim specializes in moose, grizzly bear and Kodiak brown bear hunting. During the summer and fall months, Bailey offers excellent fishing for salmon and rainbow trout in remote areas.

For more information contact: Jim Bailey, Stephan Lake Lodge, P.O. Box 770695, Eagle River, Alaska 99577, (907) 696-2163.

Bill Butler, a former guide for 20 years, has taken more than 54 trophies that qualify for Safari International Record Book, and several that make Boone & Crockett records. Among them are a Stone sheep, two antelope, a black bear, a huge bison and a barren ground caribou. He is the first man to take all of Montana's "Big Ten" game animals: mule deer, pronghorn, black bear, white-tailed deer, elk, bighorn sheep, grizzly bear, moose, mountain goat and mountain lion. Bill has taken five bighorn sheep in Montana's unlimited area, and has guided for several more. He also has taken the grand slam of North American deer.

Bill's work has appeared in numerous publications, including *Outdoor Life*, *Petersen's Hunting*, *Western Outdoors*, *Gun Digest*, *Gun Week*, *Fins and Feathers*, *Rocky Mountain Hunting and Fishing*, and Mike Eastman's *Outdoorsmen* magazines, as well as several newspapers around the Rocky Mountain region. He is an official measurer for the Boone & Crockett Club, Safari Club International, Foundation for North American Wild Sheep, Pope & Young Club, Long Hunter's Society and Roland Ward Record Books.

He started the Montana Chapter of the Safari Club International in 1980. He is a life member of the Foundation for North American Wild Sheep, the National Rifle Association and North American Deer Foundation. Bill is also a member of the Rocky Mountain Elk Foundation and the North American Hunting Club. As an NAHC member, Bill was a candidate for the 1989 President's Trophy for one of his outstanding Montana pronghorns.

Bill has hunted extensively in North America, mostly on self-guided hunts. He has conducted many seminars on trophy hunting and is quoted in several trophy hunting books. Bill and his wife, Diana, run Bill Butler's Wild Outdoors, which is a hunting consultant firm. For more information contact: P.O. Box 21, Edgar, MT 59026, or call (406) 962-3701.

Author **Darwin Carey** grew up in Watson Lake, Yukon and is the stepson of the well-known guide/ outfitter Earl Boose, who operated a highly reputable service in northern British Columbia. Earl started taking Darwin into hunting areas when he was only nine years old and, upon reaching his 18th birthday, Darwin got his first guide's license. That was followed by his pilot's license and he worked as Earl's bush pilot.

Before the dramatic, life-changing events revealed in his story, Darwin had spent the previous 12 summers working for Earl and, in doing so, gained a considerable knowledge of the sheep hunting industry and the wild creatures that share the habitat, including grizzlies. On August 9, 1980, Darwin was scheduled by fate to endure a painful but heroic experience that would add greatly to that knowledge. It's the terrifying story of the grizzly attack which Darwin shares in this special NAHC anthology.

After the murderous grizzly attack, Darwin spent 6 months in rehabilitation. However, neither Darwin nor his love for the wild outdoors would surrender, and he returned to northern British Columbia to again work with his stepfather.

Later, after a successful, prosperous career as a big game guide, Earl Boose retired. Darwin continued in the business until 1988, when he became the owner and operator of "Range Air," a flying service in Kelowna, British Columbia. "I dearly miss the hunting industry and all the good people," said Darwin. "It's a wonderful business to meet genuine people from all corners of the world. One day I will return to the guide/outfitter business."

Dan Cherry has had an intense love for hunting, an urge to roam wide-open country and see what's over the next ridge for as long as he can remember. Born in Choteau, Montana and growing up in the central part of that state gave him plenty of opportunity to pursue and cultivate that desire, and it just grew deeper with time. As a fifth-generation Montanan with a dad and great granddad who loved to hunt, some say this love ran in his blood.

The first time he remembers hunting with his dad was way back when he was four years old, and his father got a huge mule deer buck that day. From then on, Dan hunted with his father constantly, waiting for the day he could get a license himself. They became life-long hunting partners, though Dan always loved the unfettered freedom of hunting alone. Always fascinated with wildlife, whether in magazines, photos, art, or in the wild, and having a special fascination with antlers, he began dabbling with taxidermy when he was 12. That's a tender age for tanning hides, but it only served to heighten his appreciation of the natural world.

Dan's family moved to Illinois just before he turned 15 and while he finished high school there, he never could learn to call it home. He returned home to Montana each year to hunt. The Midwest was just too confining for him, so after high school he naturally gravitated back to Montana, trying to fulfill his desire to roam. Meanwhile, hoping to combine a creative streak with his love for wildlife as a way to make a living, he began to pursue a career in taxidermy. Always one for new challenge, Dan later set his sights on an outdoor writing career.

He returned to Illinois to attend a community college, but two years was all he could stand, so Dan went back to Montana to work as a guide. He spent summer and fall months as a packer and guide, transferred to the University of Missouri because it offered a magazine curriculum, and spent the winters finishing college. In 1989, Dan graduated with a journalism degree, interned with *Petersen's Hunting* magazine, then returned to Montana for his fifth year as a guide. Recently married to his college girlfriend, Dan plans to continue guiding and writing for a living, eventually hoping to work for a magazine.

Dan guides for Roland Cheek's Skyline Outfit, P.O. Box 1880, Columbia Falls, Montana 59912.

Judd Cooney was born and raised in Luverne, Minnesota, a small farm community. He grew up hunting, fishing and trapping in this area and bowhunted the first Minnesota bow season there in 1954.

He went to South Dakota State College at Brookings, South Dakota on an athletic scholarship and majored in wildlife management. Judd received his B.S. degree in 1960 while he was working for the Alaska Department of Fish & Game, so he managed to miss his own graduation. He spent the better part of two years working all over the coastal area of Alaska and then was drafted into the Army. He spent two years at Fort Carson, Colorado where he was game warden and manager of the Army base hunting and fishing program. He went to work for the Colorado Division of Wildlife in 1964 and spent 13 years as a conservation officer in Kremmling and Pagosa Springs.

In 1979, Judd quit the Division and went full time into guiding and outfitting, as well as continuing with his freelance writing and photography. He has, over the past years, guided many bowhunters and gun hunters to trophy mule deer, elk, bear and antelope. During this time, he has also managed to do some hunting on his own and presently is co-holder of the world record Pope & Young pronghorn antelope. He also has black bear, mule deer, elk, moose, cougar, caribou and five other pronghorns in the Pope & Young Record Book, and two in Boone & Crockett. Judd has been a Senior member of the Pope & Young Club since 1980.

Judd has been active in the outdoor writing and photography field since 1966. He has been a member of the Outdoor Writers Association of America for 23 years and has served two terms on the board of directors and been on numerous committees for this fine organization.

During the past 10 years Judd has been writing and photographing on a full-time basis in addition to his guiding and outfitting operation. Over the past couple of years, he has had articles and photos in numerous outdoor magazines, including *Outdoor Life, American Hunter, Southwestern Outdoor Sportsman* and *Peterson's Bowhunting*, to name just a few. He has also had photos published in a number of calenders, brochures, flyers, outdoor advertisements and various other catalogs. He was picked as one of six photographers featured in the Nikon Outdoor

Photography Gallery and calender for the third year in a row.

At present, he is a member of the NAHC's Bowhunting Advisory Council, and contributes to several other publications.

Judd is most generally on the road, photographing, fishing, hunting, guiding hunters or giving seminars on the same. As he puts it: "I spend 18 to 20 hours a day trying to avoid working an 8-5 job and wouldn't change for the world." For information on Judd's guiding services, contact: P.O. Box 808, Pagosa Springs, CO 81147.

Walt Earl grew up during World War II in the tiny settlement of Gibbonsville, Idaho, where the community well was a ditch that ran through town. Walt treed his first mountain lion with his own hounds when he was nine years old, and learned about hunting and trapping from an old Scandinavian miner who lived in a one-room log cabin.

"Hard Rock," as Walt remembers, was a hateful old miser, a big, raw-boned recluse who did most anything for a buck. One day he showed Walt how to tree a bobcat, then told the 15-year-old, "Don't you *ever* darken my doorstep again until you can do it on your own." It was more than a year later until Walt could return to Hard Rock's home with the news.

Walt started guiding big game hunters when he was 19, and hasn't missed a single year since that 1959 season. In the early '60s, he supplemented his income by working as a bounty hunter, school bus driver and sawmill worker. In 1964 he hooked up with two veteran government trappers named Jack Hanson and Jack Nancoalis. He learned from these two men for a decade, until he received his own Animal Damage Control District in the mid 1970s.

In 1978, he left his government trapping job to go full-time into guiding big game hunters. Today, Walt and wife, Una, operate Golden Bear Outfitters near Judith Gap, Montana. They guide for every legal big game animal in the state, including mule deer, white-tailed deer, elk, antelope, black bear, grizzly bear, mountain lion, moose, bighorn sheep and mountain goat.

A long-time supporter of the NAHC, Walt has donated nearly a dozen hunts to the NAHC Membership Drive Contest and is an NAHC

Approved Outfitter & Guide. He reports that more than 80 percent of his hunters are NAHC members. For more information, contact: Walt Earl, Golden Bear Outfitters, H.C. 60, Box 348, Judith Gap, MT 59453, or call (406) 473-2312.

Ken Fanning's background is about as well-rounded as they come. He is a full-time registered guide, former Alaska legislator, past director of the National Rifle Association and past director for the Alaska Professional Hunters Association. He has owned and operated Alaska Guide Service for more than two decades.

Ken came to Alaska in 1967 and worked for the Alaska Department of Fish & Game while pursuing a degree in wildlife and fisheries management. He married his wife, Jill, in 1969 and, soon after, both moved to Fairbanks. In 1970, Ken ran a fishing service on the Gulkana, and operated a taxidermy receiving station. He received his registered guide's license in 1974, and now hunts the Yakutat area and Alaska Range.

Ken has a reputation for producing excellent sheep trophies for his clients. He says his hunts are 100 percent successful, if his sheep hunters are in good physical condition. He's guided sheep hunters as old as 73 years old, and two hunters with wooden legs. All were successful because the hunters planned the extra time necessary for success, and they were in shape.

Ken hunts from one of seven sheep camps at elevations ranging from 3,500 to 4,500 feet. The base camps are rock/concrete or tent cabins and one small log cabin. In some areas, hunting is done from spike camps. He also offers caribou, sheep and moose combinations.

Ken conducts brown bear hunts in the Yakutat Jungles, as well as successful hunts for goats, black bear and glacial bear. He offers some of the most exciting brown bear hunting in the state. This is thick brush hunting, with most shots usually taken within 50 yards. Ken hunts the major river systems, where bears are feeding on salmon. Most bears, on the average, square eight to nine feet.

For more information, contact: Ken Fanning, Alaska Guide Service, Box 287, Yakutat, AK 99689, or call (907) 784-3232.

Mike Kraetsch is a native of Southwestern Minnesota. Primarily growing up in and around Luverne, Minnesota, he was an avid outdoorsman from early on. The local populations of rabbits and gophers lived in a general state of fear, at least until the summer baseball leagues started or a pick-up basketball game commenced. Mike first began bowhunting whitetails at the ripe old age of 10, and took his first deer at 13. Slightly side-tracked for a couple of years by high school sports, Mike still managed to get in a fair amount of pheasant, partridge and duck hunting.

Upon graduation from Luverne High School in 1981, Mike attended the University of Minnesota-Morris. Majoring in biology, geology, football and hunting, he graduated in 1985 with a B.A. degree. Following a short stint with the Dallas Cowboys football team, Mike spent three months with his arm in a cast, writing letters and applying to graduate schools. A timely visit from fellow Luverne native and present Colorado outfitter Judd Cooney saved Mike from graduate school and set him on the road to being a professional big game hunting guide, writer and photographer.

Upon arriving in Colorado in the spring of 1986, Mike began his tutelage under Judd in the finer arts of hauling bear bait garbage, digging antelope pit blinds and the state-of-the-art techniques of how to pack an elk out on one's back. In other words, he became a professional hunting guide. Together with Judd, Mike guides spring bear, antelope, deer and elk hunters in Colorado.

Working closely with Judd in other aspects of his business exposed Mike to the fields of outdoor writing and photography. Photography was an interest Mike had from youth and no prompting was necessary for it to develop. The writing was a natural outlet for all the anecdotes and stories accumulated while guiding hunters, and on the numerous photo and hunting trips he and Judd have been on together. Mike qualified for Outdoor Writers Association of America membership in 1988 and has numerous published photos and stories to his credit.

Mike currently lives with his wife, Lisa (Judd's daughter), and two young sons, Zane and Cole, in Pagosa Springs, Colorado. He guides for Judd Cooney, P.O. Box 808, Pagosa Springs, CO 81147.

Patrick Meitin was raised in New Mexico, where he learned to hunt at an early age. He has been bowhunting exclusively for more than 10 years. His personal list of bowhunting trophies include, Rocky Mountain elk, pronghorn antelope, mule deer, white-tailed deer, Coues' deer, black bear, javelina, turkey and many species of varmints and exotic game. Many of these animals are large enough to exceed the minimums established by Pope & Young.

Patrick began guiding professionally at age 17 and still spends six months each year in the mountains. He specializes most frequently in trophy elk and Coues' whitetail hunts, and has led many of his hunters to Boone & Crockett animals. Patrick says that, while Coues' are his favorite game animal, he loves each species for its own uniqueness.

Patrick pursues his own bowhunting, big-game challenges, whenever he can find the time. In addition he's an expert turkey hunter and stays sharp in the off season through his interest in bowfishing. A versatile bowhunter, Patrick emphasizes matching the proper bow to the task at hand. He's become a specialist in the backcountry-benefits of takedown bows.

As a freelance writer/photographer, Patrick's works have appeared in *Archery World*, *Bowhunting World*, *Bowhunter Magazine*, *Petersen's Bowhunting*, *North American Bowhunting*, *Bow and Arrow Hunting*, *The Western Bowhunter* (where Meitin has a monthly column), *Sportsman's Bowhunting*, *The Southwestern Sportsman* and *Buckmasters* among others.

To enhance his skills as a hunter, hunting guide and outdoor communicator, Patrick is earning a degree in journalism, photography and wildlife management at Texas Tech University in Lubbock, Texas. That is the city he is forced to call "home" when he is not hunting in his beloved mountains.

Patrick is also currently acting as a hunting advisor for High Country Archery. He plans to continue pursuing a career as a freelance writer and to hunt wherever he is able.

For more information contact: Patrick Meitin, Rt. 8, Box 70-A-2, Lubbock, TX 79407, or call (806) 793-8388.

Ron Moore was born January 26, 1942 in Seminole, Oklahoma. As a youth, he spent every moment free from school and chores roaming the Canadian River bottoms, armed with an old Western Field .22 rifle, in relentless search of rabbits, quail and ducks.

When he was 12 years old, Ron's family relocated to Colorado. This fortunate move sparked and kindled what has become Ron's never-ending love affair with the mountains and big game hunting. From the first breath of mountain air, he never seriously entertained thoughts of anything but a hunting career.

Until the spring of 1969, Ron concentrated on putting horse and hound tracks in most of the canyons of Colorado, Utah and Nevada.

In the spring of 1969, he accepted a position as Bear Damage Control Hunter for the Washington Forest Protection Association and relocated to Kalama, Washington. He worked with the association for three seasons and stayed in Washington hunting bear, lion and elk until 1979.

In 1979, Ron relocated to remote Young, Arizona, where he hunted and ranched until his retirement from the hunting business in 1987.

In a hunting career spanning nearly three decades, Ron hunted in Colorado, Utah, Arizona, New Mexico, California, Nevada, Oregon, Old Mexico, and Belize, Central America. In a career combining work as a government hunter and a professional hunting guide Ron and his clients have been directly responsible for the demise of more than 500 mountain lions and more than 1,000 bears, along with deer, elk, bobcat, and predator kills too numerous to mention.

Looking back, Ron considers himself privileged to have had the opportunity to host and hunt with clients from three foreign countries and all the states except Alaska.

Since retiring from the hunting business, Ron has been writing and working on an art career. He has had several articles published and is currently working on a book of his own guiding and hunting experiences. Several original pieces of his art and a series of limited edition prints have been sold.

Ron has been married to his wife, Christie, since 1966 and they have three children. They now make their home in Texas.

Gary Peters was born in Alymer, Ontario in 1949. As a youth, Gary guided his grade school teachers on hunts for small game and varmints. Despite a good rapport with his teachers, he felt more at home in the woods than in a classroom. Rabbits and squirrels he harvested helped feed his eight brothers and sisters. "We had a good life," he says, "but hard."

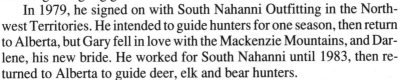

His appreciation for the outdoors blossomed through his teen years. When his mother died in 1972, Gary moved the family to Southern Alberta. After bagging elk, moose, deer, sheep and bear, Gary started guiding big game hunters.

In 1979, he signed on with South Nahanni Outfitting in the Northwest Territories. He intended to guide hunters for one season, then return to Alberta, but Gary fell in love with the Mackenzie Mountains, and Darlene, his new bride. He worked for South Nahanni until 1983, then returned to Alberta to guide deer, elk and bear hunters.

The Mackenzie Mountains, however, could not be scratched from his memory. Gary guided hunters in both Alberta and the Northwest Territories. For information, contact: Gary Peters, Box 31, Mountain View, Alberta, TOK1NO, or call (403) 653-2546.

Al Pletzke has lived in Bruce Crossing all his life. Located in Ontonogan County, Michigan, his camp is in one of the state's top areas for bear and deer. He has been guiding bear hunts since 1970 as well as operating a charter boat on Lake Superior during the summer months. When he's not on the lake, he's in the woods scouting for new bear country.

Aside from his bear hunts, Al has extended his guiding to whitetail and provides a bucks-only hunt in October.

During the winter months, Al sells and repairs snowmobiles, scouts new country and studies wind currents for the upcoming seasons.

He is also in the process of writing a series of short stories of hunts that he has guided which he feels will be of interest to sportspeople.

Aside from his busy schedule, Al manages to spend two weeks per year in British Columbia, hunting, relaxing and putting pressure on other guides.

Al is married and has one child. His wife, Kathy, does all the cooking for their hunters.

The Michigan bear season starts in September. Al conducts three bear hunts a year. For more information contact: Al Pletzke's Bear Guiding Service, Bruce Crossing, MI 49912, or call (906) 827-3466.

Billy Stockton has been guiding hunters for more than 25 years in the East and West Pioneer Mountains of the Pender Wilderness area outside Butte, Montana. He's lived his entire life in this area and even the natives will tell you no one knows this country better than Billy.

Stockton Outfitters operates six camps and has access to over 100 square miles of prime elk, mule deer and bear habitat. Billy can put hunters onto good whitetail at lower elevations and also guides hunters fortunate enough to draw special tags for sheep, mountain goats and moose. Success rates for elk during the bowhunting season run as high as 80 percent, with later-season rifle hunters successful 60 percent of the time under Billy's tutelage.

Spring bear is one of Billy's best hunts, with almost 100 percent of his hunters taking bear. In this country, bear are seldom overharvested and will average six feet square. Many are taken in various cinnamon and blonde color phases.

A bonus for any hunt with the Stockton Outfitters includes blue ribbon trout fishing in the nearby Big Hole River, one of America's premier trout streams.

Billy provides comfortable accommodations for his hunters whether they hunt out of his lodge or one of his many spike camps. For more information, write to: Billy Stockton, Stockton Outfitters, Wise River, Montana 59762, or call (406) 832-3138.

Charlie Stricker is perhaps North America's most experienced sheep outfitter. He began his career hunting bighorns in Alberta many years ago, and has also owned a highly successful Stone sheep operation in British Columbia. Currently, Charlie outfits for Dall sheep and other big game in Yukon's famed Bonnet Plume region.

Charlie is well known for his ever-present smile, and most clients remember him for his sense of humor as well as his prowess as a guide and outfitter. While he now makes his permanent home in the Yukon, Alberta will always be in his blood: that's where both of his stories for this anthology take place.

Charlie operates Bonnet Plume Outfitters, Ltd., Box 5963, Whitehorse, Yukon, Canada Y1A 5L7, (403) 633-3366.

Tommy Thompson received his Bachelor's Degree in Range Animal Husbandry in 1960 and a Masters of Arts in Biology in 1965, both from Sul Ross State University, Alpine, Texas.

After several years of employment as a golf course superintendent, he worked for a large Texas hunting ranch as a guide. But during the spring of 1982, Tommy started his own guide/outfitting business known as Central Texas Hunts.

With access to 30 ranches in the Edwards Plateau area of Texas, he has placed over 300 trophies in the Exotic Wildlife Association's New Burkett System record book for his hunters since 1978. He received the Outfitter/Guide Award for 1987-88 for most record book trophies taken during that period. Tommy is a member of the board of directors of the Exotic Wildlife Association.

For further information on Central Texas Hunts, contact: Route 1, Box 52, Medina, TX 78055, (210) 589-7703.

Larry Trimber (LC to his friends) has been guiding and outfitting hunters for more than 15 years through the western states.

He learned his trade in Colorado, under the tutelage of other outfitters, then put in six years of guiding cat hunters in Nevada, Arizona and New Mexico. Upon moving to Montana, he first worked for outfitters there and in Idaho, before starting his own operation.

As head of High Country Connection, he handles big game hunts for bear, elk and deer.

His one-week packer school is geared to teaching the do-it-yourself hunter. His guide school trains professional hunting guides. Other summer programs include pack-in fishing of alpine lakes for trout and grayling and a bowhunting school.

For full details, contact: High Country Connection, 4085 Illinois Bench, Stevensville, MT 59870, (406) 777-3631.

In 1971, **Duane Wiltse** gave up a prosperous contracting business in Flint, Michigan, and moved his wife and family to an old log ranch in the shadows of the Beartooth Mountains of northern Wyoming.

Duane's interest in hunting is a family heritage honed for him on outdoor adventures on the peninsula of Michigan and in several Canadian provinces. Now, with more than 18 years of guiding under his belt, Duane and his family regularly guide hunters from around the world to the trophy bull elk that inhabit the Yellowstone region west of Cody, Wyoming.

Duane is the author of magazine articles, co-author of the NAHC's *All About Elk* and has been featured in outdoor television productions. Duane operates Cabin Creek Outfitters, 3411 Yellowstone Hwy., Cody, WY 82414, (307) 527-7030.